Disney · PIXAR

MONSTERS, INC.

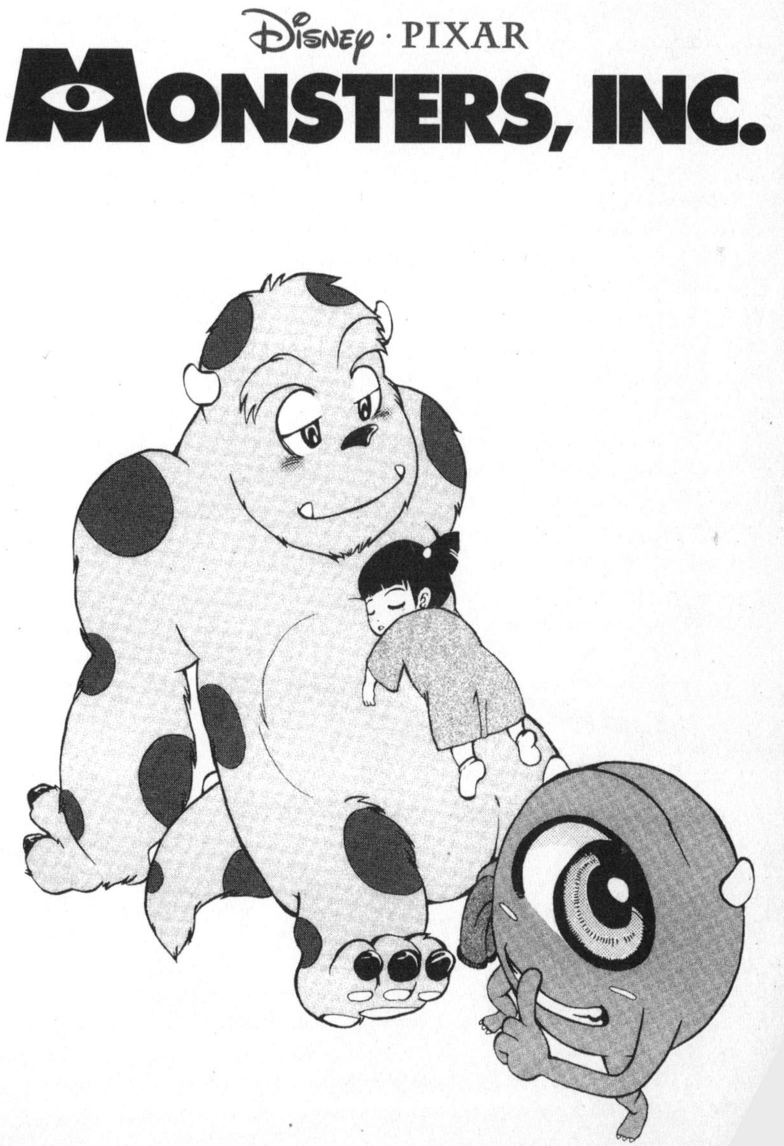

Also Available from TOKYOPOP®:

Angelic Layer
Cardcaptor Sakura
Cardcaptor Sakura: Master of the Clow
Clover
Corrector Yui
Cowboy Bebop
Dragon Knights
Gundam Blue Destiny
Gundam Wing
Gundam Wing - The Last Outpost
Gundam Technical Manual
Juline
Kare Kano
Kodocha
Magic Knight Rayearth
Marmalade Boy
Mars
Miracle Girls
Planet Ladder
Ragnarok
Real Bout High School
Sailor Moon
Saint Tail
Sushi Girl
Wish

Coming Soon:

Digital Digimon Monsters™

Stray Sheep

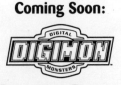

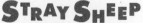

Kim Possible
Lizzie McGuire

DISNEY · PIXAR

MONSTERS, INC.

**Written and Illustrated
by Hiromi Yamafuji**

Los Angeles – Tokyo

14078703

Original comic by Hiromi Yamafuji

Retouch and Lettering - Tami Ortenau and Lauren Alpert Magnin
English Adaptation - Cylin Busby Ross
Senior Editor - Julie Taylor
Production Manager - Jennifer Wagner
Cover Layout - Anna Kernbaum
Art Director - Matt Alford
VP of Production - Ron Klamert
Publisher - Stuart Levy

Email: editor@TOKYOPOP.com
Come visit us online at www.TOKYOPOP.com

A  manga
TOKYOPOP® is an imprint of Mixx Entertainment, Inc.
5900 Wilshire Blvd. Ste 2000, Los Angeles, CA 90036
TOKYOPOP is a registered trademark
of Mixx Entertainment, Inc.

Disney · PIXAR

Original Comic by Hiromi Yamafuji / Kodansha
Copyright©2002 Disney Enterprises, Inc./Pixar Animation Studios
Monsters, Inc.© Disney Enterprises, Inc./Pixar Animation Studios

All rights reserved. No portion of this book may be reproduced or
transmitted in any form or by any means without written permission
from the copyright holders. This graphic novel is a work of fiction.
Any resemblance to actual events or locales or persons, living or dead,
is entirely coincidental.

ISBN: 1-591820-75-8

First TOKYOPOP® printing: September 2002

10 9 8 7 6 5 4 3 2 1

Manufactured in Canada

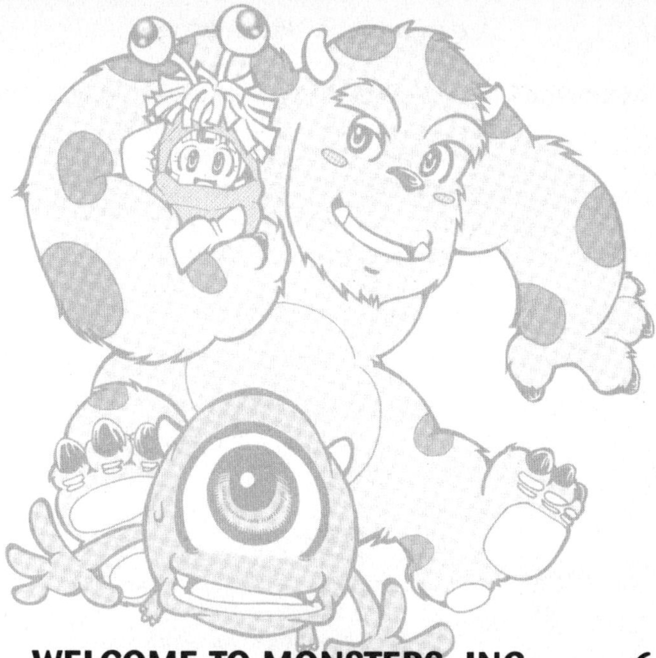

What is Manga?

This book is called a manga. Manga is the Japanese word for comic book. Manga used to only be available to readers in Japan, but now it's popular all over the world. Manga is almost the same as a cartoon you watch on TV, but instead it's in the form of a book. Think of this as a freeze-framed cartoon! This means it's a book that you read, yet the pictures are just as important as what your favorite characters are saying. Some people even think of manga as a movie that you can hold in your hands.

This book is the manga version of *Monsters, Inc.*, the movie that you love so much. Have fun reading this monstrously fun manga!

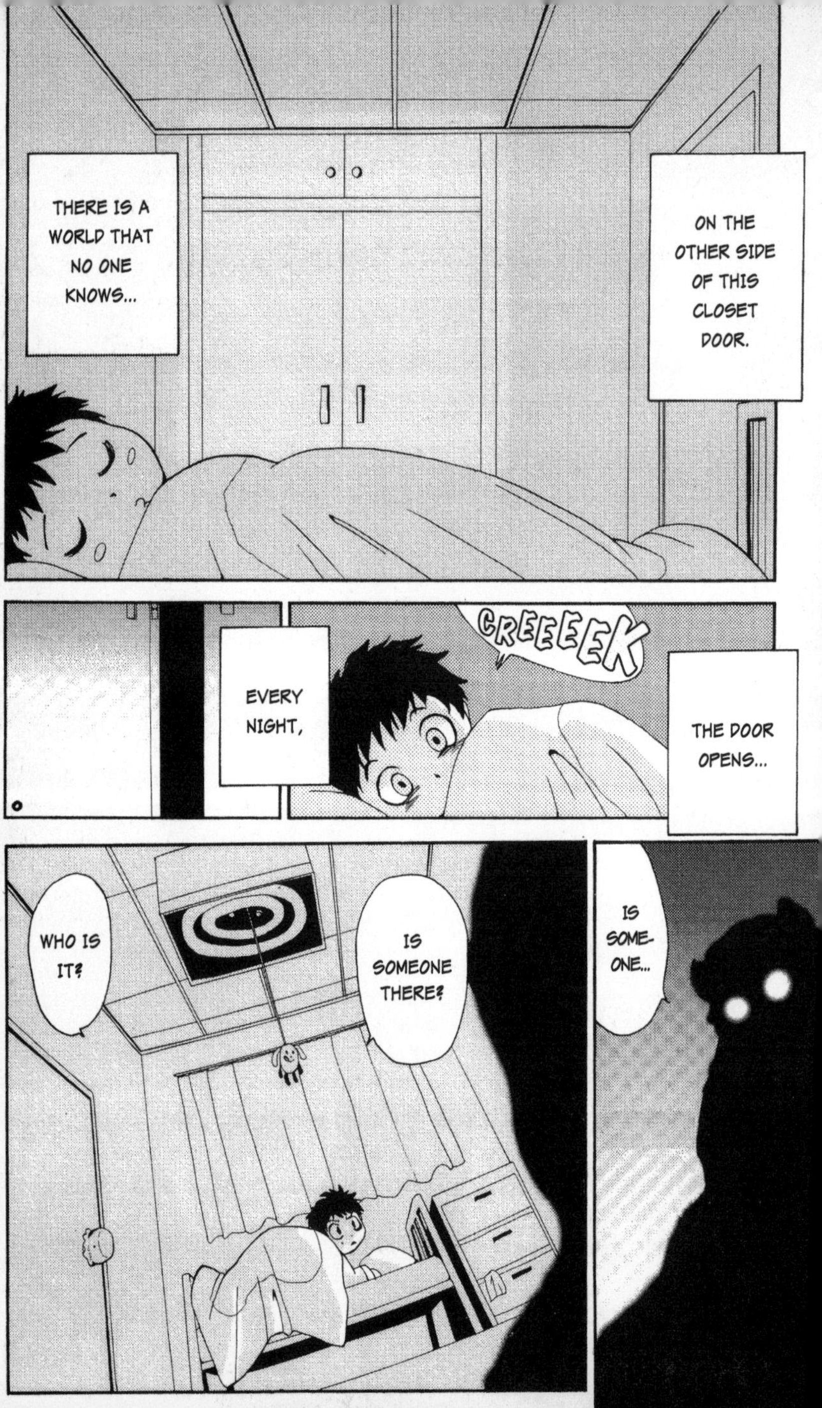
THERE IS A WORLD THAT NO ONE KNOWS...
ON THE OTHER SIDE OF THIS CLOSET DOOR.
EVERY NIGHT,
CREEEEEK
THE DOOR OPENS...
WHO IS IT?
IS SOMEONE THERE?
IS SOME-ONE...

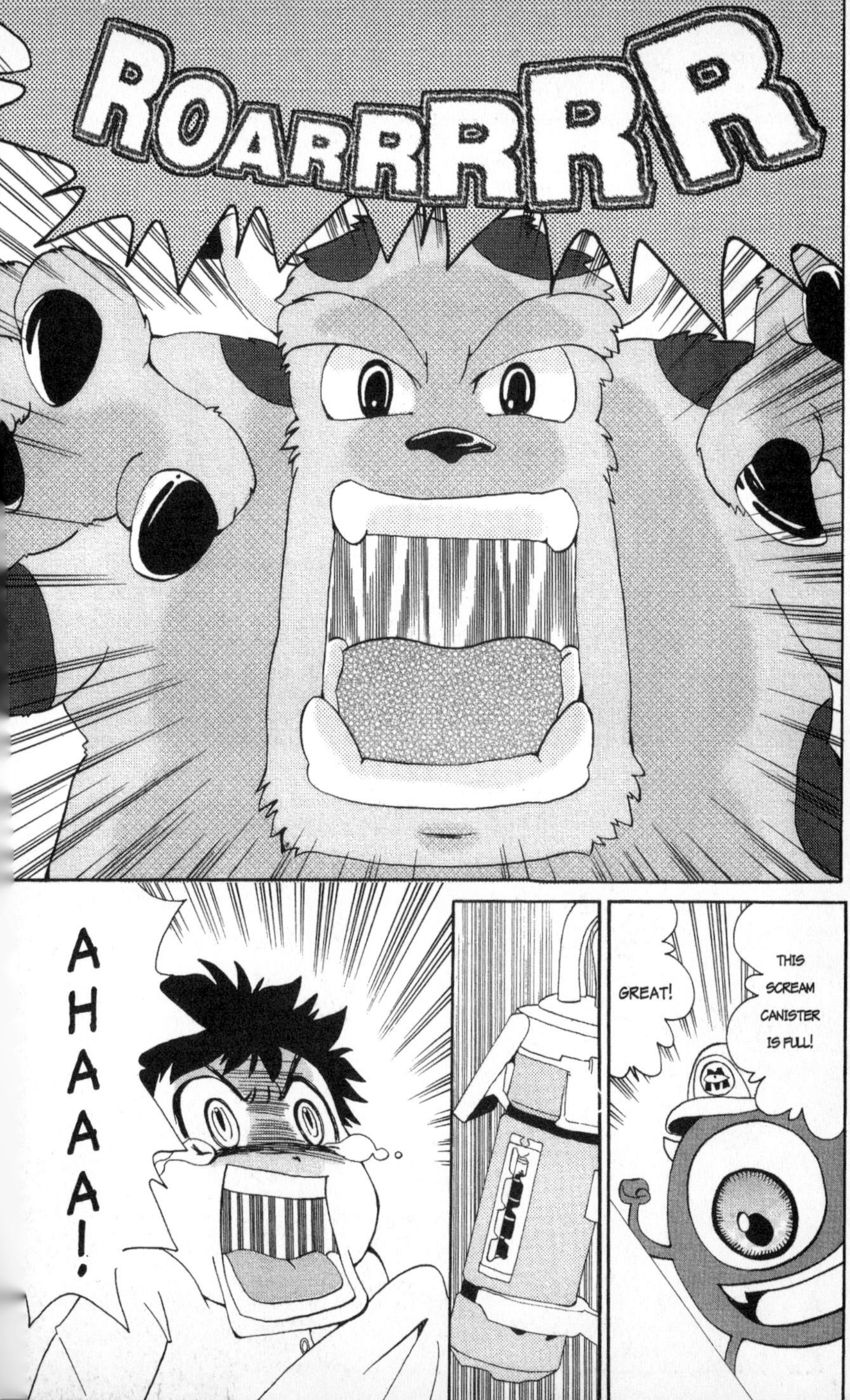
ROARRRRRR
AHAAAA!
GREAT!
THIS SCREAM CANISTER IS FULL!

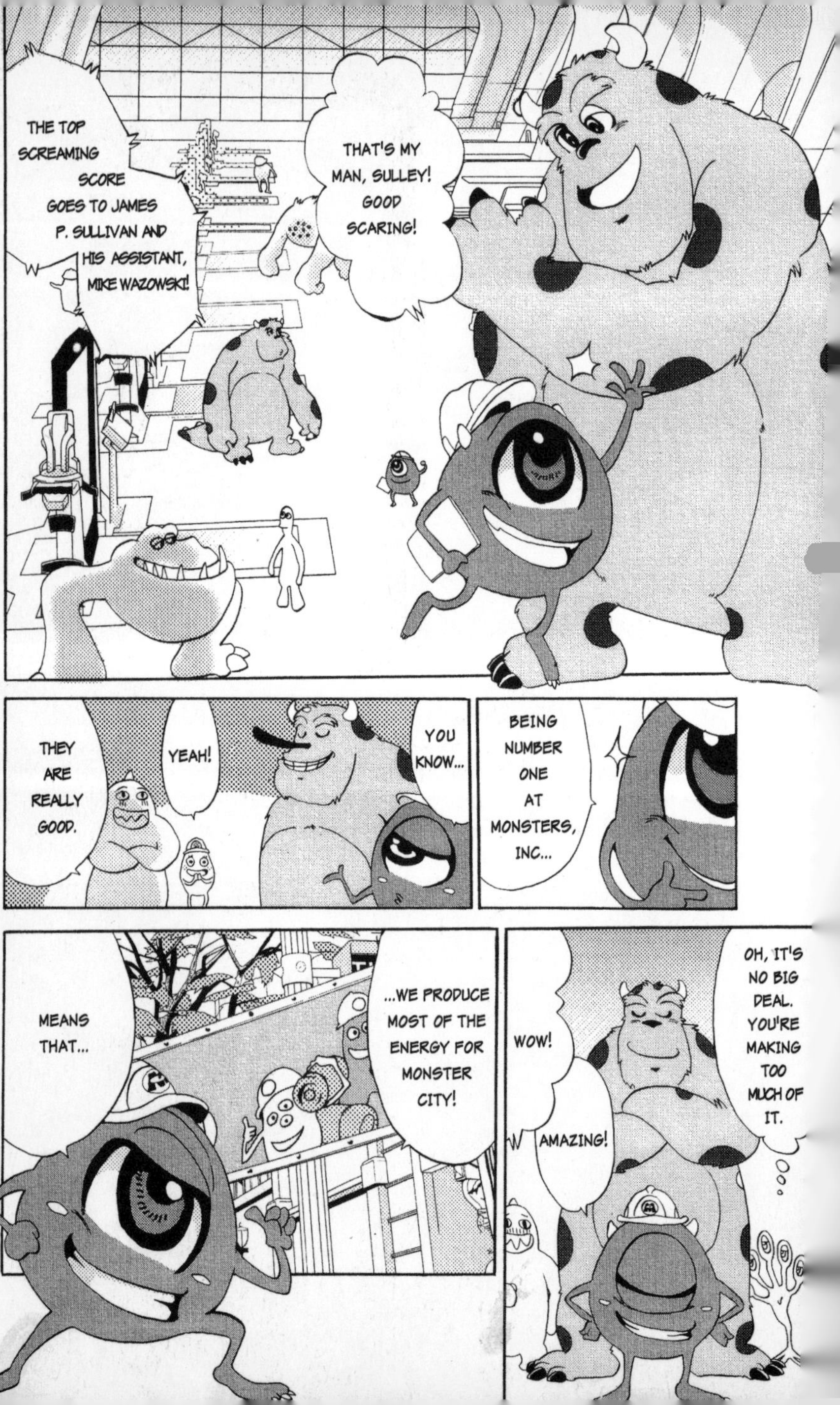
THE TOP SCREAMING SCORE GOES TO JAMES P. SULLIVAN AND HIS ASSISTANT, MIKE WAZOWSKI!
THAT'S MY MAN, SULLEY! GOOD SCARING!
THEY ARE REALLY GOOD.
YEAH!
YOU KNOW...
BEING NUMBER ONE AT MONSTERS, INC...
MEANS THAT...
...WE PRODUCE MOST OF THE ENERGY FOR MONSTER CITY!
WOW!
AMAZING!
OH, IT'S NO BIG DEAL. YOU'RE MAKING TOO MUCH OF IT.

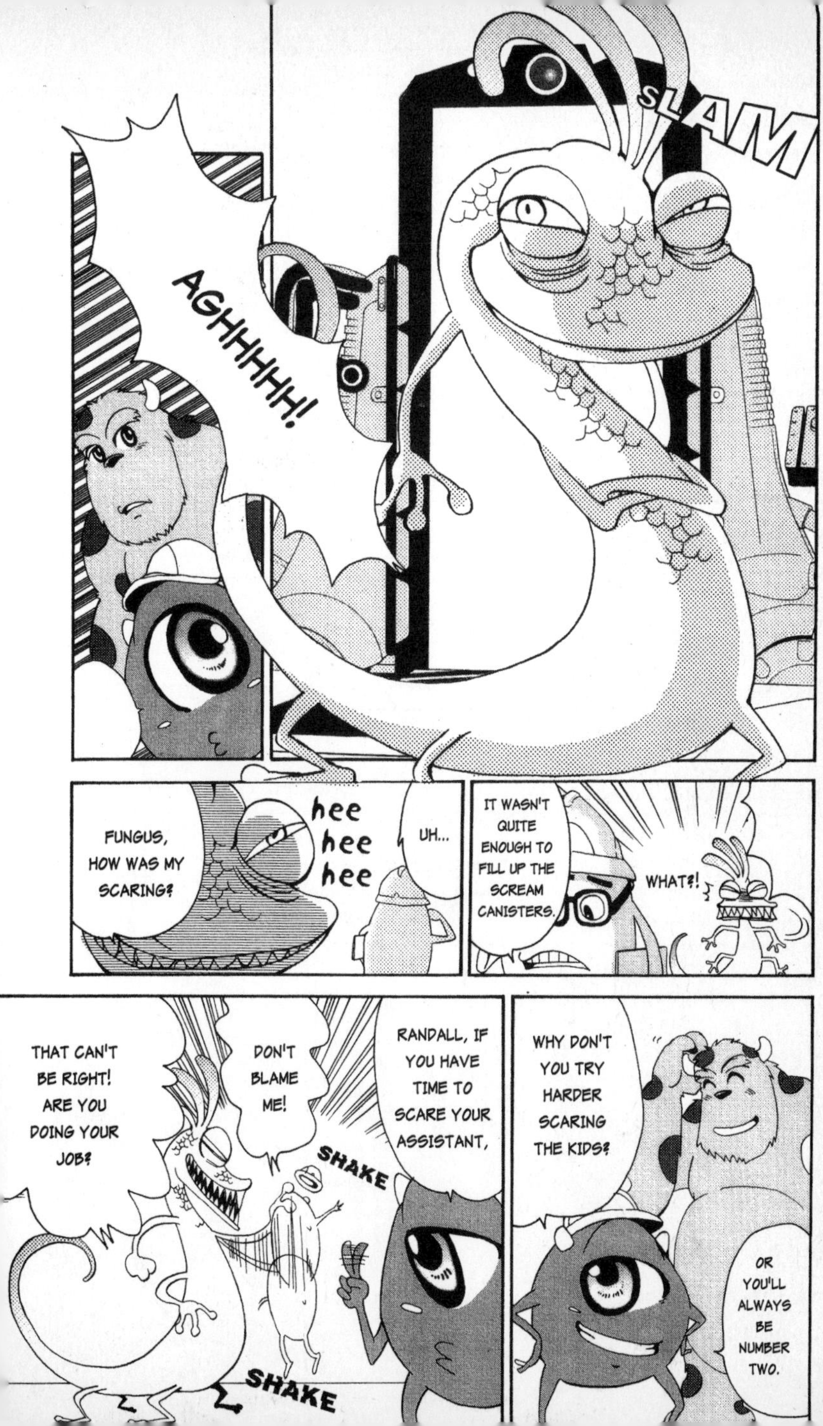
AGHHHHHH!
SLAM
FUNGUS, HOW WAS MY SCARING?
hee hee hee
UH...
IT WASN'T QUITE ENOUGH TO FILL UP THE SCREAM CANISTERS.
WHAT?!
THAT CAN'T BE RIGHT! ARE YOU DOING YOUR JOB?
DON'T BLAME ME!
SHAKE
SHAKE
RANDALL, IF YOU HAVE TIME TO SCARE YOUR ASSISTANT,
WHY DON'T YOU TRY HARDER SCARING THE KIDS?
OR YOU'LL ALWAYS BE NUMBER TWO.

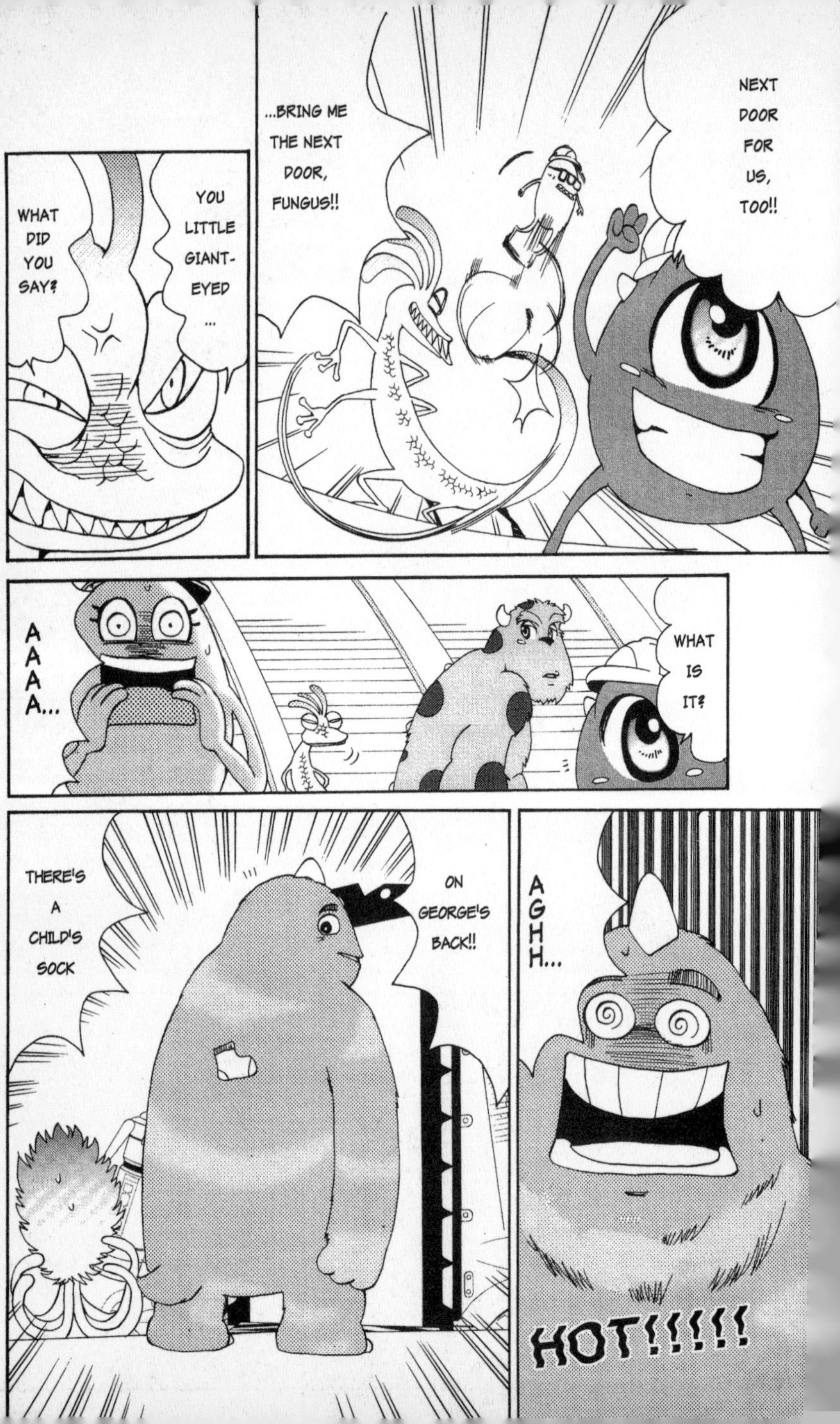
WHAT DID YOU SAY?
YOU LITTLE GIANT-EYED ...
...BRING ME THE NEXT DOOR, FUNGUS!!
NEXT DOOR FOR US, TOO!!
AAAA...
WHAT IS IT?
THERE'S A CHILD'S SOCK
ON GEORGE'S BACK!!
AGHH...
HOT!!!!!!

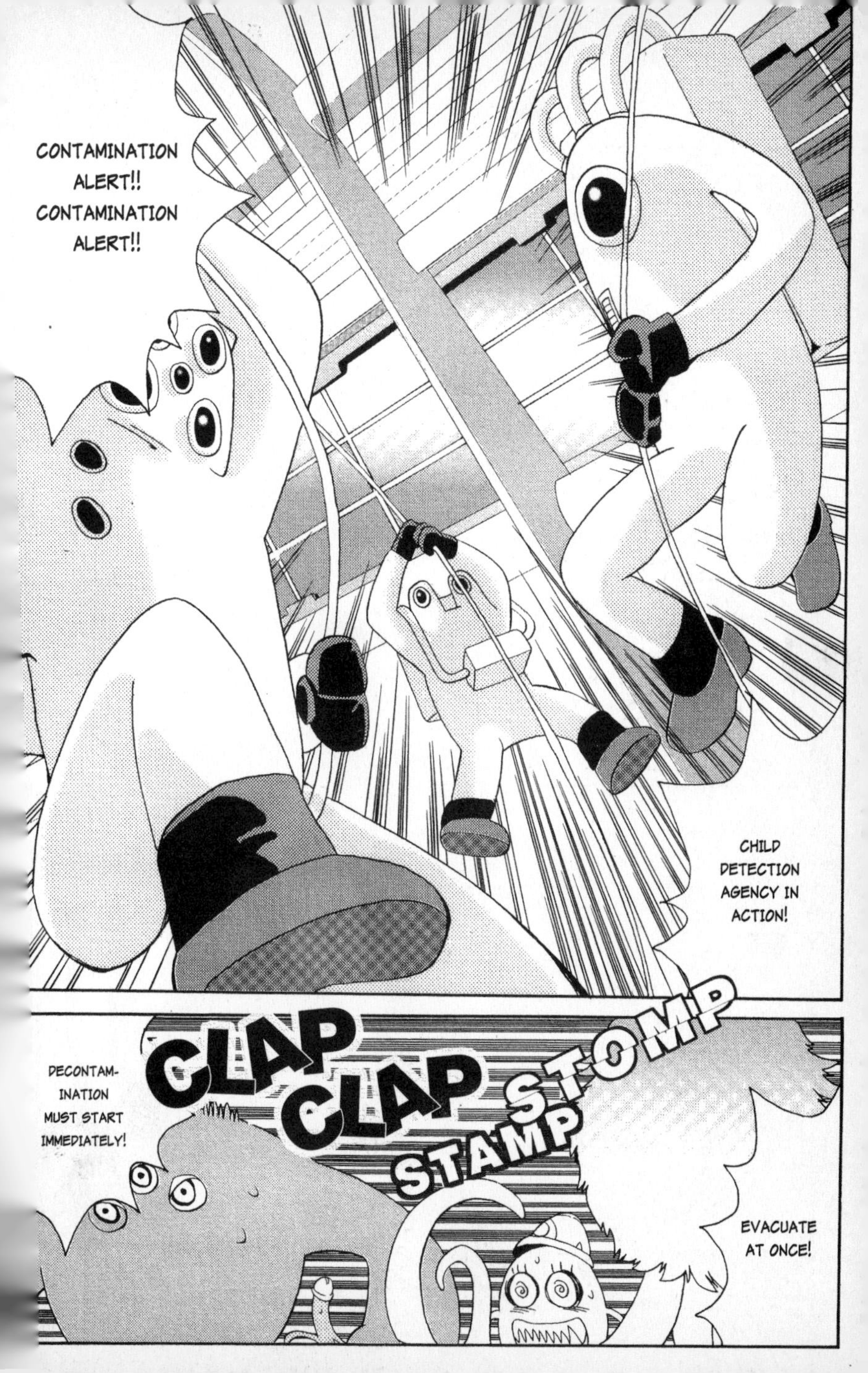
CONTAMINATION ALERT!! CONTAMINATION ALERT!!
CHILD DETECTION AGENCY IN ACTION!
DECONTAMINATION MUST START IMMEDIATELY!
CLAP CLAP
STAMP STOMP
EVACUATE AT ONCE!

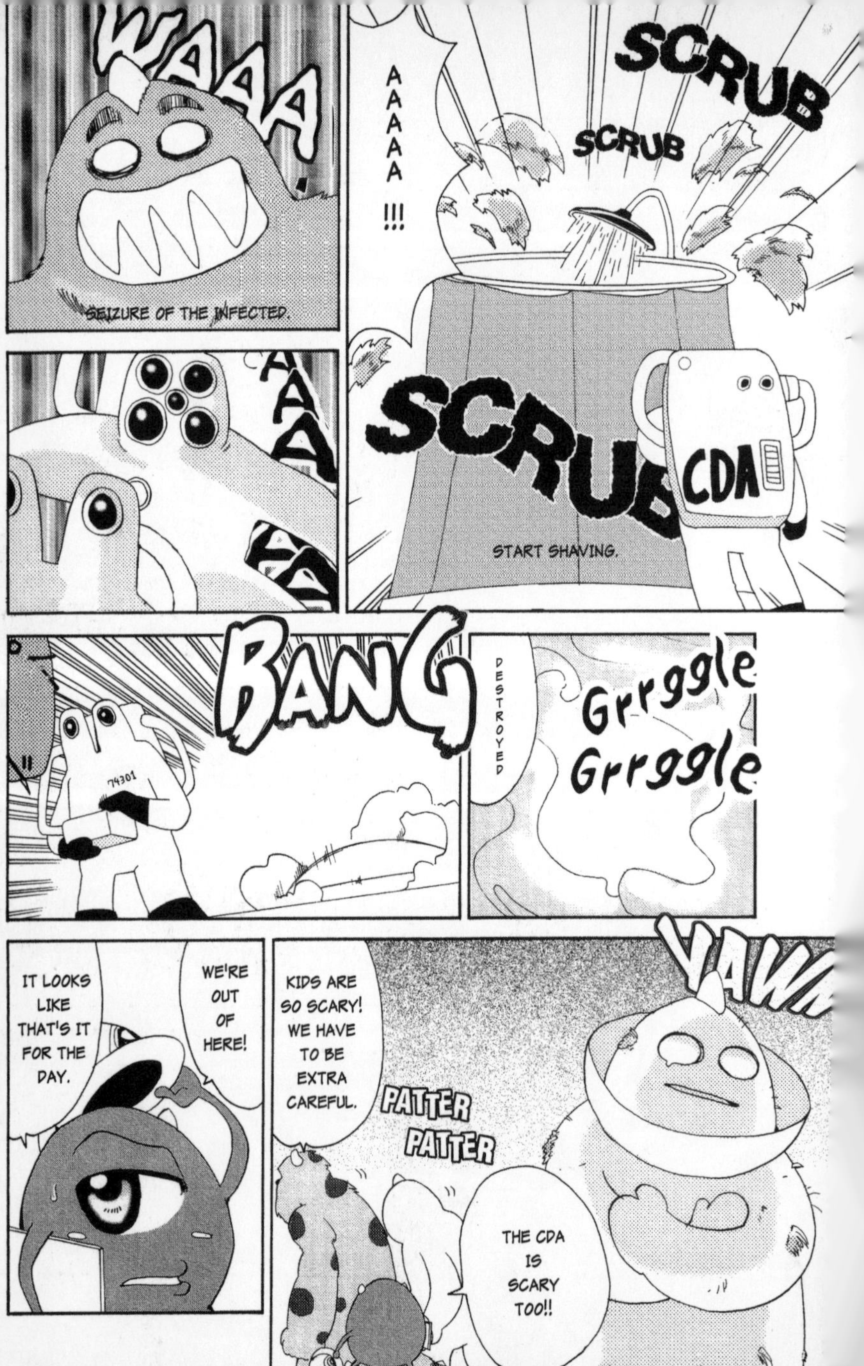
WAAAA.
SEIZURE OF THE INFECTED.
AAA
AAAAA!!!
SCRUB
SCRUB
SCRUB
CDA
START SHAVING.
BANG
74301
DESTROYED
Grrggle Grrggle
IT LOOKS LIKE THAT'S IT FOR THE DAY.
WE'RE OUT OF HERE!
KIDS ARE SO SCARY! WE HAVE TO BE EXTRA CAREFUL.
PATTER PATTER
THE CDA IS SCARY TOO!!

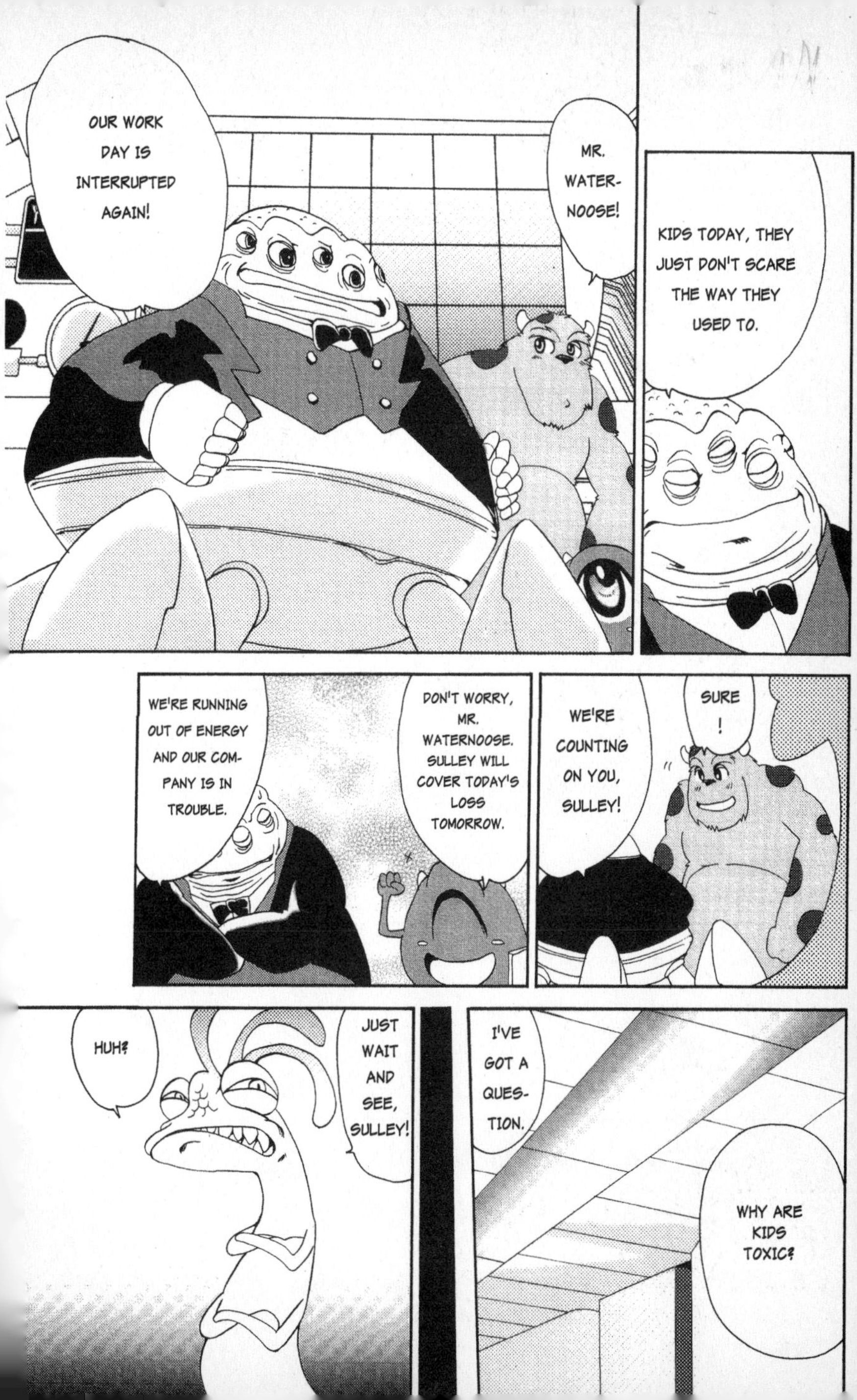
OUR WORK DAY IS INTERRUPTED AGAIN!
MR. WATER-NOOSE!
KIDS TODAY, THEY JUST DON'T SCARE THE WAY THEY USED TO.
WE'RE RUNNING OUT OF ENERGY AND OUR COM-PANY IS IN TROUBLE.
DON'T WORRY, MR. WATERNOOSE. SULLEY WILL COVER TODAY'S LOSS TOMORROW.
WE'RE COUNTING ON YOU, SULLEY!
SURE!
HUH?
JUST WAIT AND SEE, SULLEY!
I'VE GOT A QUES-TION.
WHY ARE KIDS TOXIC?

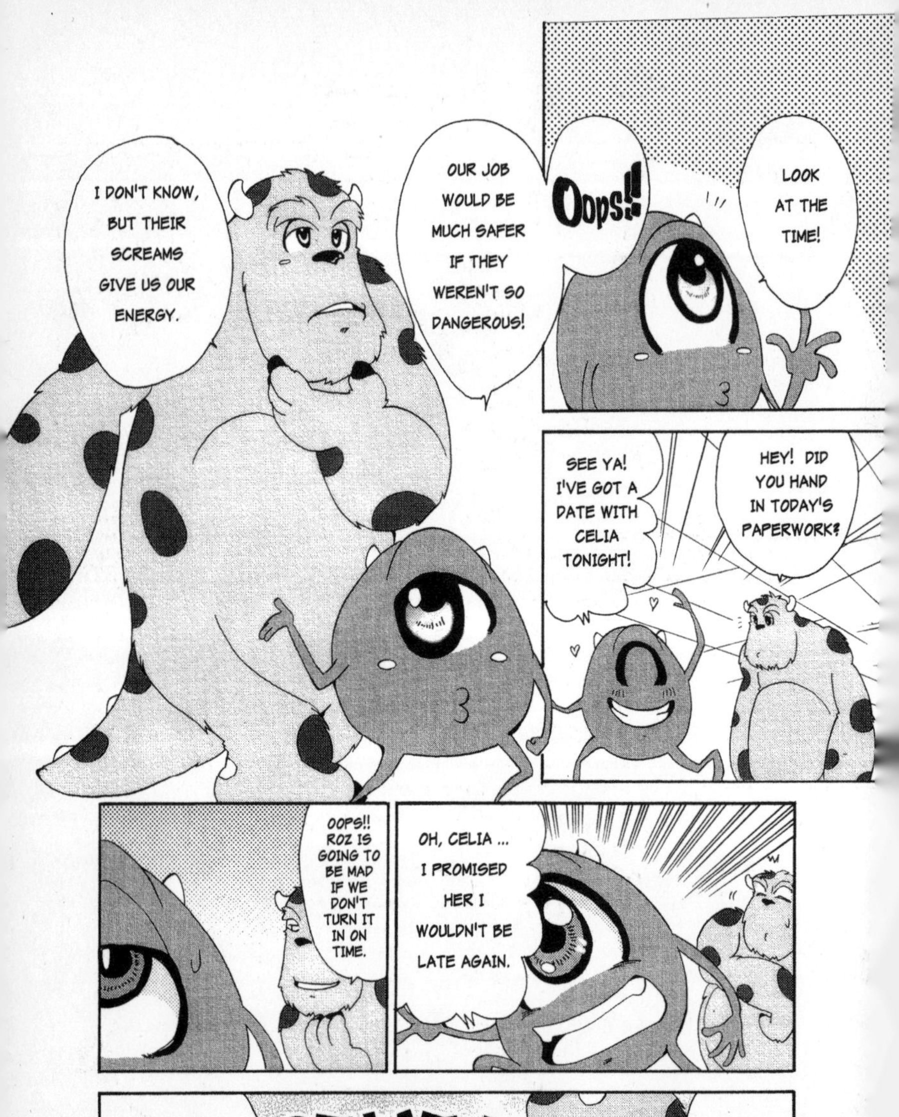

I DON'T KNOW, BUT THEIR SCREAMS GIVE US OUR ENERGY.
OUR JOB WOULD BE MUCH SAFER IF THEY WEREN'T SO DANGEROUS!
Oops!!
LOOK AT THE TIME!
SEE YA! I'VE GOT A DATE WITH CELIA TONIGHT!
HEY! DID YOU HAND IN TODAY'S PAPERWORK?
OOPS!! ROZ IS GOING TO BE MAD IF WE DON'T TURN IT IN ON TIME.
OH, CELIA ... I PROMISED HER I WOULDN'T BE LATE AGAIN.
...BUT I GUESS OUR LOVE JUST WASN'T MEANT TO BE.
GRUMBLE
GRUMBLE
DO YOU WANT ME TO HAND IT IN FOR YOU?

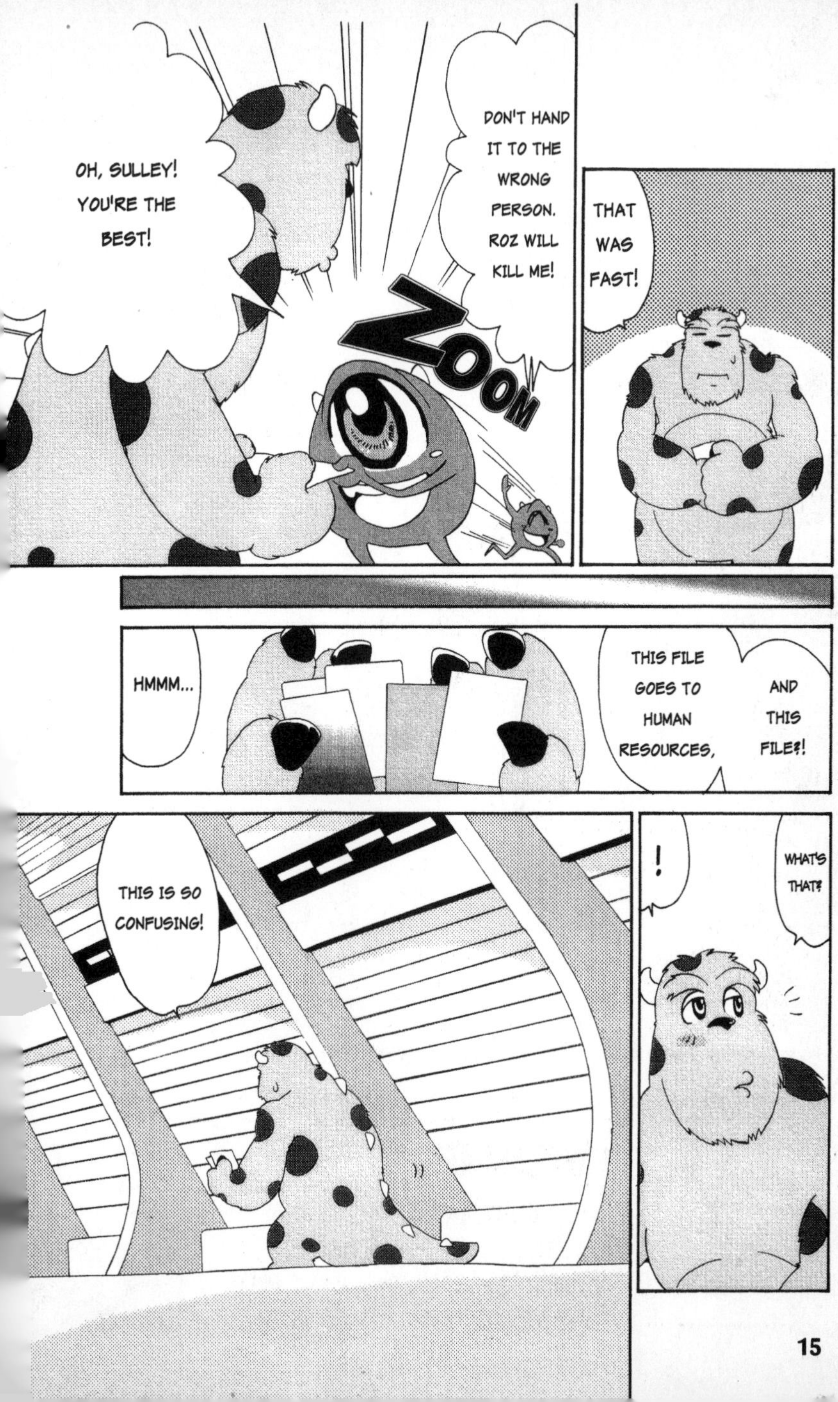
OH, SULLEY! YOU'RE THE BEST!
DON'T HAND IT TO THE WRONG PERSON. ROZ WILL KILL ME!
ZOOM
THAT WAS FAST!
HMMM...
THIS FILE GOES TO HUMAN RESOURCES,
AND THIS FILE?!
THIS IS SO CONFUSING!
!
WHAT'S THAT?

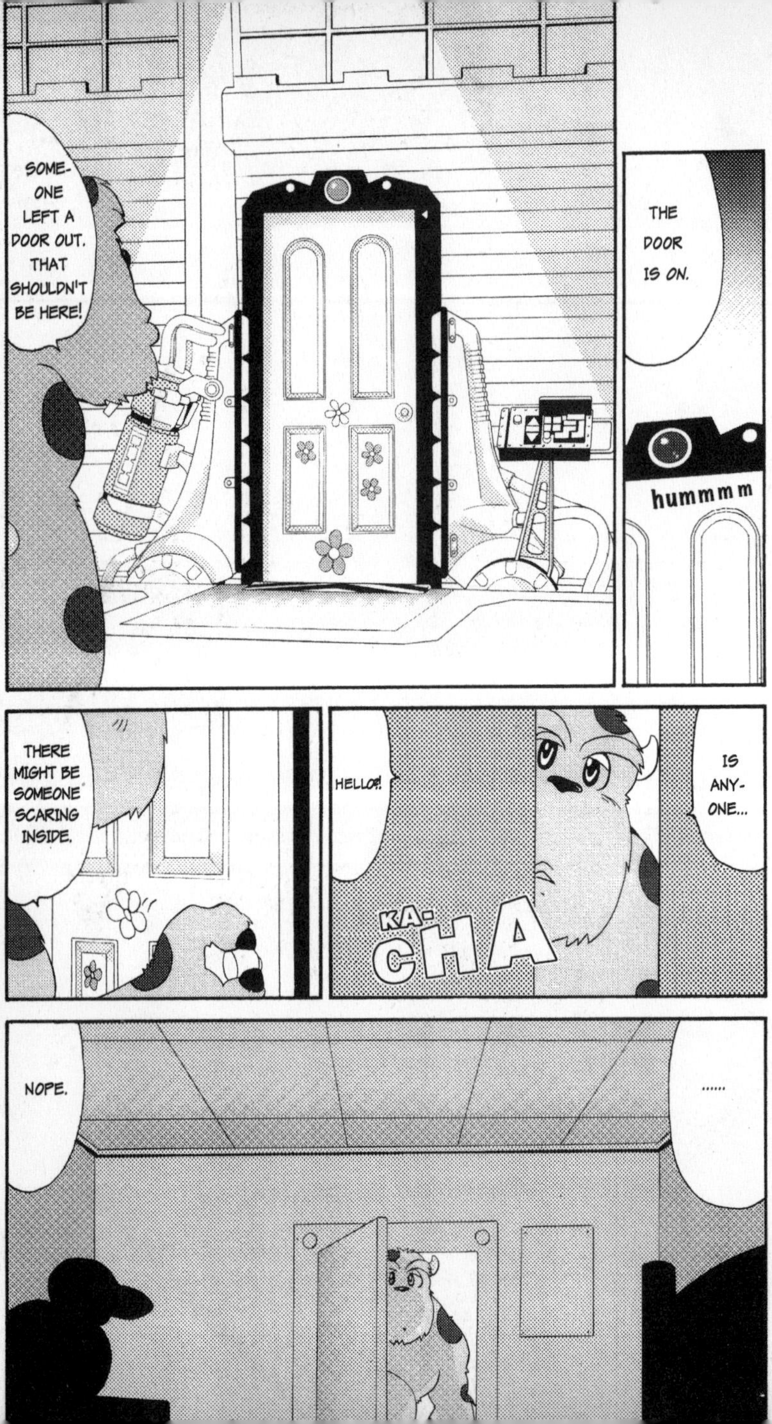
SOME-ONE LEFT A DOOR OUT. THAT SHOULDN'T BE HERE!
THE DOOR IS ON.
hummmm
THERE MIGHT BE SOMEONE SCARING INSIDE.
HELLO?!
IS ANY-ONE...
KA-CHA
NOPE.
......

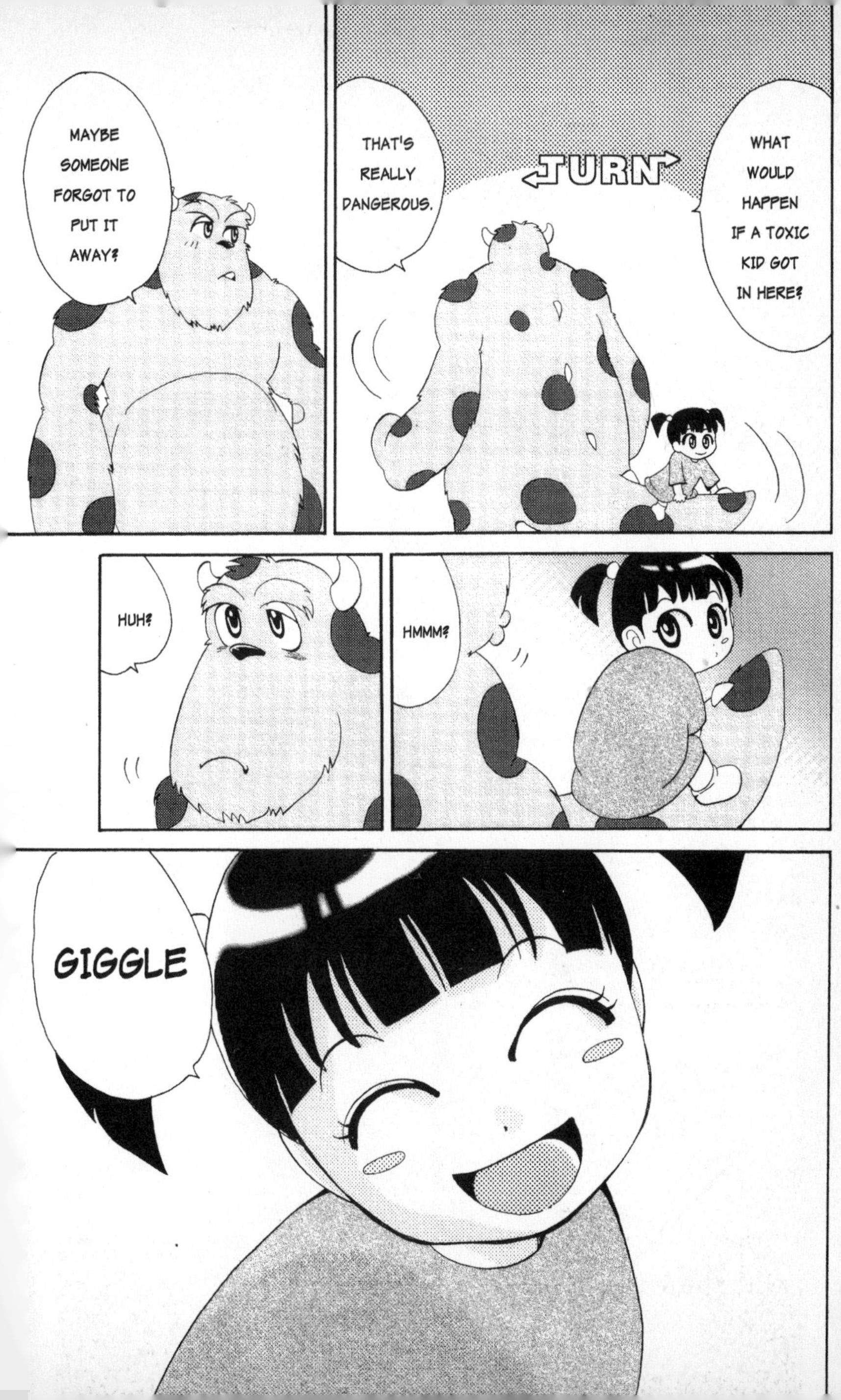
MAYBE SOMEONE FORGOT TO PUT IT AWAY?
THAT'S REALLY DANGEROUS.
TURN
WHAT WOULD HAPPEN IF A TOXIC KID GOT IN HERE?
HUH?
HMMM?
GIGGLE

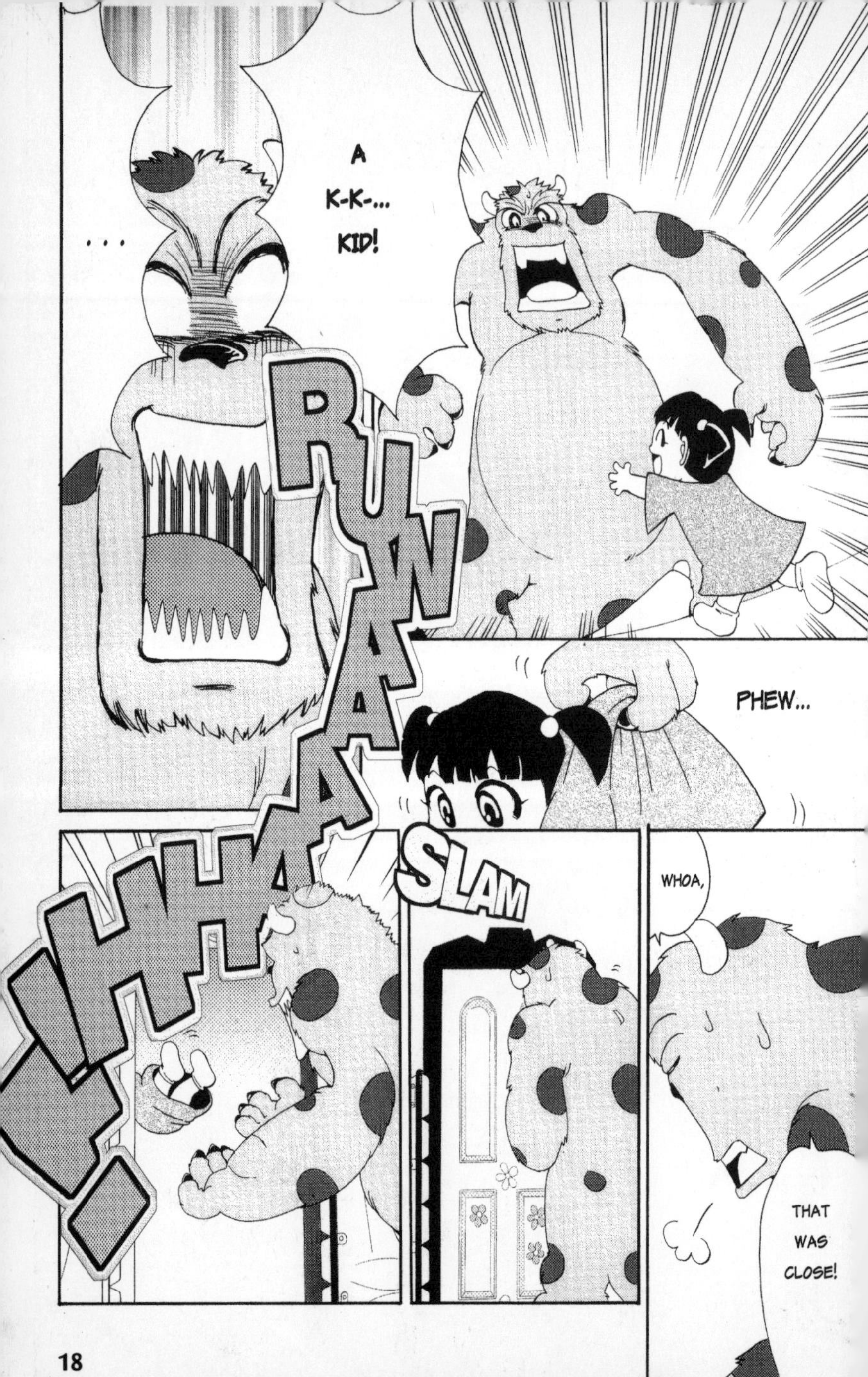
. . .
RWAAAAHH!!
A K-K-... KID!
PHEW...
SLAM
WHOA,
THAT WAS CLOSE!

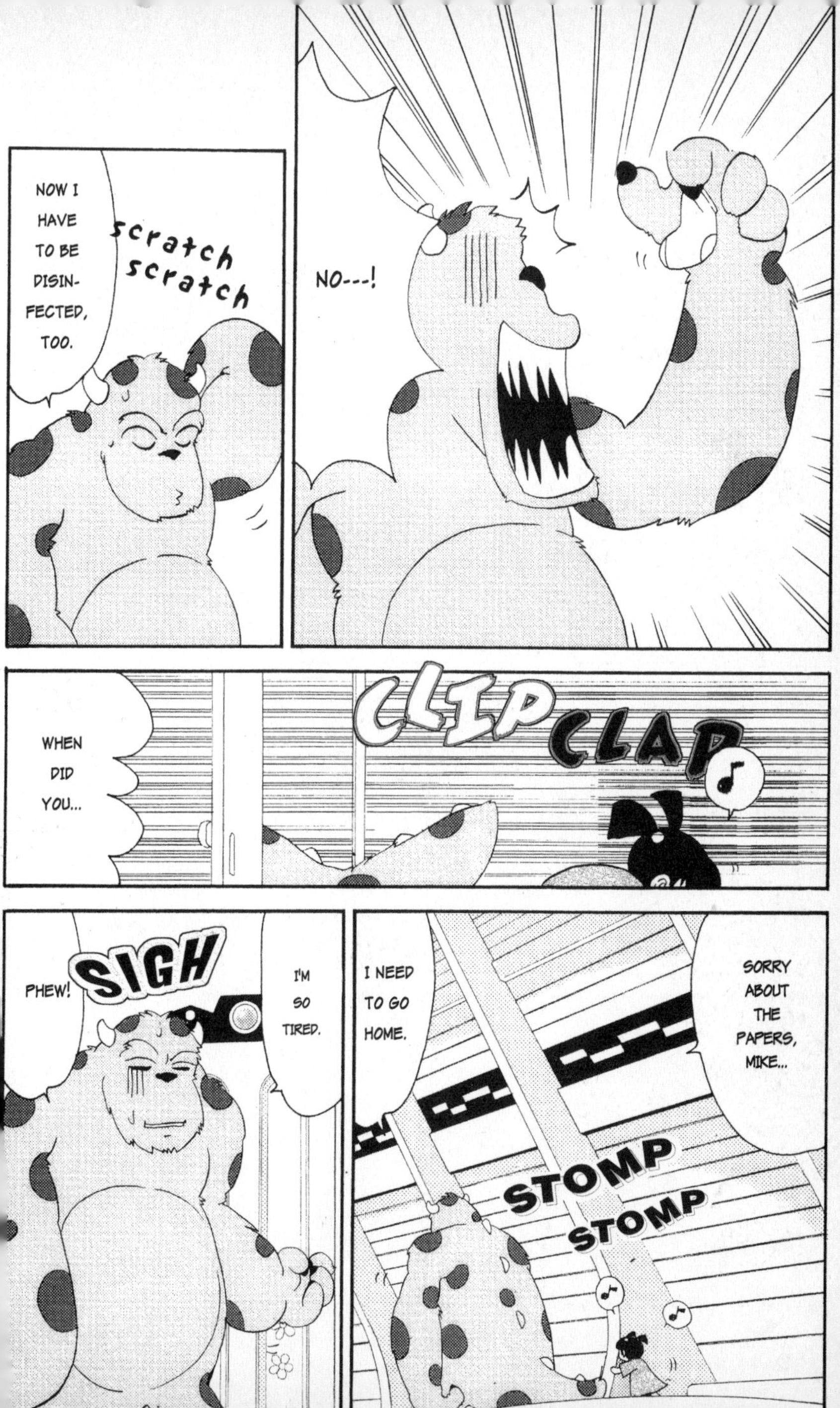
NOW I HAVE TO BE DISIN-FECTED, TOO.
scratch scratch
NO---!
WHEN DID YOU...
CLIP CLAP
PHEW!
SIGH
I'M SO TIRED.
I NEED TO GO HOME.
SORRY ABOUT THE PAPERS, MIKE...
STOMP
STOMP

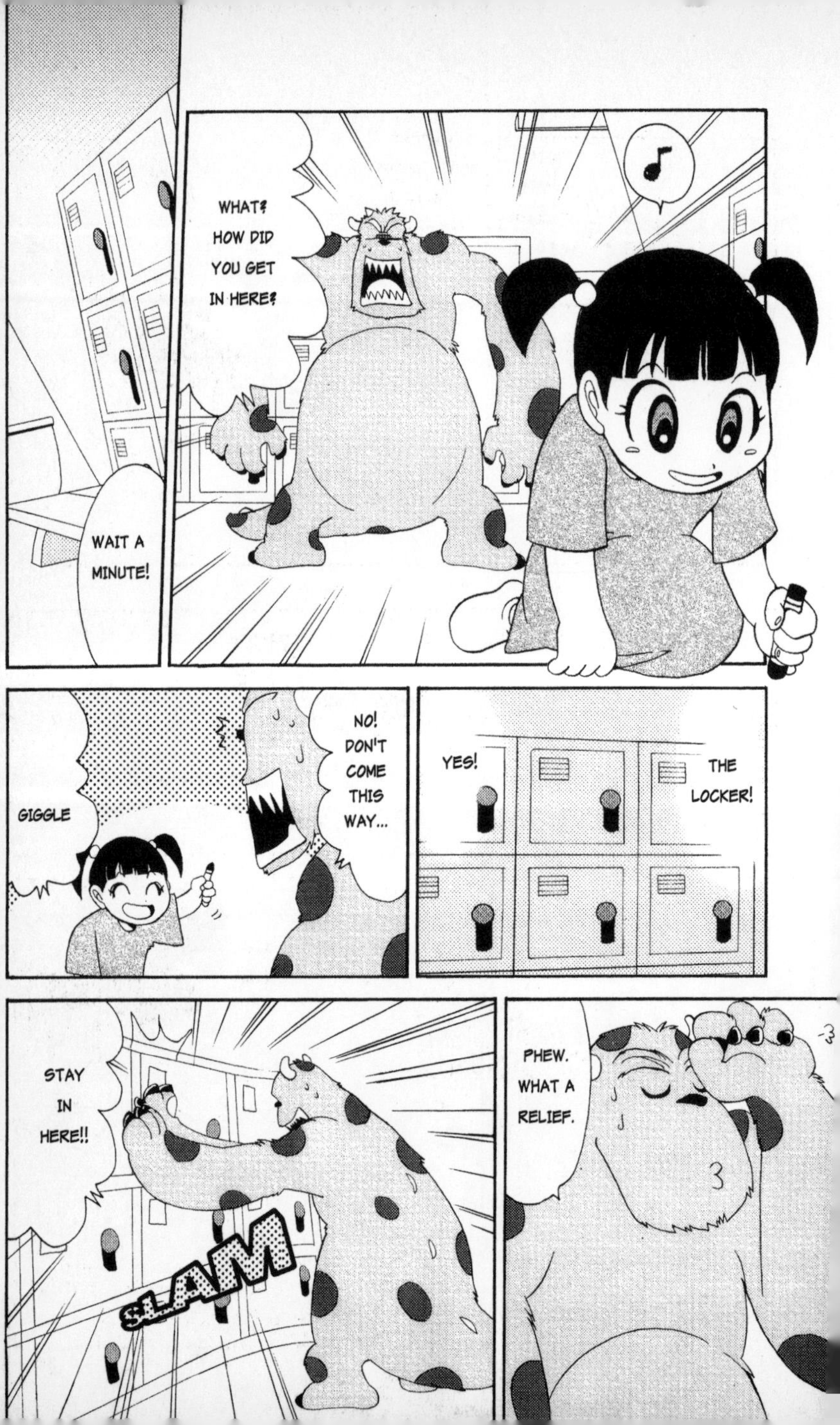
WAIT A MINUTE!
WHAT? HOW DID YOU GET IN HERE?
GIGGLE
NO! DON'T COME THIS WAY...
YES!
THE LOCKER!
STAY IN HERE!!
SLAM
PHEW. WHAT A RELIEF.

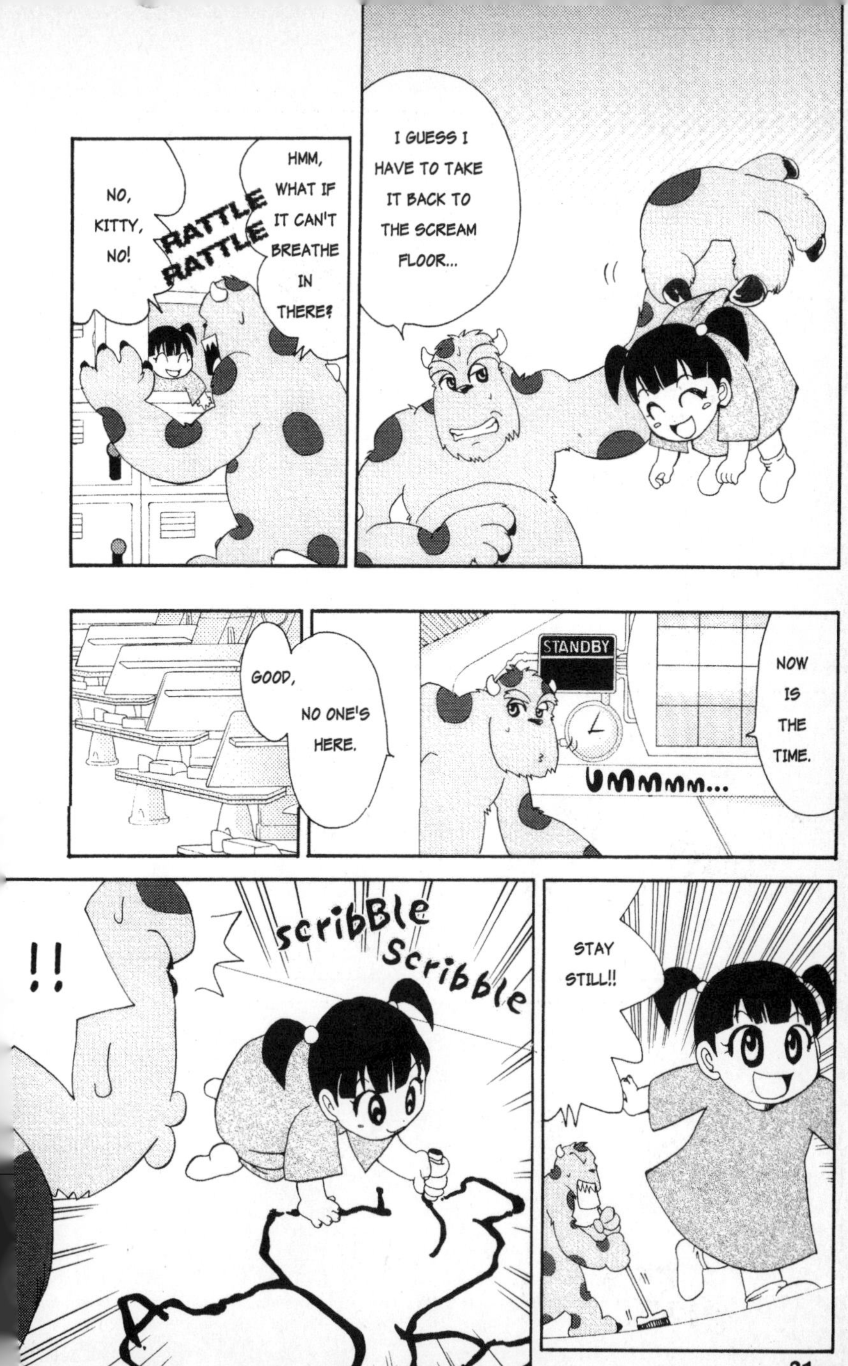
NO, KITTY, NO!
RATTLE RATTLE
HMM, WHAT IF IT CAN'T BREATHE IN THERE?
I GUESS I HAVE TO TAKE IT BACK TO THE SCREAM FLOOR...
GOOD, NO ONE'S HERE.
STANDBY
UMMMM...
NOW IS THE TIME.
!!
scribble Scribble
STAY STILL!!

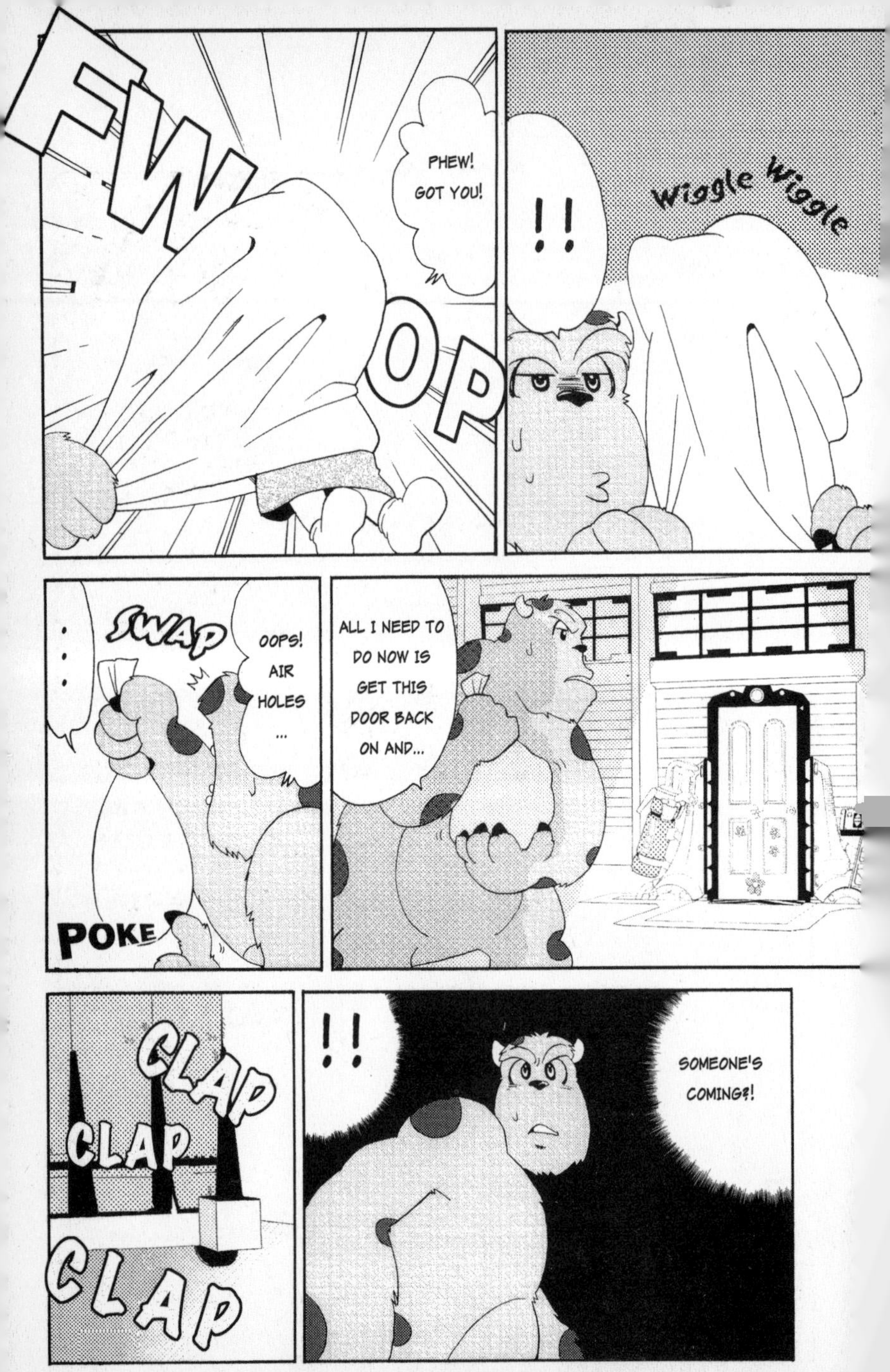
FWOP
PHEW! GOT YOU!
!!
Wiggle Wiggle
...
SWAP
OOPS! AIR HOLES ...
POKE
ALL I NEED TO DO NOW IS GET THIS DOOR BACK ON AND...
CLAP
CLAP
CLAP
!!
SOMEONE'S COMING?!

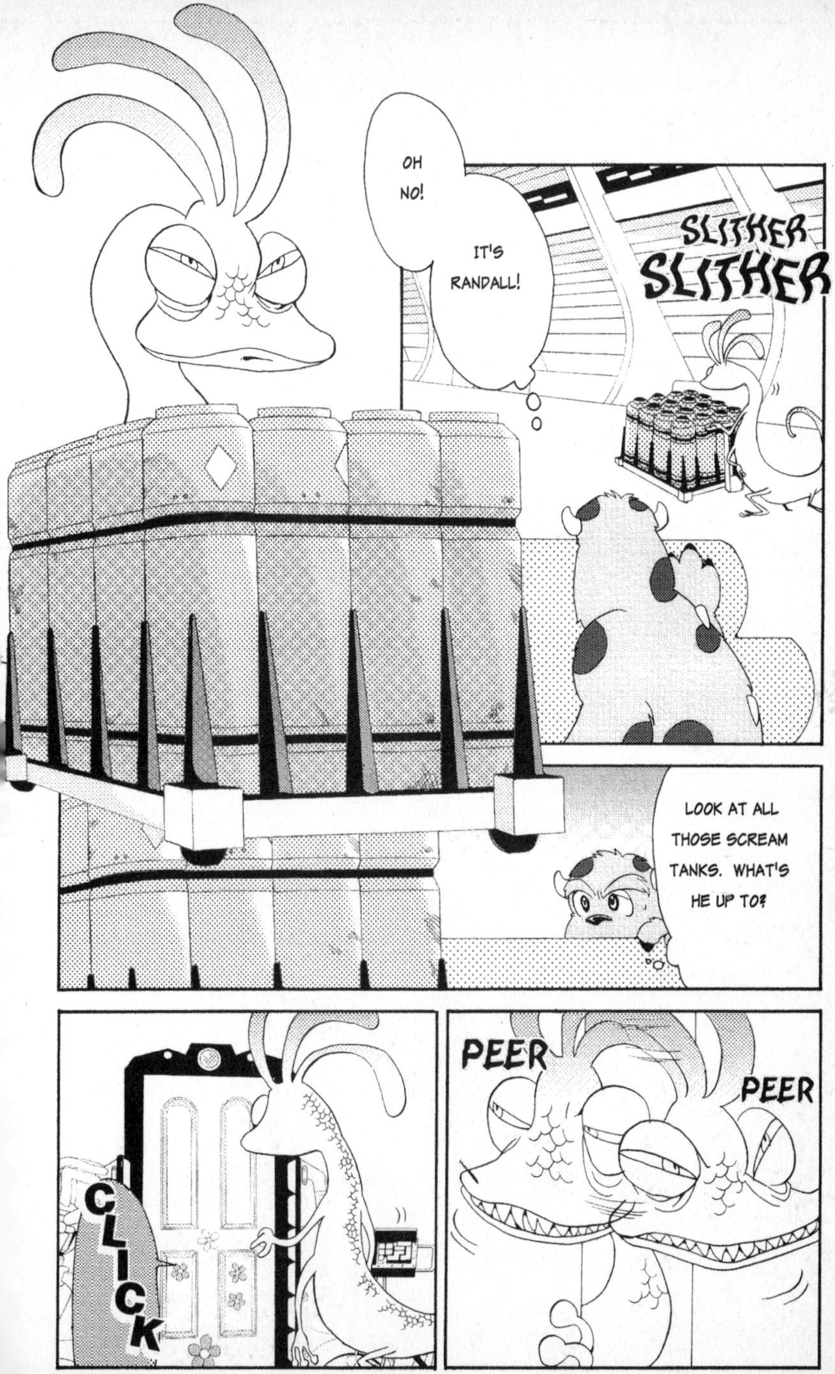
OH NO!
IT'S RANDALL!
SLITHER SLITHER
LOOK AT ALL THOSE SCREAM TANKS. WHAT'S HE UP TO?
CLICK
PEER
PEER

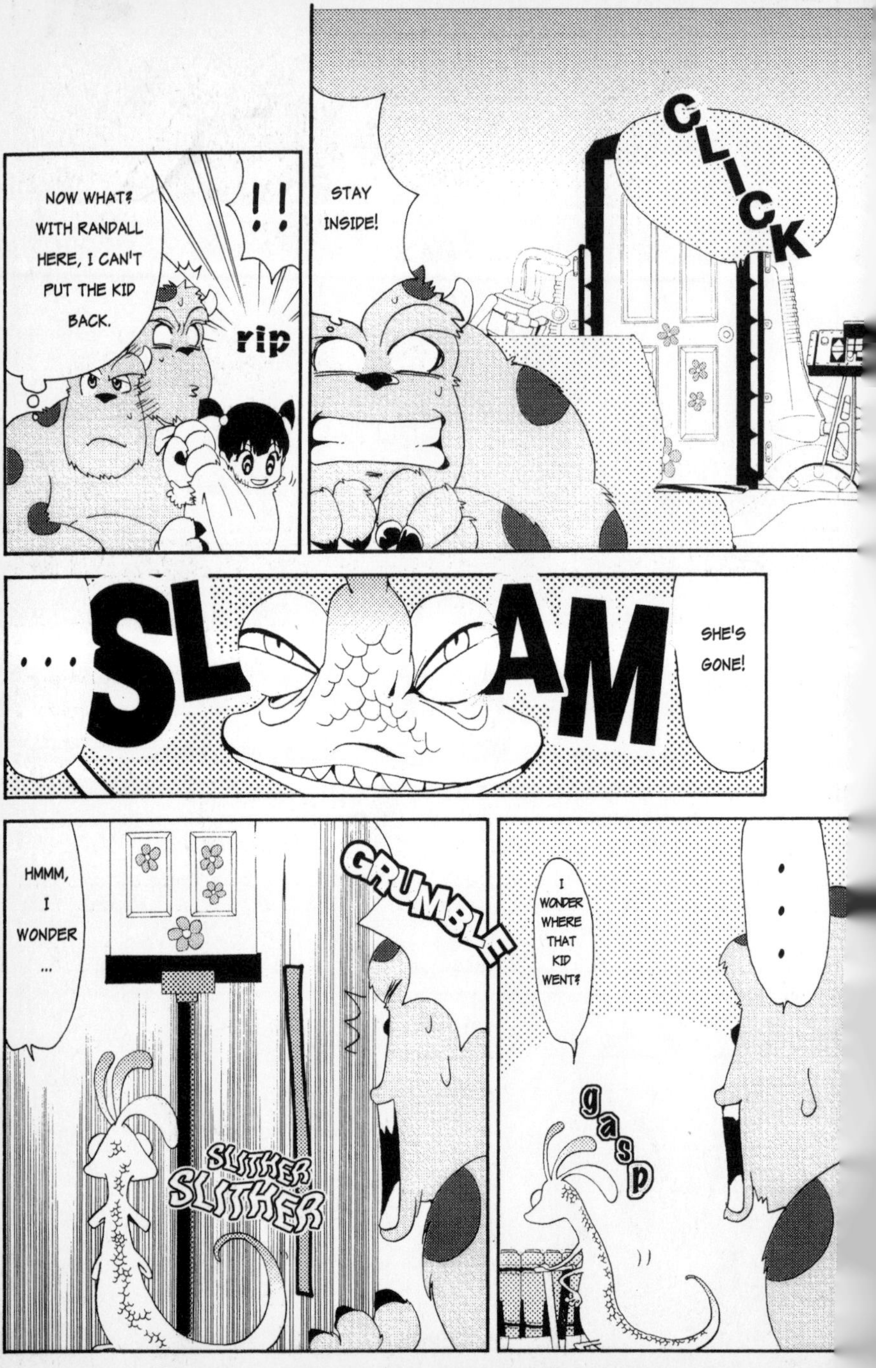
CLICK
STAY INSIDE!
!!
NOW WHAT? WITH RANDALL HERE, I CAN'T PUT THE KID BACK.
rip
SHE'S GONE!
SLAM
...
...
I WONDER WHERE THAT KID WENT?
gasp
GRUMBLE
HMMM, I WONDER ...
SLITHER SLITHER

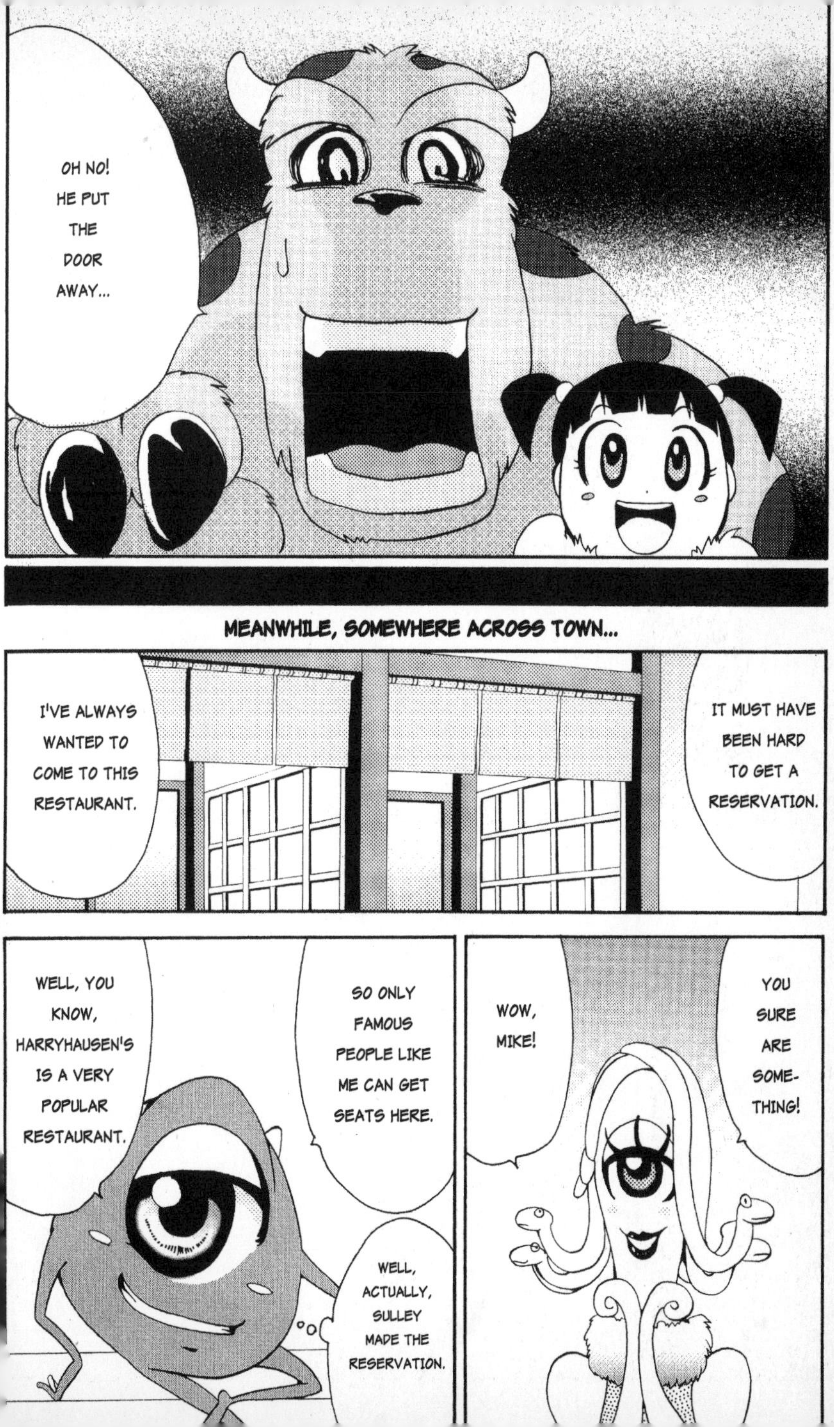
OH NO! HE PUT THE DOOR AWAY...
MEANWHILE, SOMEWHERE ACROSS TOWN...
I'VE ALWAYS WANTED TO COME TO THIS RESTAURANT.
IT MUST HAVE BEEN HARD TO GET A RESERVATION.
WELL, YOU KNOW, HARRYHAUSEN'S IS A VERY POPULAR RESTAURANT.
SO ONLY FAMOUS PEOPLE LIKE ME CAN GET SEATS HERE.
WELL, ACTUALLY, SULLEY MADE THE RESERVATION.
WOW, MIKE!
YOU SURE ARE SOME-THING!

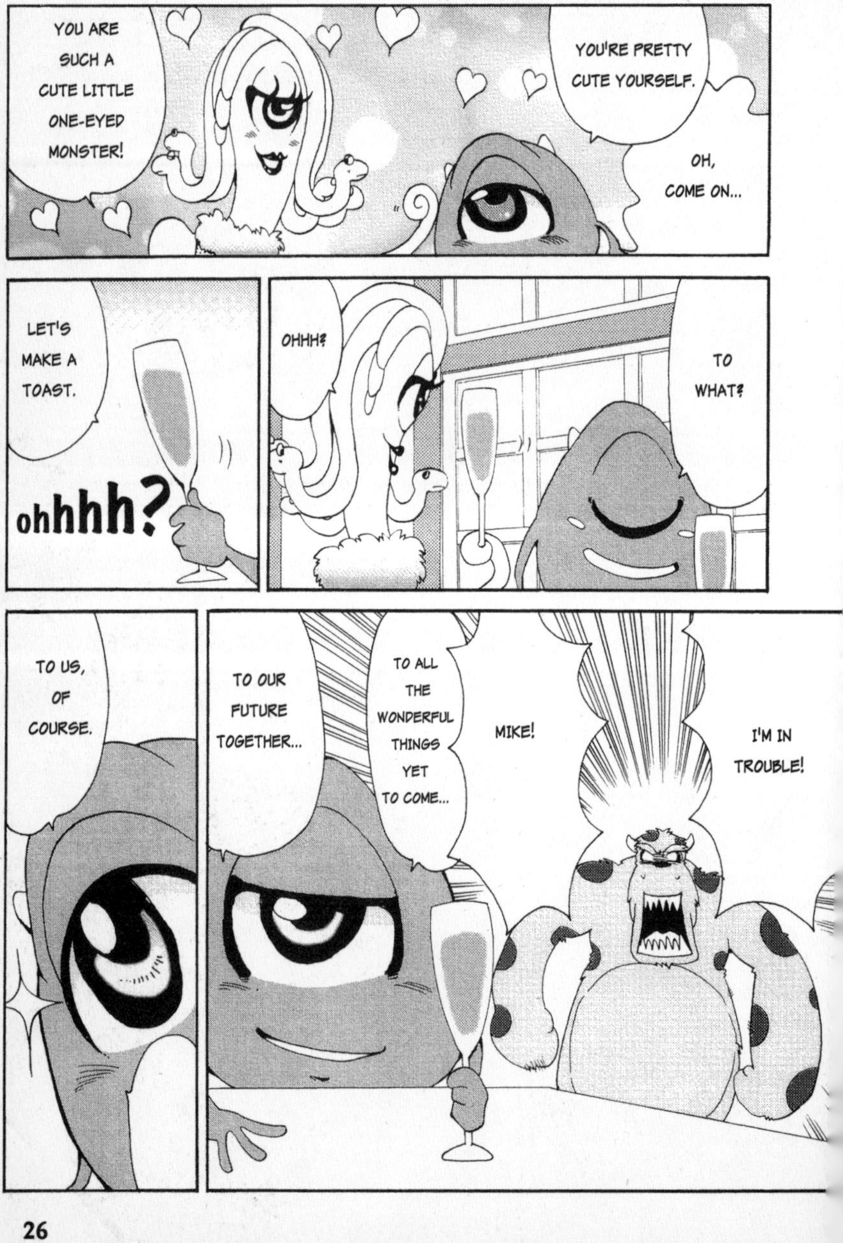
YOU ARE SUCH A CUTE LITTLE ONE-EYED MONSTER!
YOU'RE PRETTY CUTE YOURSELF.
OH, COME ON...
LET'S MAKE A TOAST.
ohhhh?
OHHH?
TO WHAT?
TO US, OF COURSE.
TO OUR FUTURE TOGETHER...
TO ALL THE WONDERFUL THINGS YET TO COME...
MIKE!
I'M IN TROUBLE!

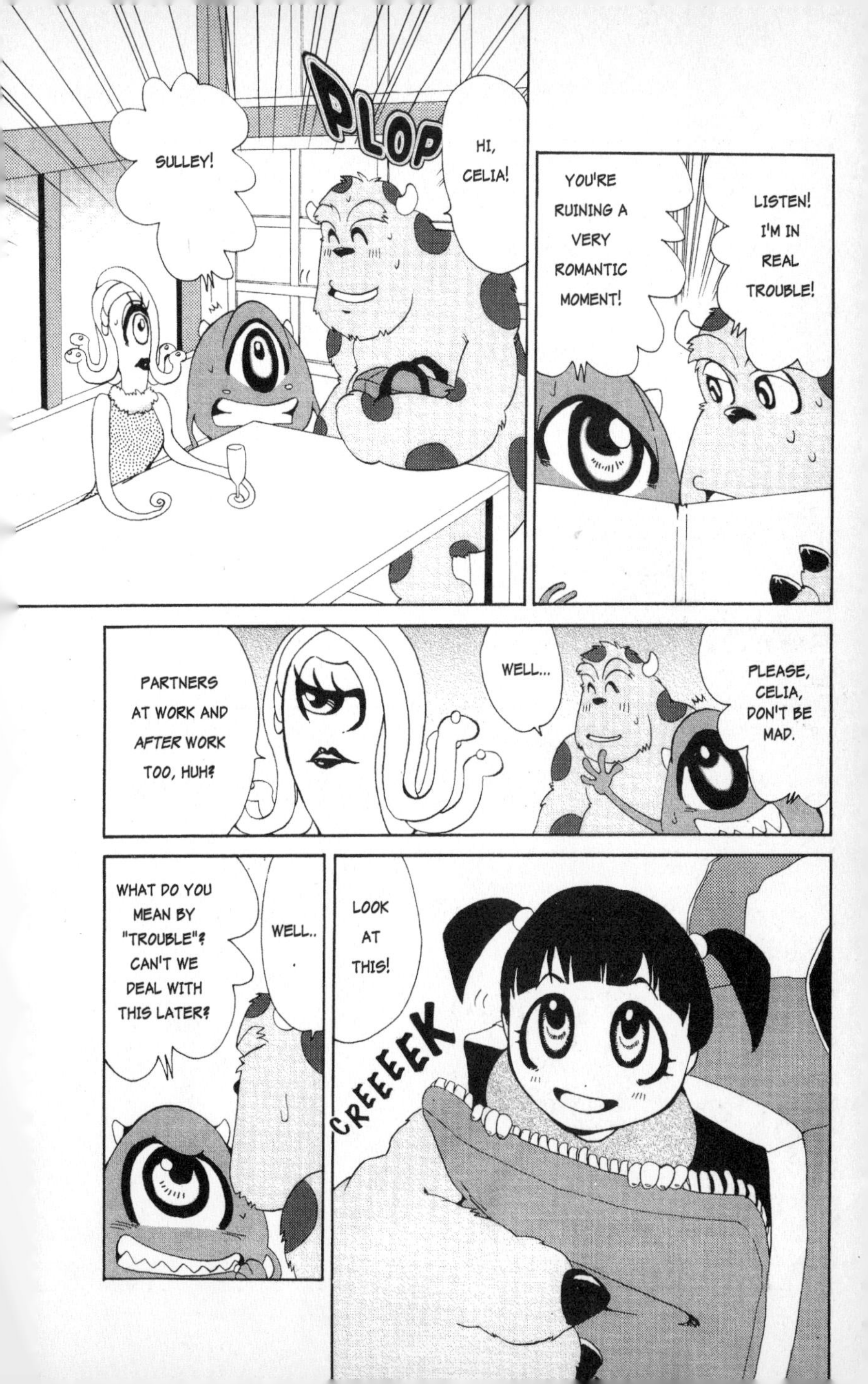
PLOP
SULLEY!
HI, CELIA!
YOU'RE RUINING A VERY ROMANTIC MOMENT!
LISTEN! I'M IN REAL TROUBLE!
PARTNERS AT WORK AND AFTER WORK TOO, HUH?
WELL...
PLEASE, CELIA, DON'T BE MAD.
WHAT DO YOU MEAN BY "TROUBLE"? CAN'T WE DEAL WITH THIS LATER?
WELL...
LOOK AT THIS!
CREEEEK

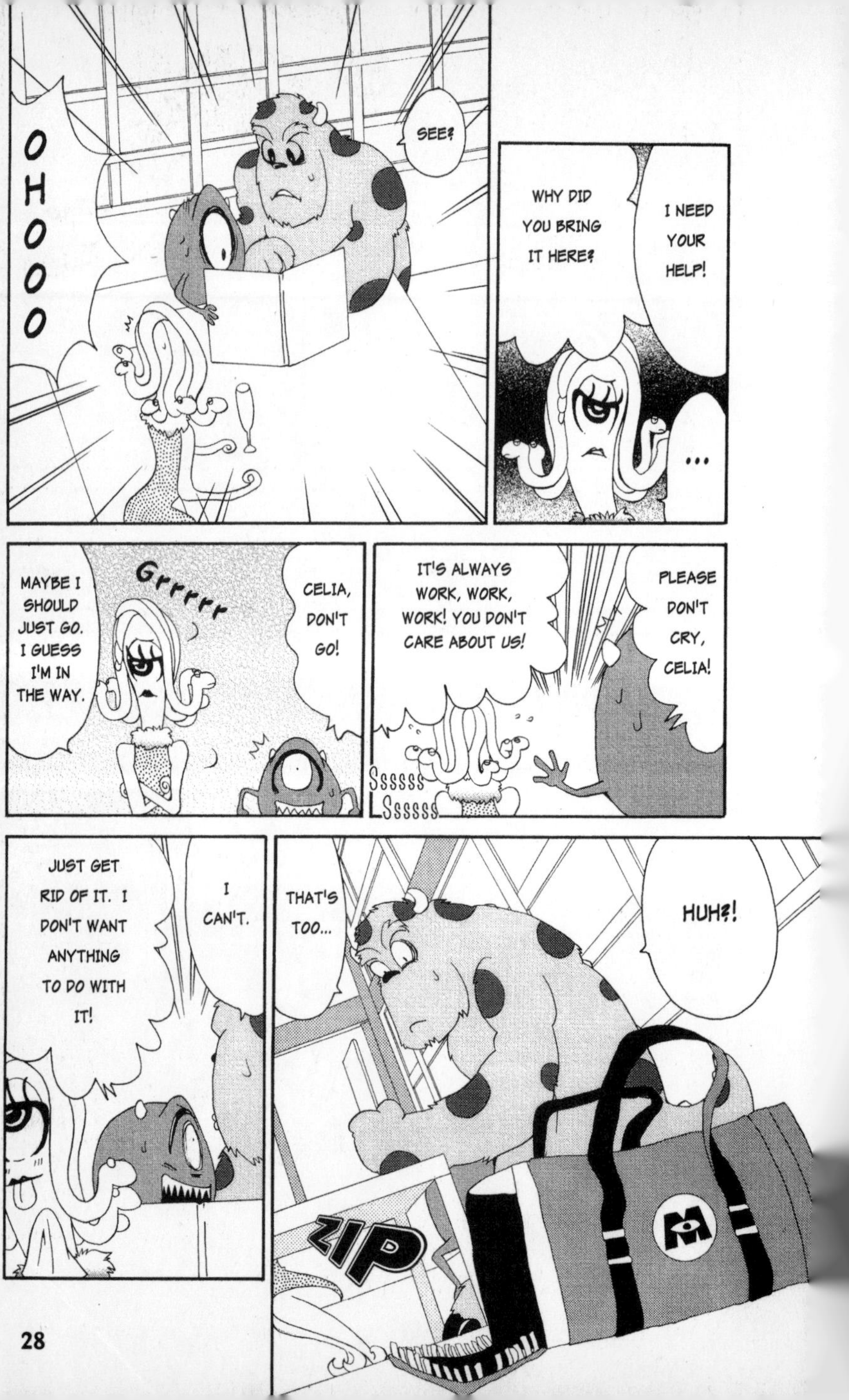
OHOOO
SEE?
WHY DID YOU BRING IT HERE?
I NEED YOUR HELP!
...
MAYBE I SHOULD JUST GO. I GUESS I'M IN THE WAY.
Grrrrr
CELIA, DON'T GO!
IT'S ALWAYS WORK, WORK, WORK! YOU DON'T CARE ABOUT US!
PLEASE DON'T CRY, CELIA!
Ssssss Ssssss
JUST GET RID OF IT. I DON'T WANT ANYTHING TO DO WITH IT!
I CAN'T.
THAT'S TOO...
HUH?!
ZIP

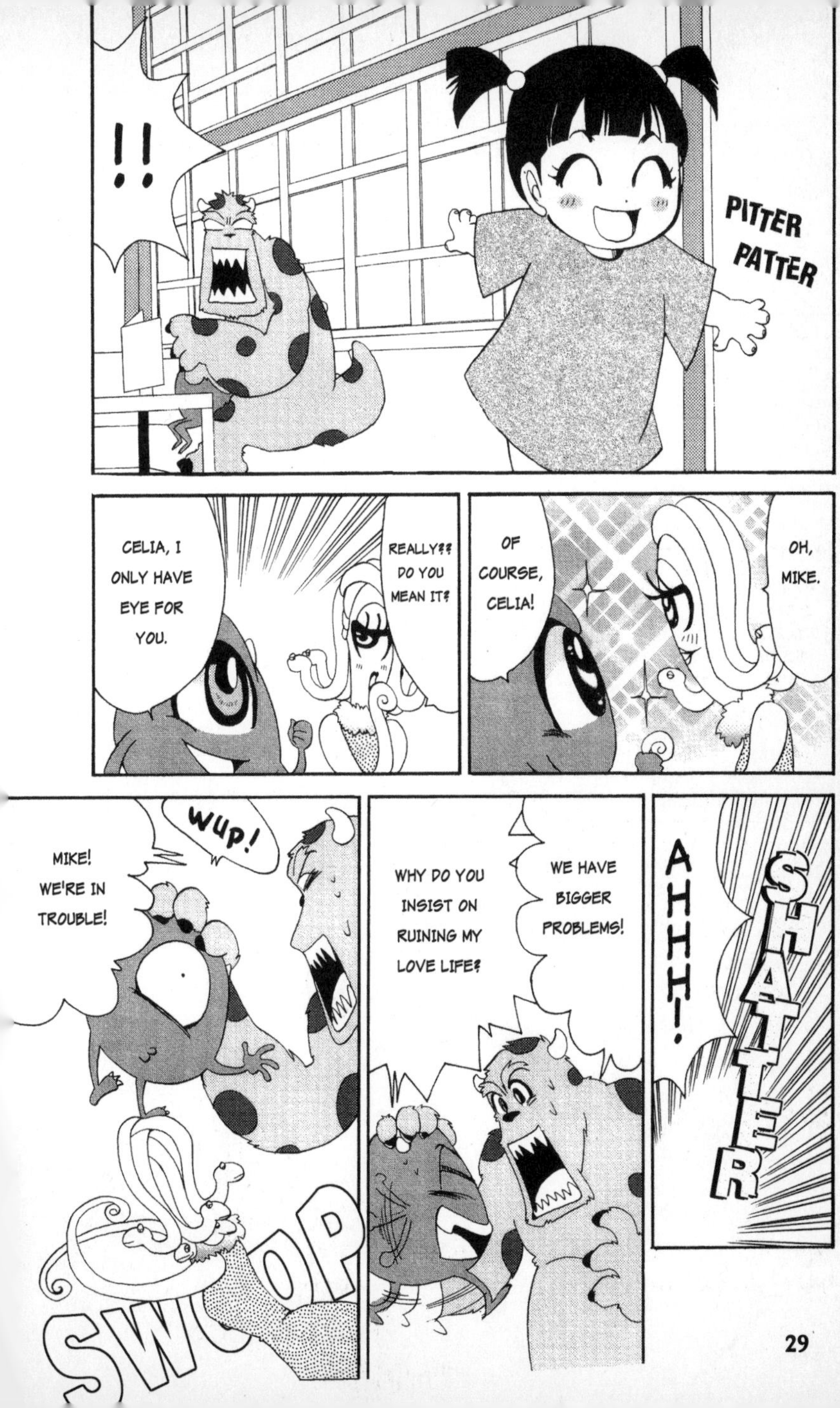
!!
PITTER PATTER
CELIA, I ONLY HAVE EYE FOR YOU.
REALLY?? DO YOU MEAN IT?
OF COURSE, CELIA!
OH, MIKE.
MIKE! WE'RE IN TROUBLE!
wup!
SWOOP
WHY DO YOU INSIST ON RUINING MY LOVE LIFE?
WE HAVE BIGGER PROBLEMS!
AHHH!
SHATTER

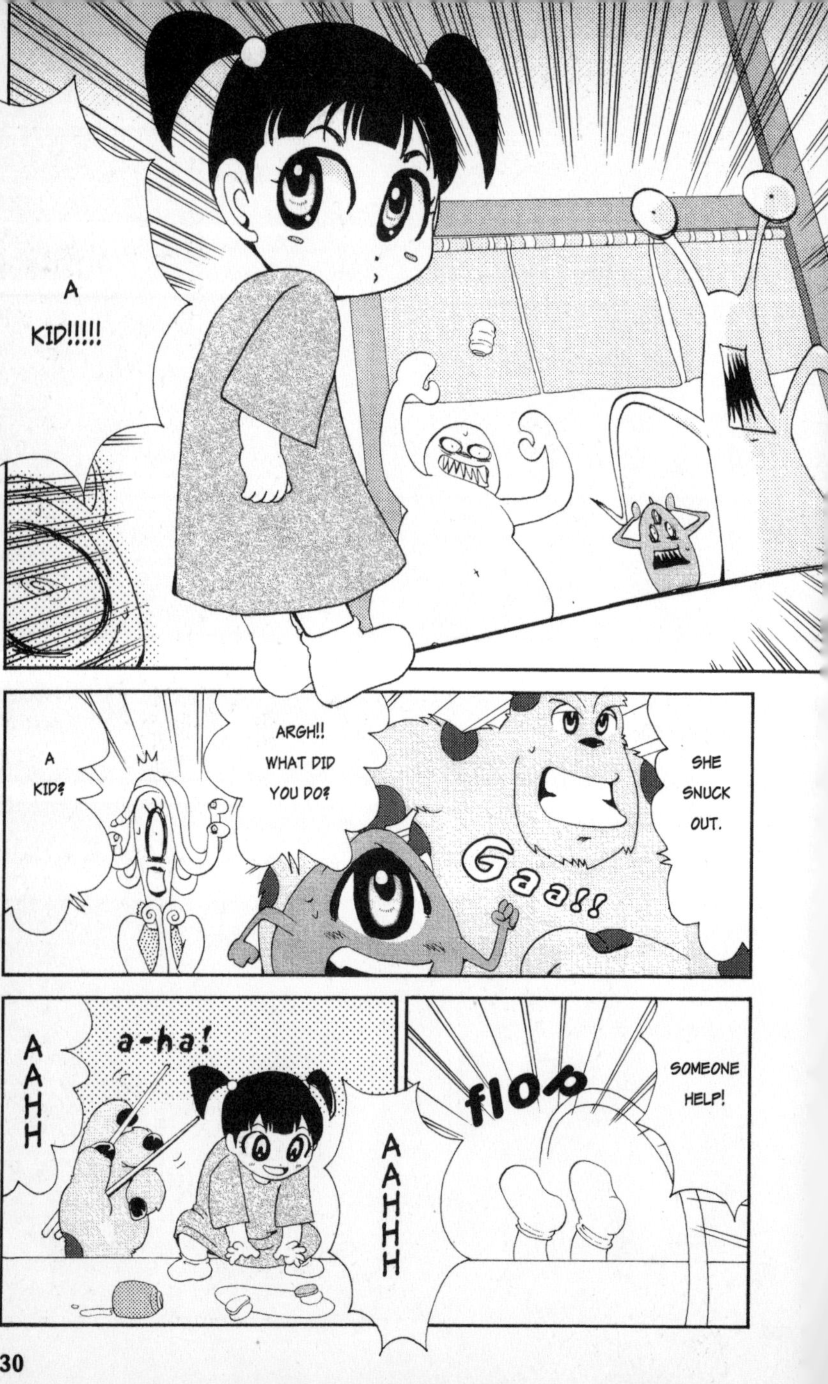
A KID!!!!!
A KID?
ARGH!! WHAT DID YOU DO?
SHE SNUCK OUT.
Gaa!!
AAHH
a-ha!
AAHHH
flop
SOMEONE HELP!

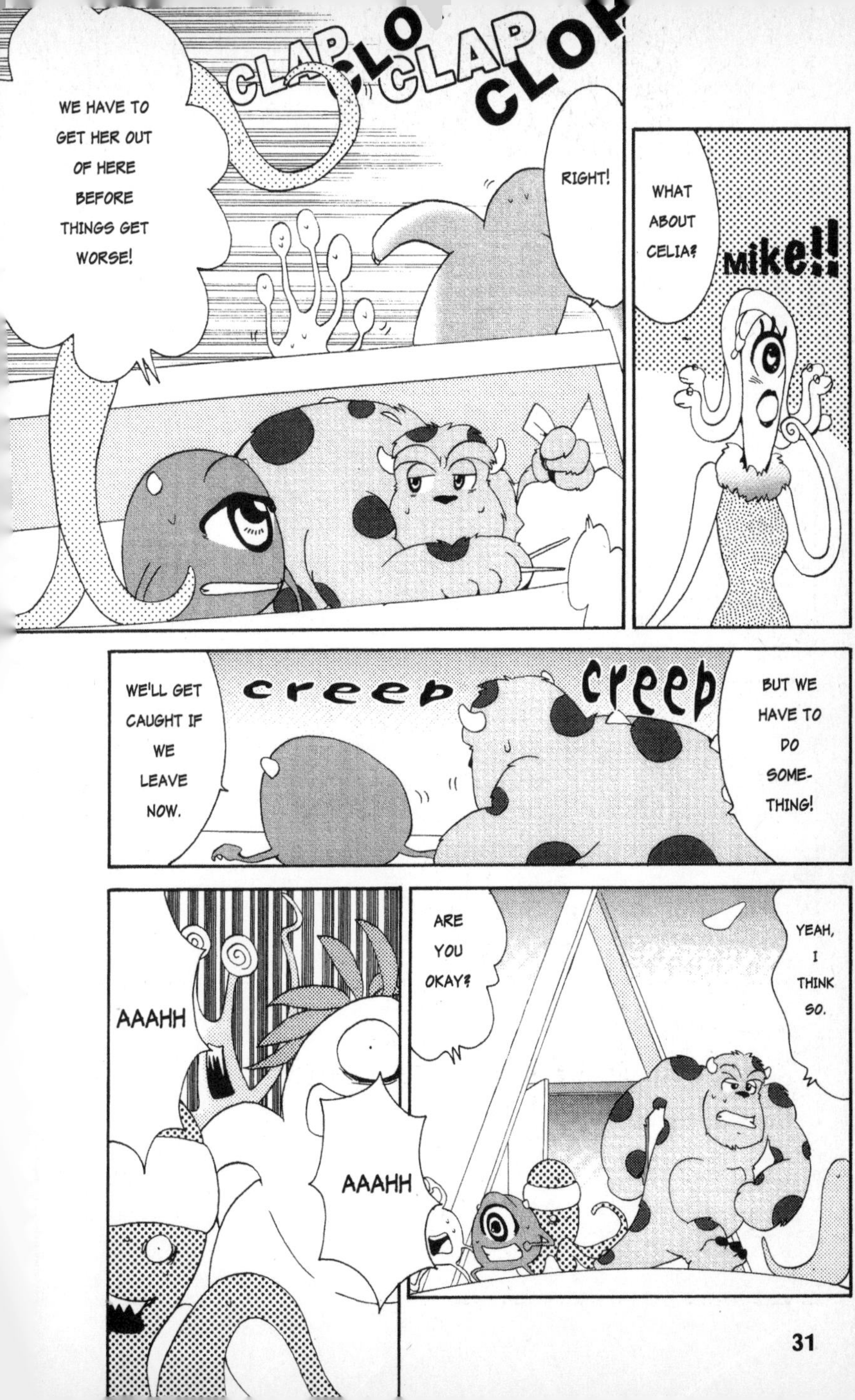
CLAP CLOP CLAP CLOP
WE HAVE TO GET HER OUT OF HERE BEFORE THINGS GET WORSE!
RIGHT!
WHAT ABOUT CELIA?
MIKE!!
WE'LL GET CAUGHT IF WE LEAVE NOW.
creep creep
BUT WE HAVE TO DO SOME-THING!
AAAHH
AAAHH
ARE YOU OKAY?
YEAH, I THINK SO.

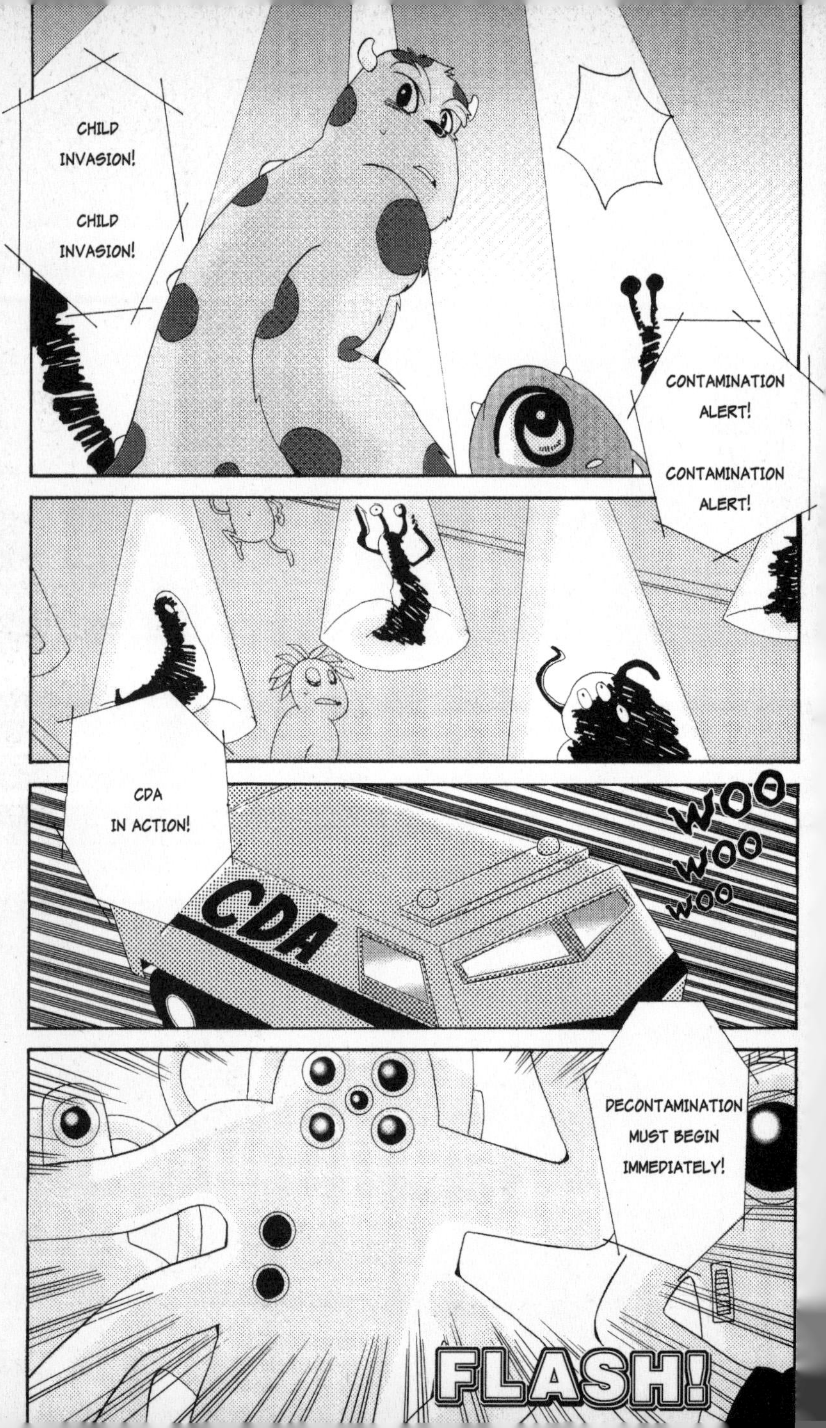
CHILD INVASION!
CHILD INVASION!
CONTAMINATION ALERT!
CONTAMINATION ALERT!
CDA IN ACTION!
CDA
WOO WOO WOO
DECONTAMINATION MUST BEGIN IMMEDIATELY!
FLASH!

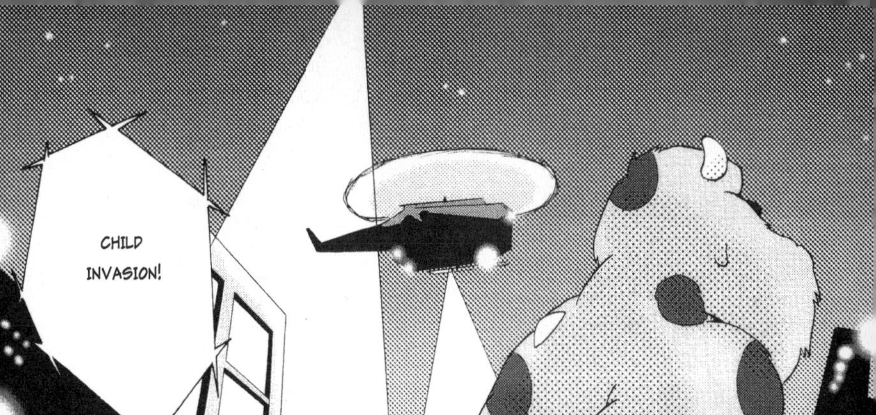
CHILD INVASION!

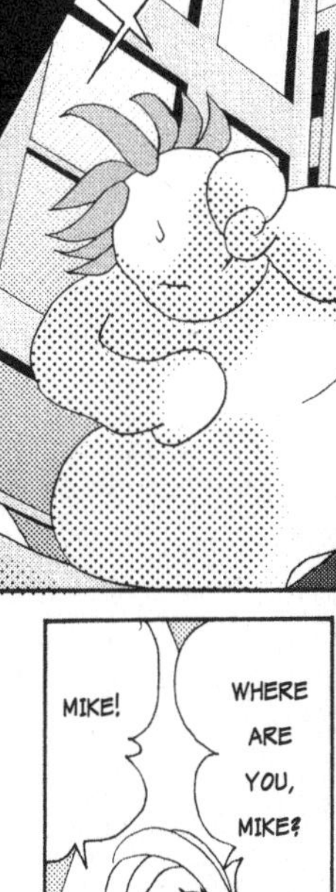
MIKE!
WHERE ARE YOU, MIKE?
Uh-oh!!

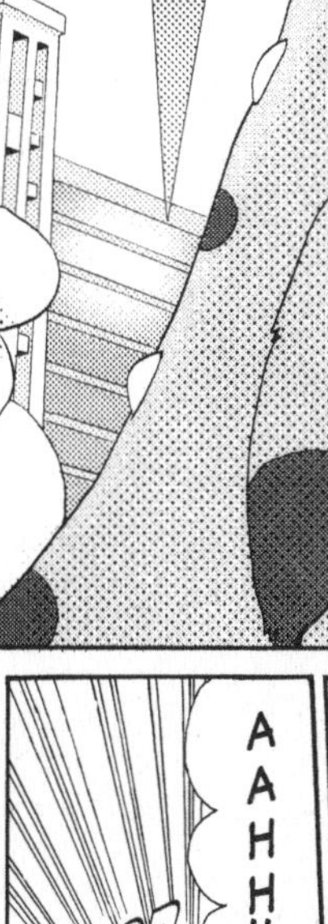
GASP
AAHH!!
CDA
A

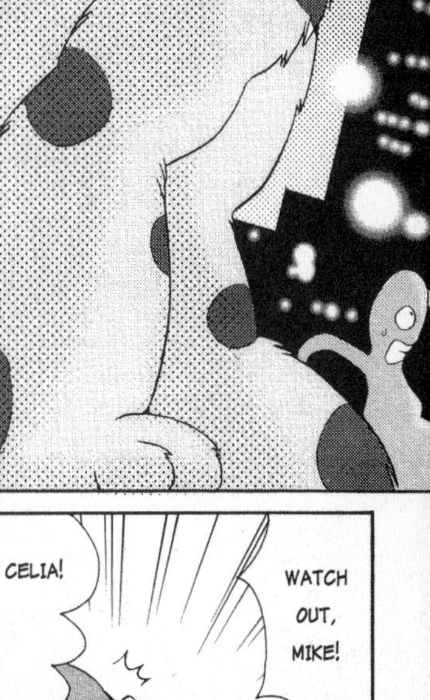
CELIA!
WATCH OUT, MIKE!

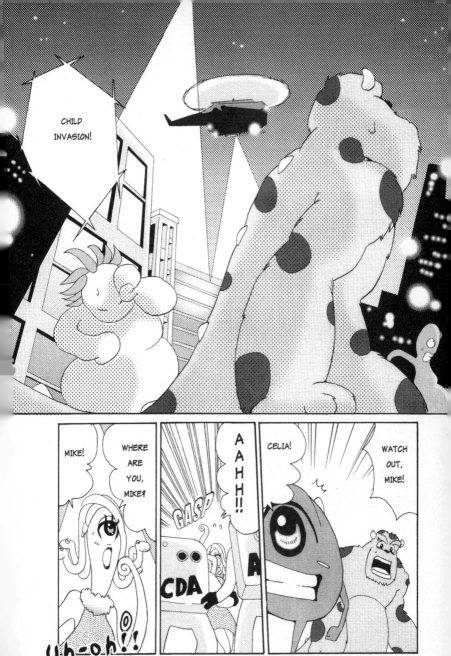

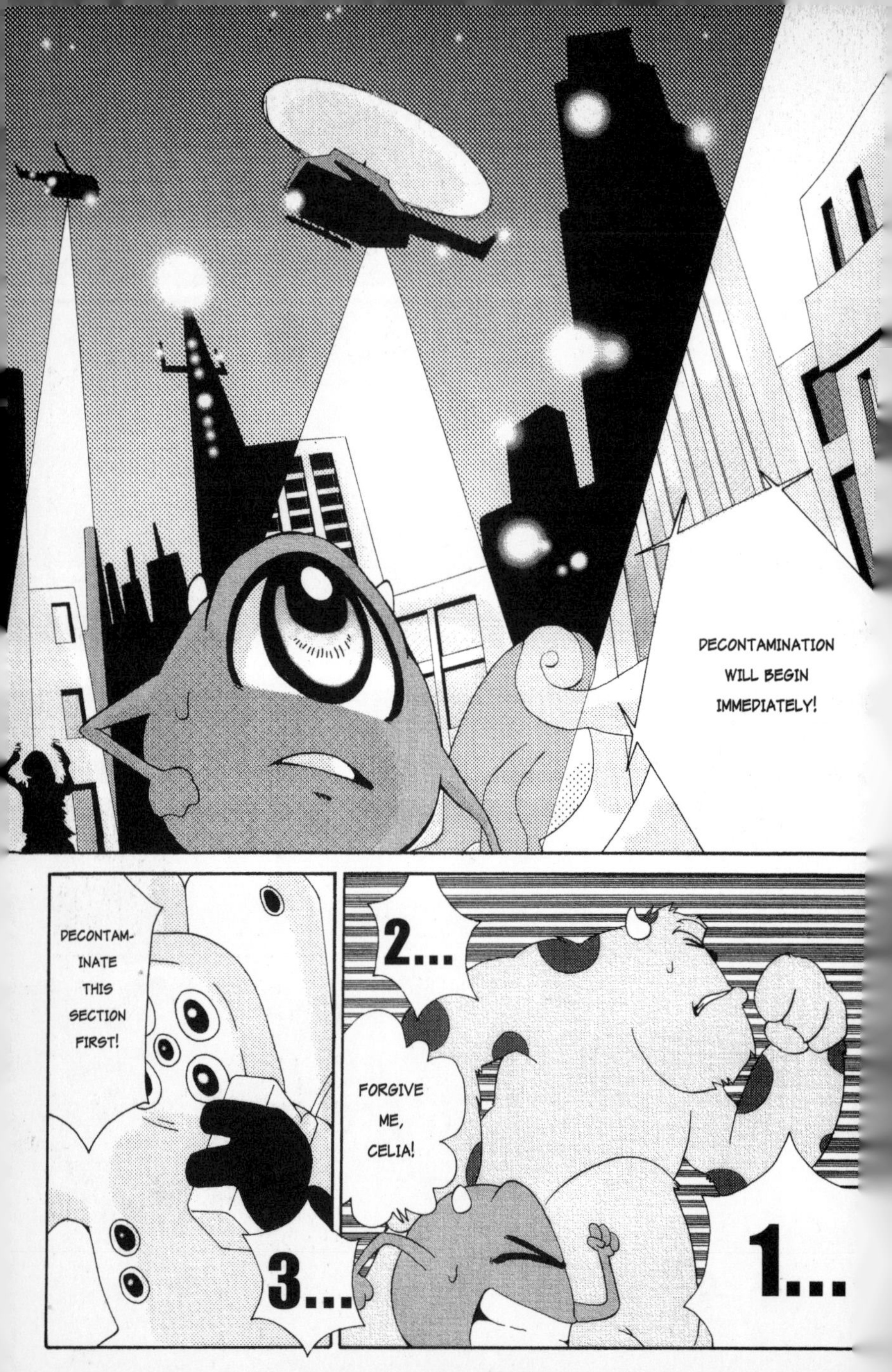
DECONTAMINATION WILL BEGIN IMMEDIATELY!
DECONTAMINATE THIS SECTION FIRST!
3...
2...
FORGIVE ME, CELIA!
1...

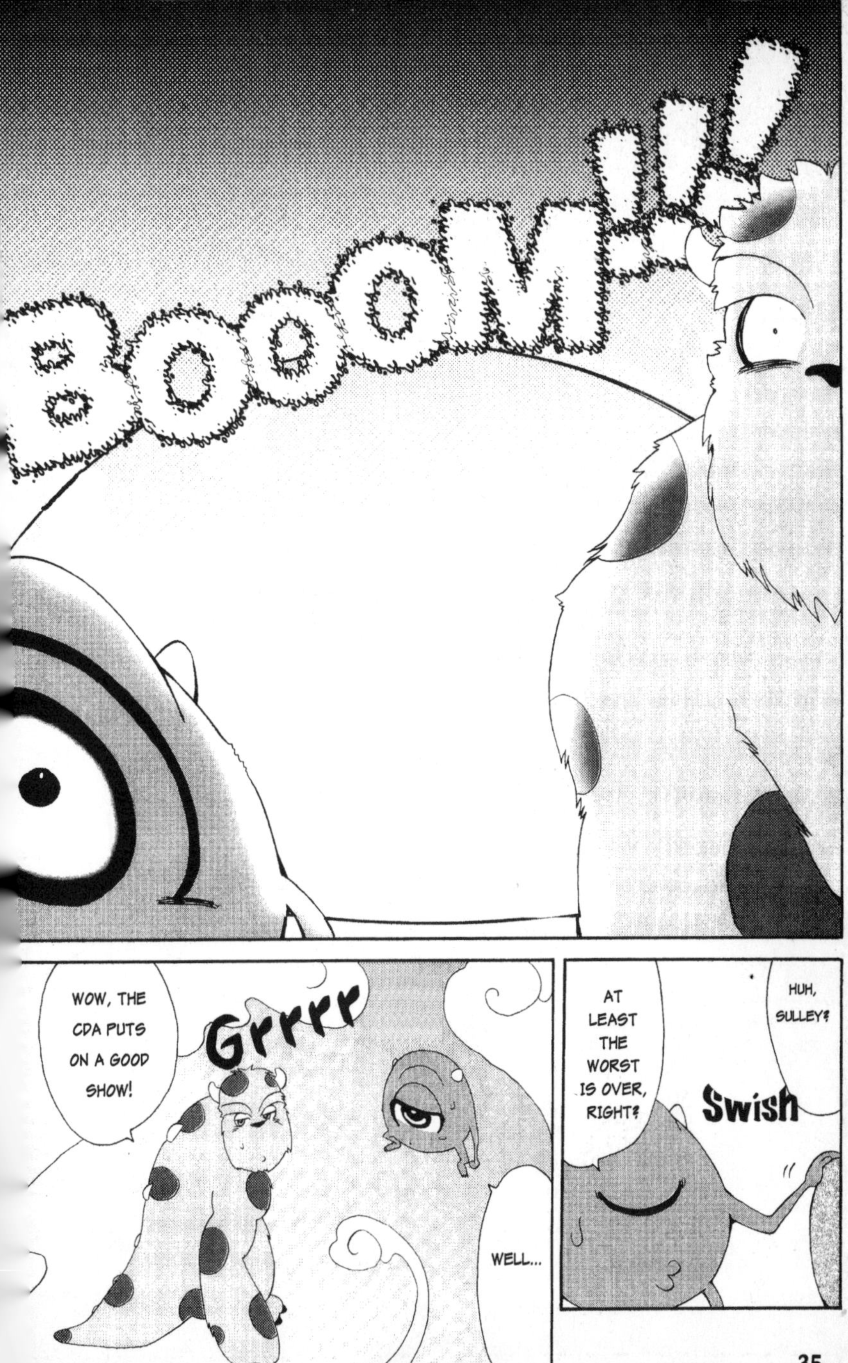
BOOOOOM!!!!
WOW, THE CDA PUTS ON A GOOD SHOW!
Grrrr
WELL...
AT LEAST THE WORST IS OVER, RIGHT?
HUH, SULLEY?
Swish

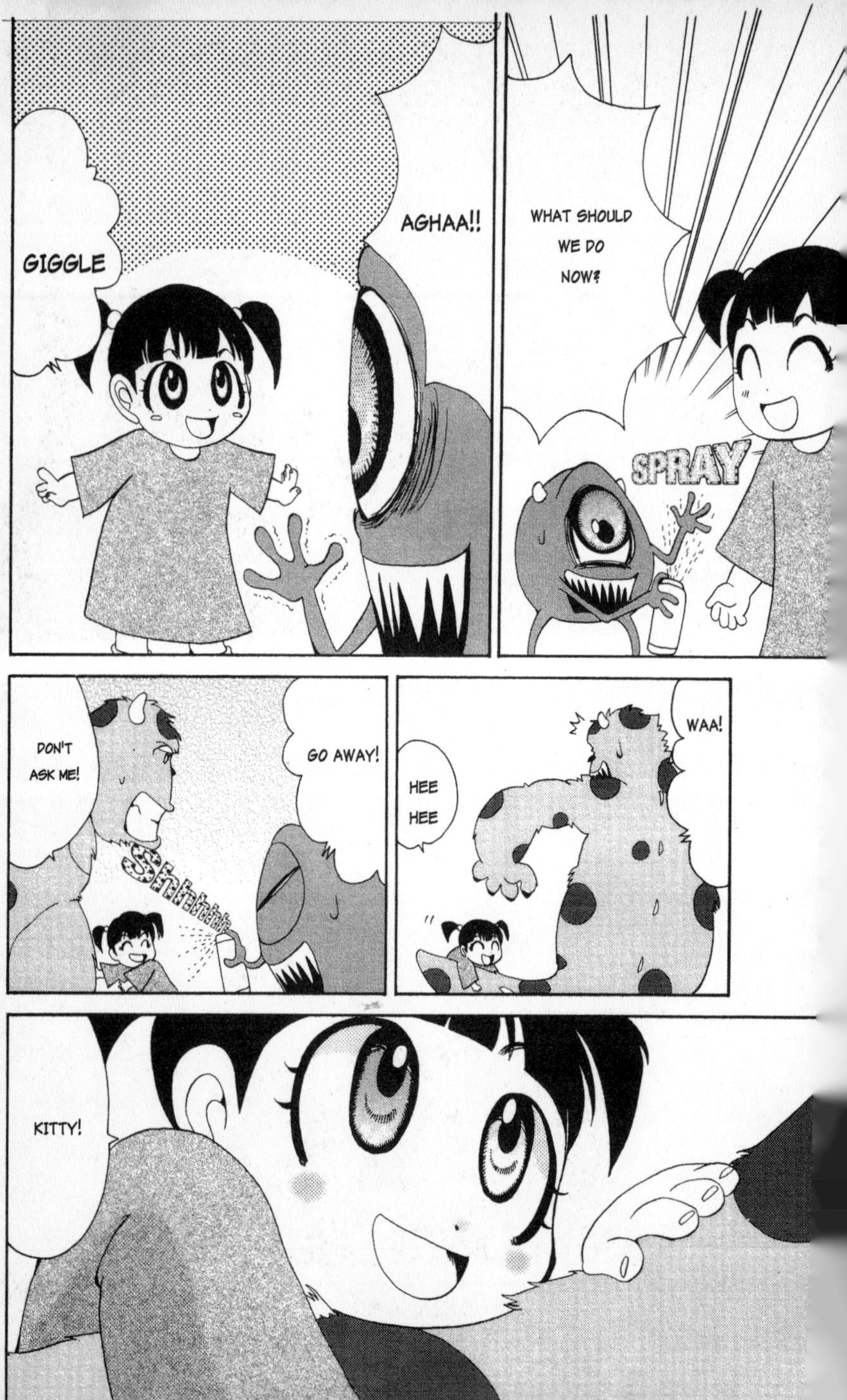
GIGGLE
AGHAA!!
WHAT SHOULD WE DO NOW?
SPRAY
DON'T ASK ME!
GO AWAY!
HEE HEE
WAA!
KITTY!

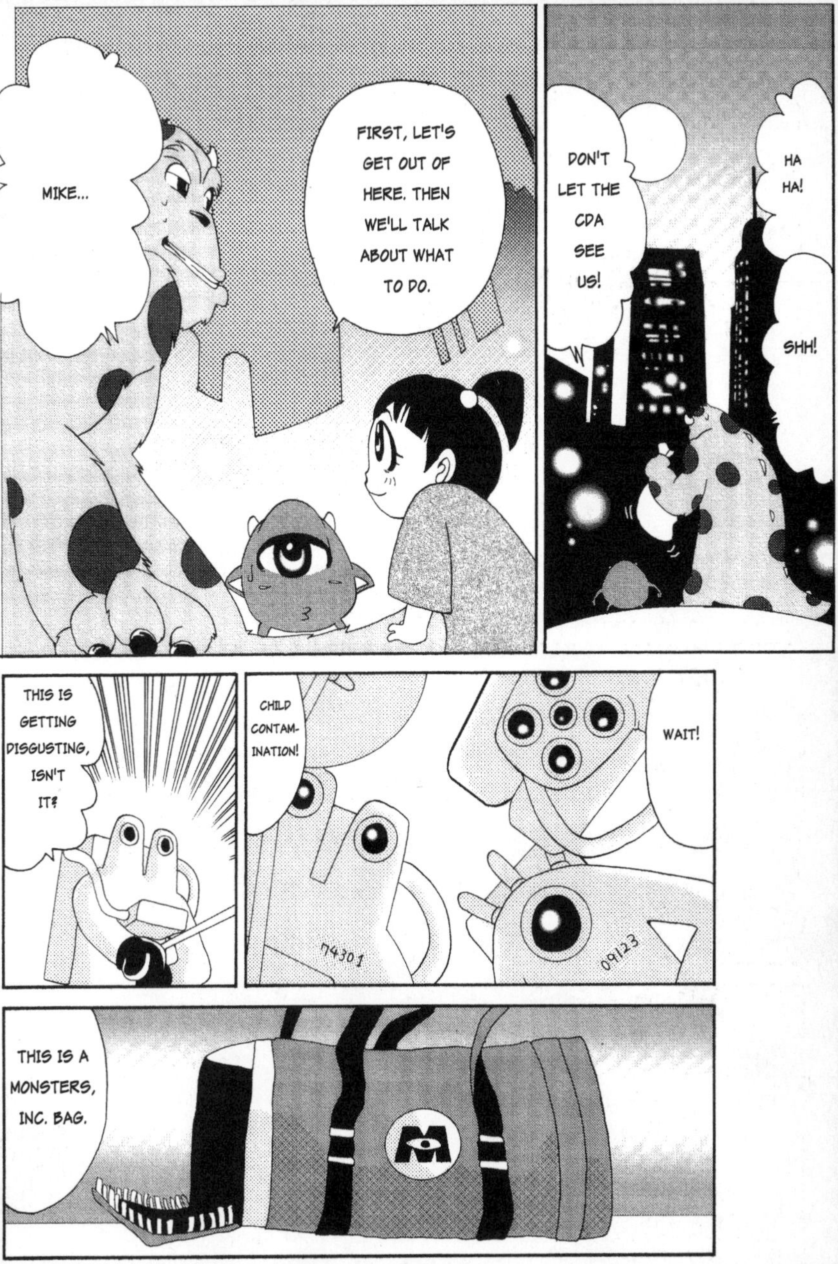
MIKE...
FIRST, LET'S GET OUT OF HERE. THEN WE'LL TALK ABOUT WHAT TO DO.
DON'T LET THE CDA SEE US!
HA HA!
SHH!
THIS IS GETTING DISGUSTING, ISN'T IT?
CHILD CONTAM-INATION!
WAIT!
74301
09123
THIS IS A MONSTERS, INC. BAG.

TO BE CONTINUED...

BOO MEETS WORLD

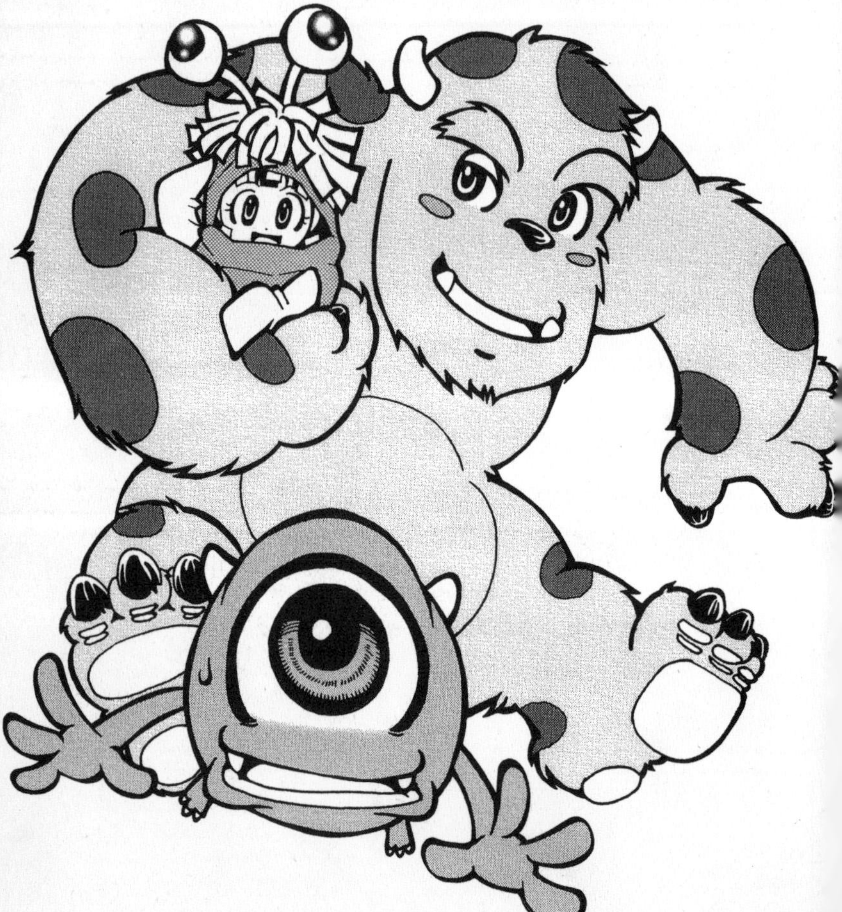

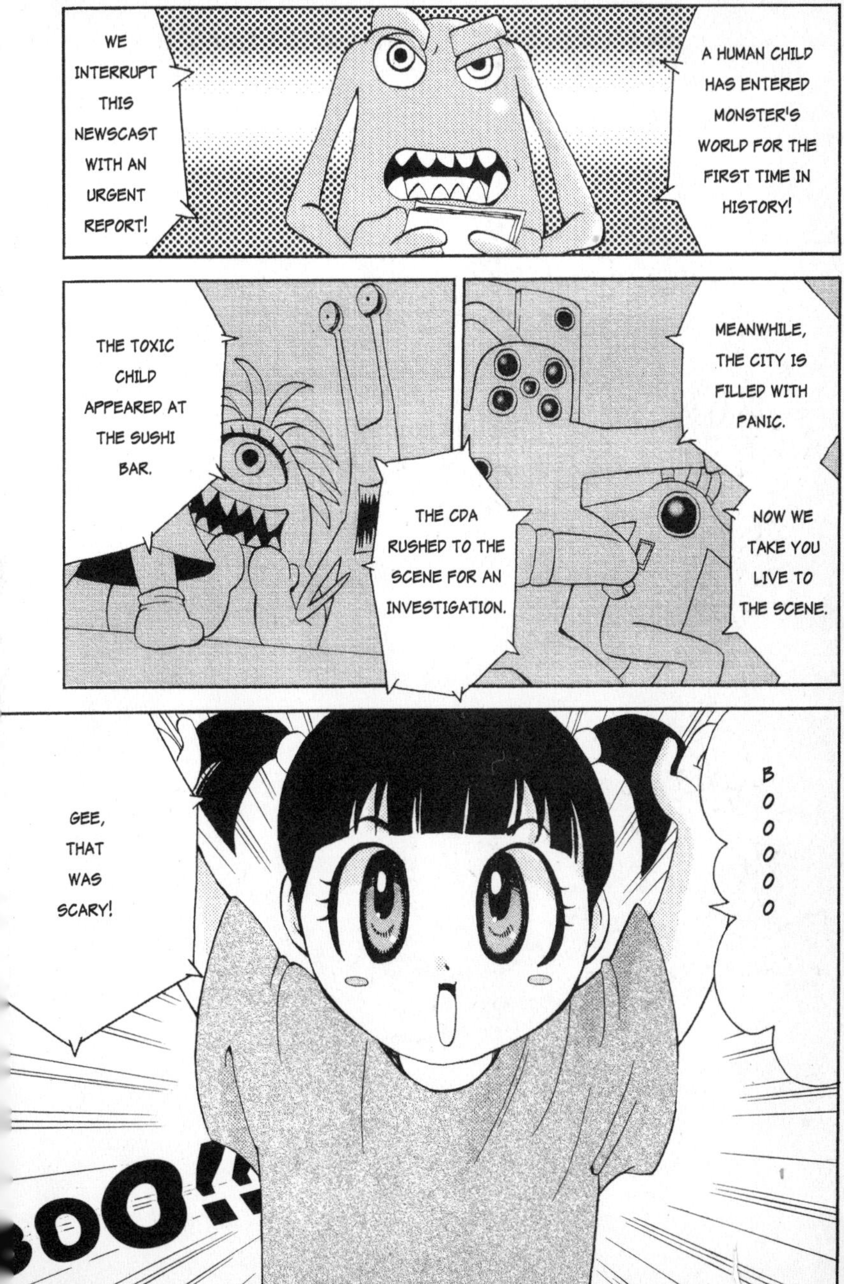
WE INTERRUPT THIS NEWSCAST WITH AN URGENT REPORT!
A HUMAN CHILD HAS ENTERED MONSTER'S WORLD FOR THE FIRST TIME IN HISTORY!
THE TOXIC CHILD APPEARED AT THE SUSHI BAR.
THE CDA RUSHED TO THE SCENE FOR AN INVESTIGATION.
MEANWHILE, THE CITY IS FILLED WITH PANIC.
NOW WE TAKE YOU LIVE TO THE SCENE.
GEE, THAT WAS SCARY!
BOOOOOO
BOO!!

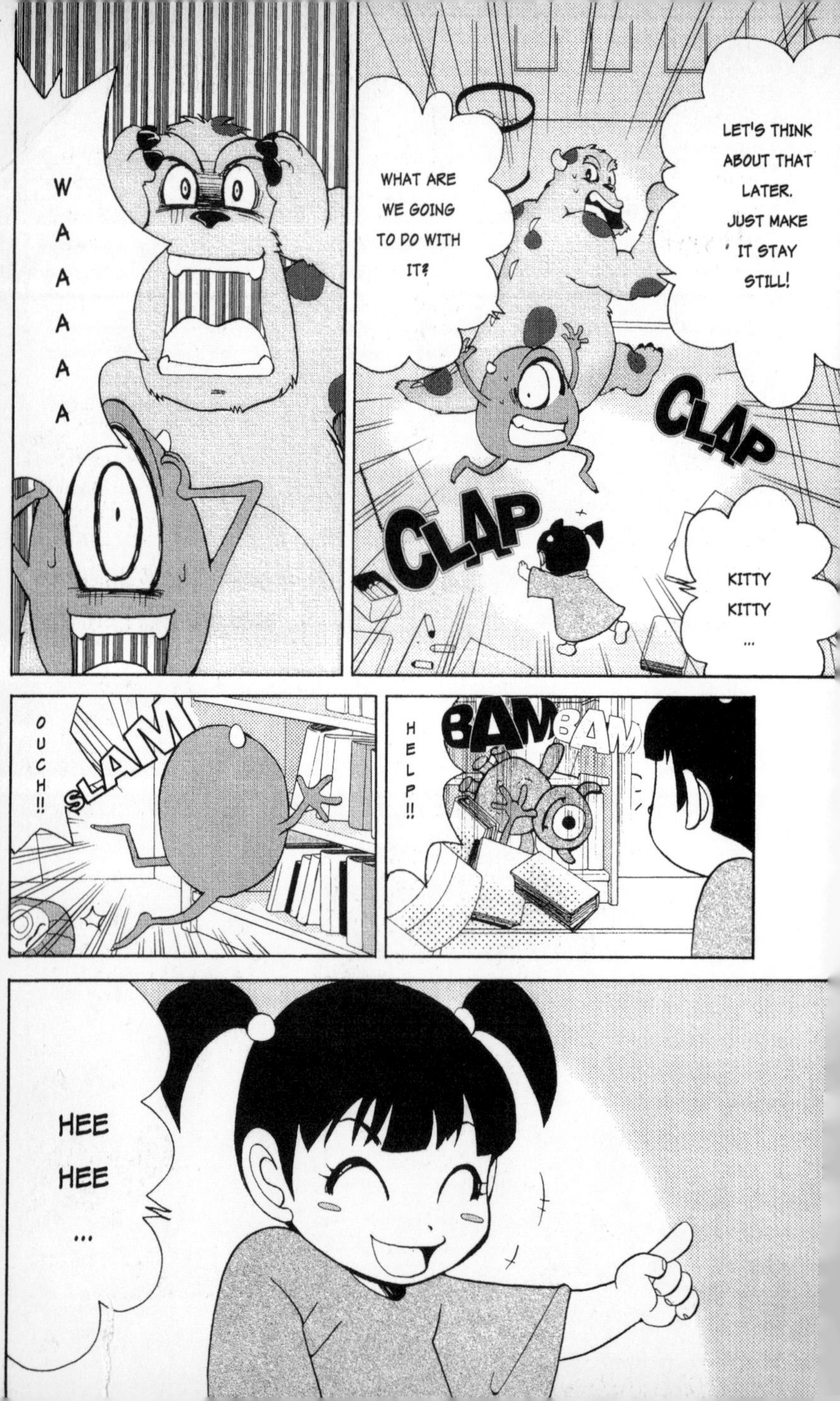
WAAAAAA
WHAT ARE WE GOING TO DO WITH IT?
LET'S THINK ABOUT THAT LATER. JUST MAKE IT STAY STILL!
CLAP
CLAP
KITTY KITTY ...
OUCH!!
SLAM
HELP!!
BAM
BAM
HEE HEE ...

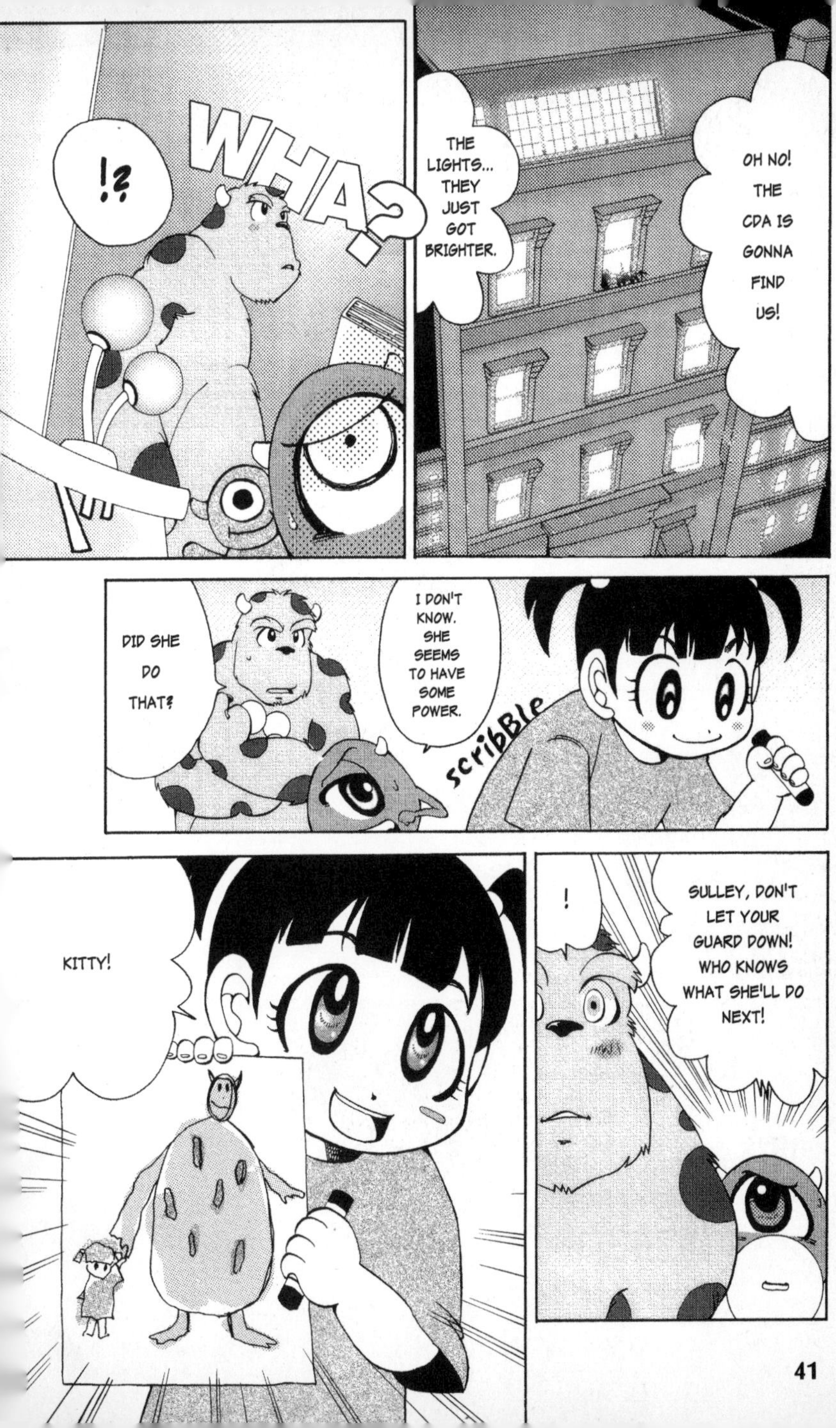
!?
WHA?
THE LIGHTS... THEY JUST GOT BRIGHTER.
OH NO! THE CDA IS GONNA FIND US!
DID SHE DO THAT?
I DON'T KNOW. SHE SEEMS TO HAVE SOME POWER.
scribble
KITTY!
!
SULLEY, DON'T LET YOUR GUARD DOWN! WHO KNOWS WHAT SHE'LL DO NEXT!

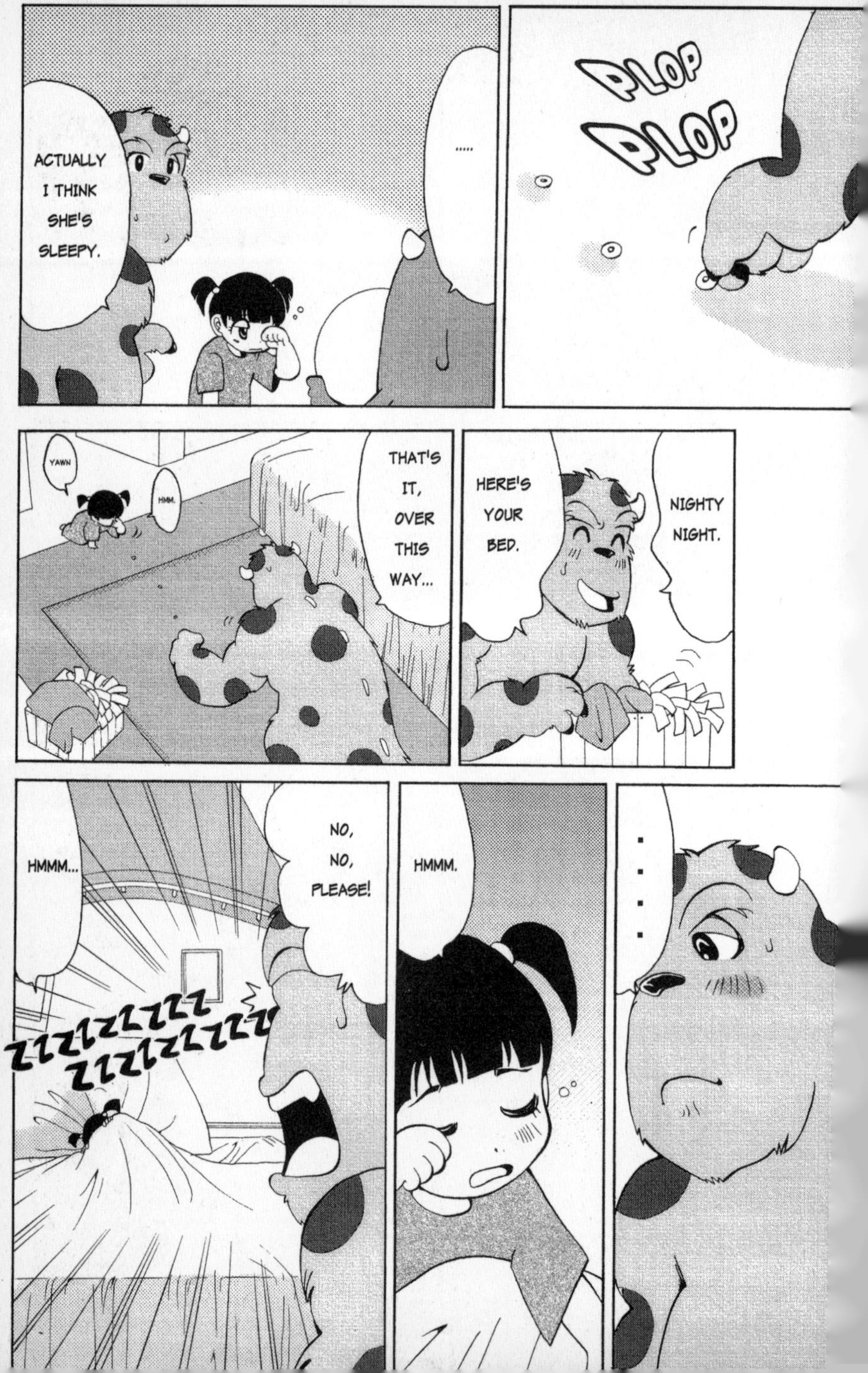
ACTUALLY I THINK SHE'S SLEEPY.
.....
PLOP
PLOP
YAWN
HMM.
THAT'S IT, OVER THIS WAY...
HERE'S YOUR BED.
NIGHTY NIGHT.
HMMM...
ZZZZZZZZZ
ZZZZZZZZZZ
NO, NO, PLEASE!
HMMM.
....

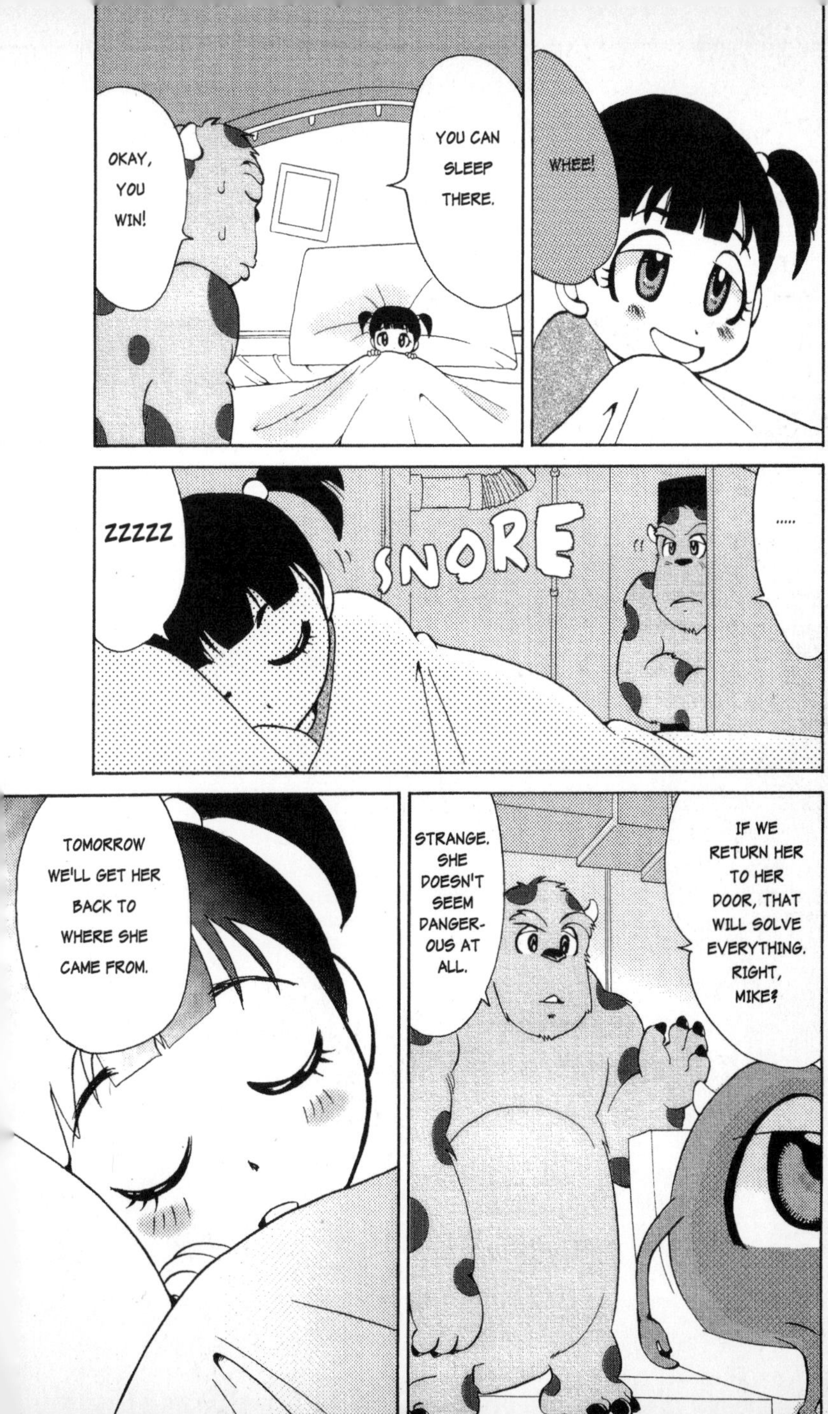
OKAY, YOU WIN!
YOU CAN SLEEP THERE.
WHEE!
ZZZZZ
SNORE
.....
TOMORROW WE'LL GET HER BACK TO WHERE SHE CAME FROM.
STRANGE. SHE DOESN'T SEEM DANGER-OUS AT ALL.
IF WE RETURN HER TO HER DOOR, THAT WILL SOLVE EVERYTHING. RIGHT, MIKE?

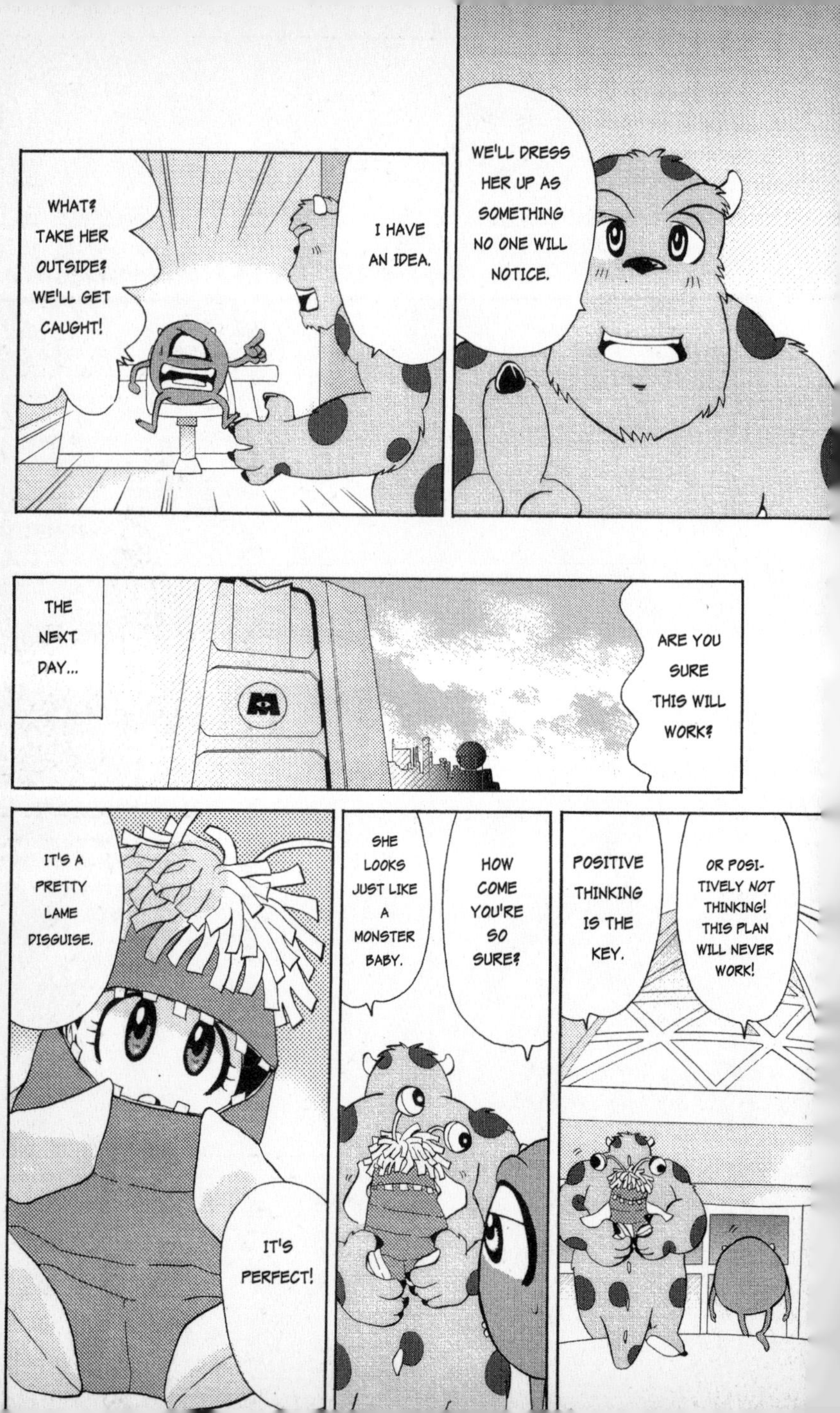
WHAT? TAKE HER OUTSIDE? WE'LL GET CAUGHT!
I HAVE AN IDEA.
WE'LL DRESS HER UP AS SOMETHING NO ONE WILL NOTICE.
THE NEXT DAY...
ARE YOU SURE THIS WILL WORK?
IT'S A PRETTY LAME DISGUISE.
IT'S PERFECT!
SHE LOOKS JUST LIKE A MONSTER BABY.
HOW COME YOU'RE SO SURE?
POSITIVE THINKING IS THE KEY.
OR POSI-TIVELY NOT THINKING! THIS PLAN WILL NEVER WORK!

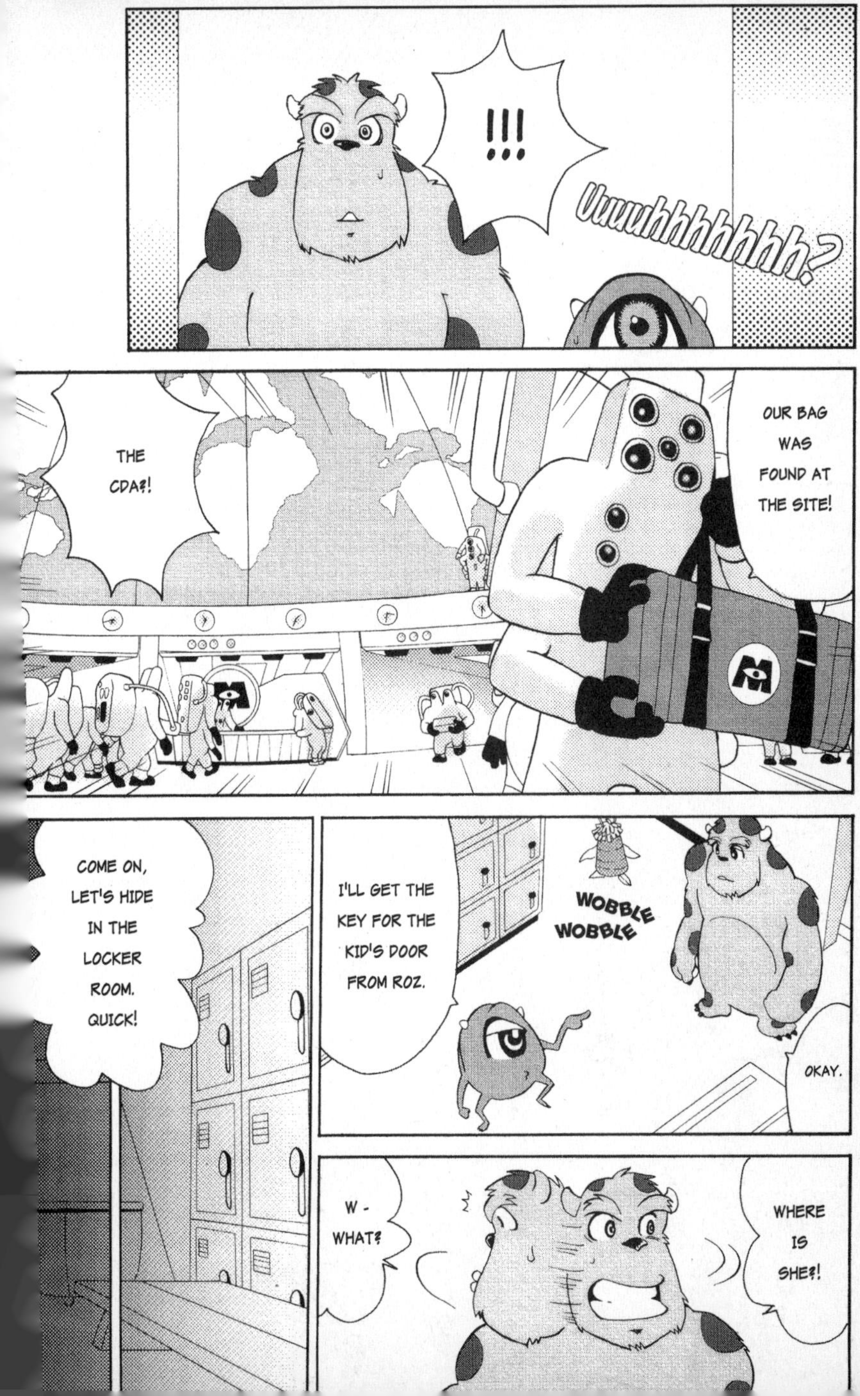
!!!
Uuuuhhhhhhh?
THE CDA?!
OUR BAG WAS FOUND AT THE SITE!
COME ON, LET'S HIDE IN THE LOCKER ROOM. QUICK!
I'LL GET THE KEY FOR THE KID'S DOOR FROM ROZ.
WOBBLE WOBBLE
OKAY.
W - WHAT?
WHERE IS SHE?!

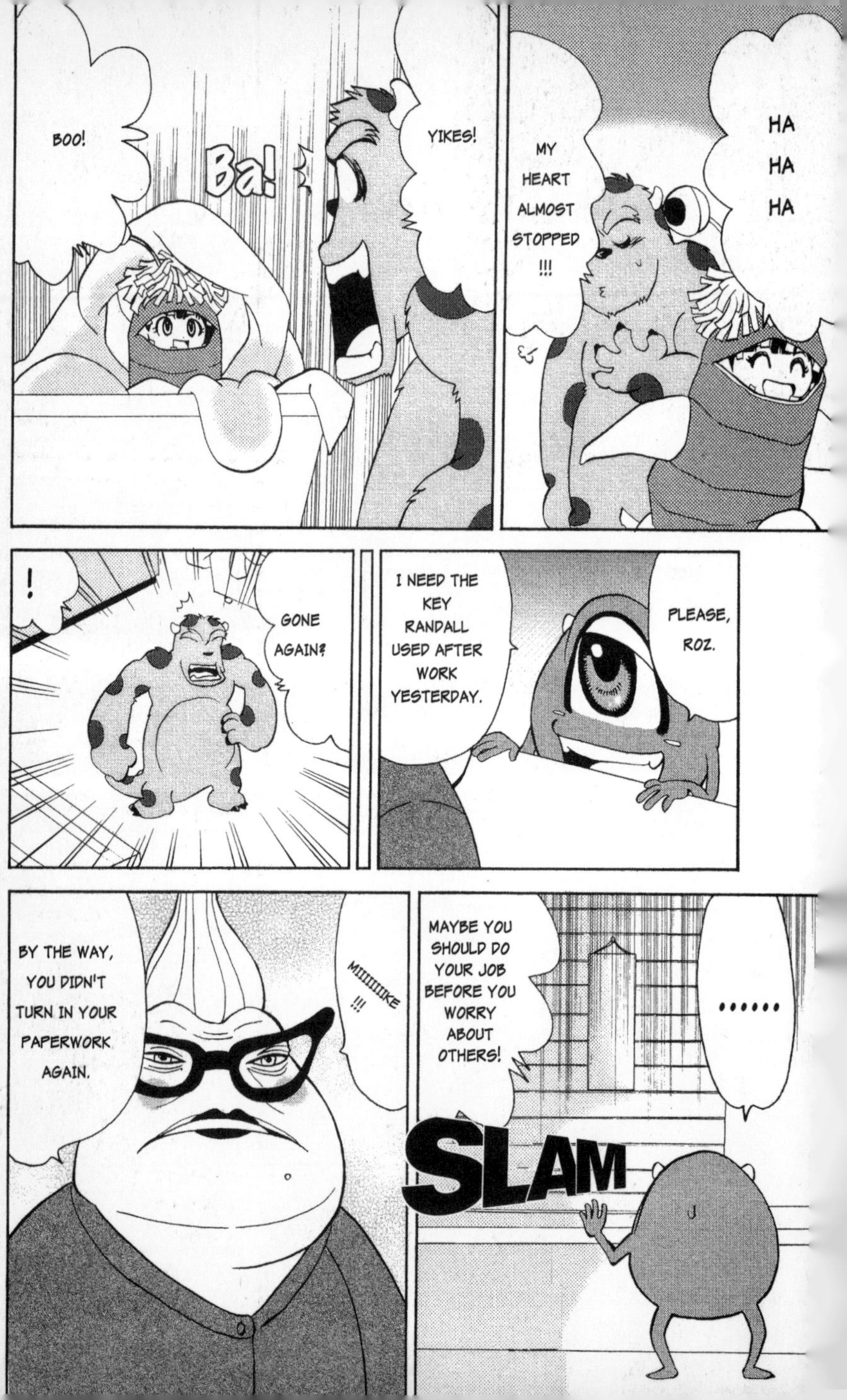
BOO!
Ba!
YIKES!
MY HEART ALMOST STOPPED !!!
HA HA HA
!
GONE AGAIN?
I NEED THE KEY RANDALL USED AFTER WORK YESTERDAY.
PLEASE, ROZ.
BY THE WAY, YOU DIDN'T TURN IN YOUR PAPERWORK AGAIN.
MIIIIIIIKE !!!
MAYBE YOU SHOULD DO YOUR JOB BEFORE YOU WORRY ABOUT OTHERS!
SLAM
......

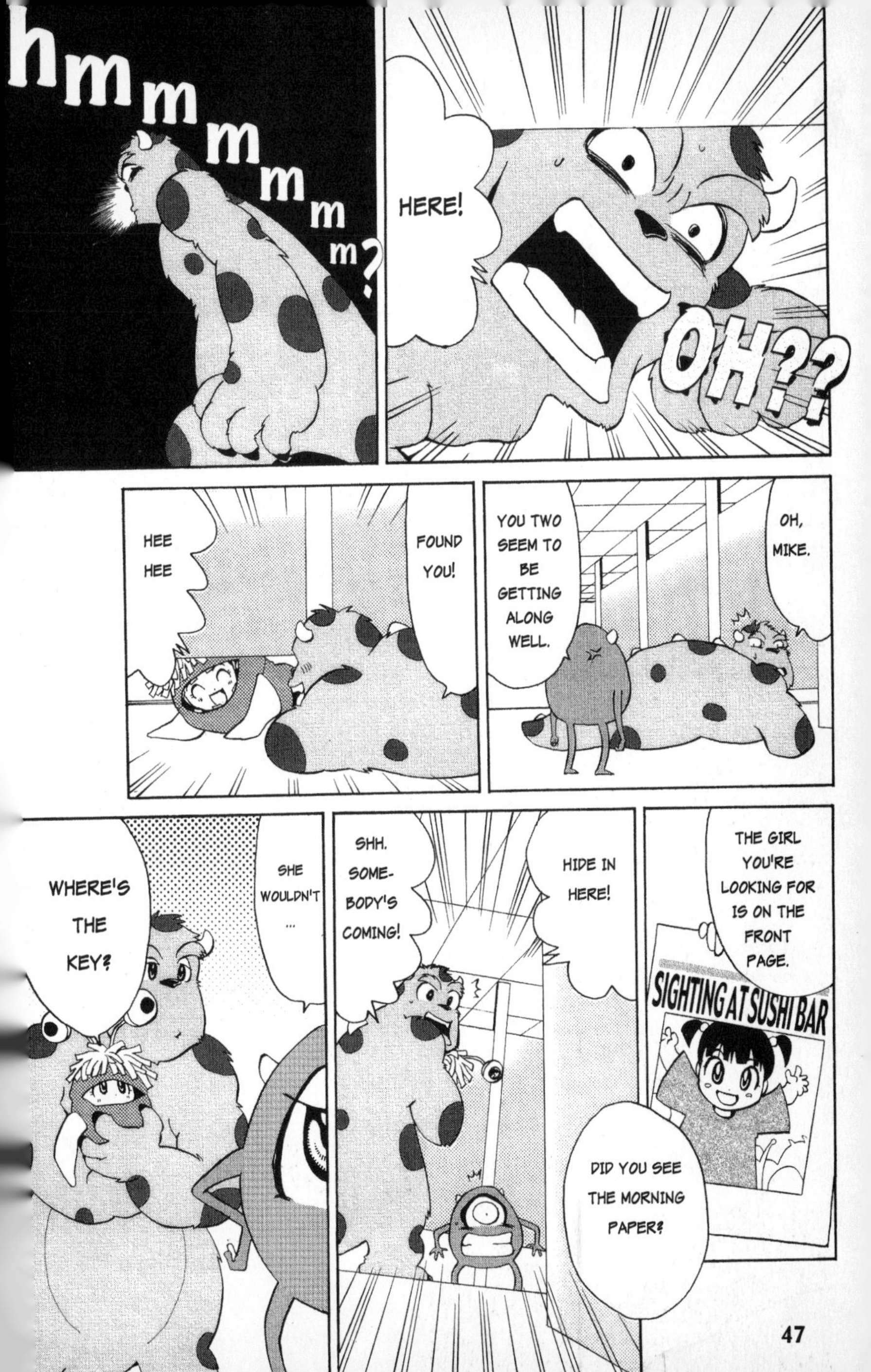
hmmmmmmm?
HERE!
OH??
HEE HEE
FOUND YOU!
YOU TWO SEEM TO BE GETTING ALONG WELL.
OH, MIKE.
WHERE'S THE KEY?
SHE WOULDN'T ...
SHH. SOME-BODY'S COMING!
HIDE IN HERE!
THE GIRL YOU'RE LOOKING FOR IS ON THE FRONT PAGE.
SIGHTING AT SUSHI BAR
DID YOU SEE THE MORNING PAPER?

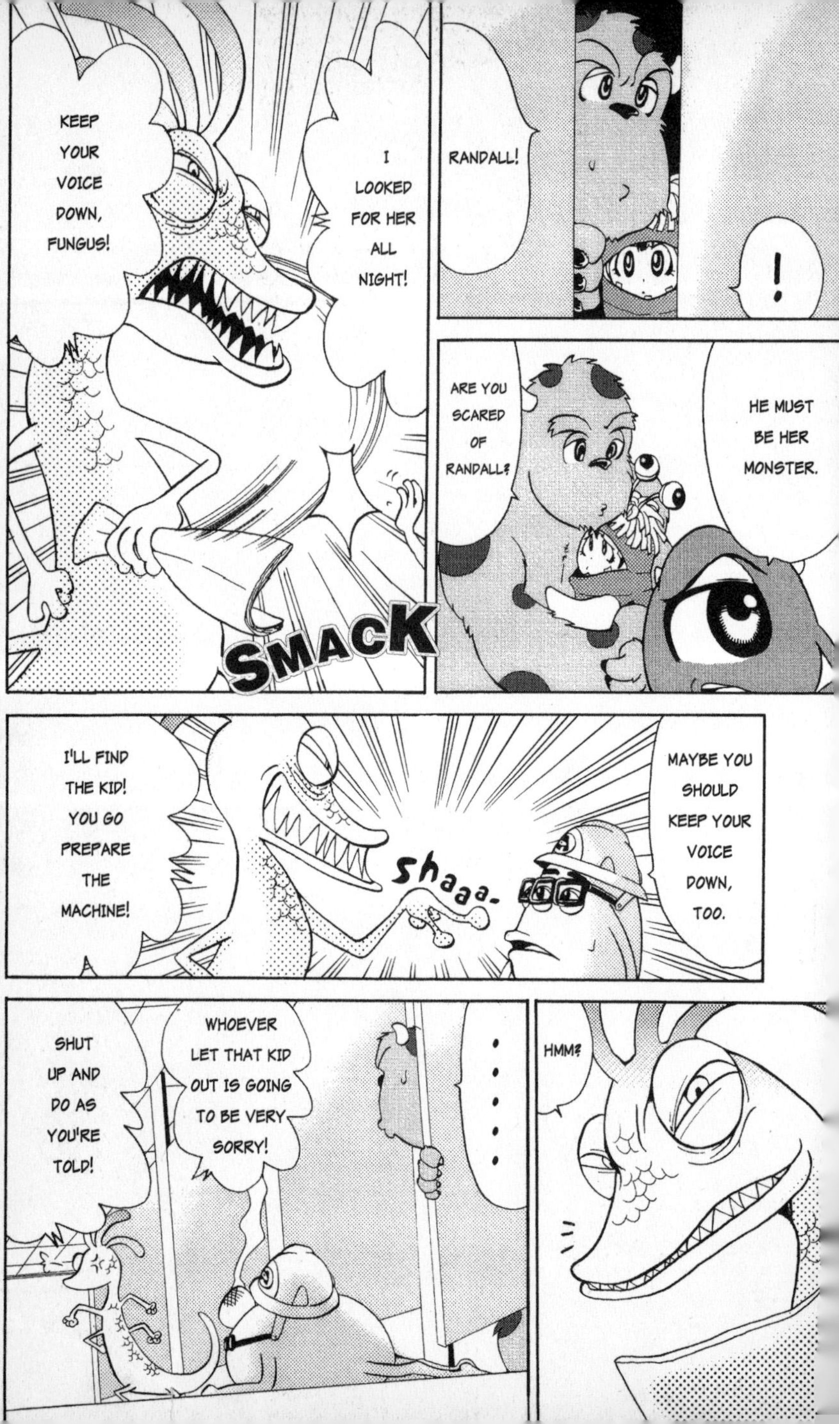

KEEP YOUR VOICE DOWN, FUNGUS!
I LOOKED FOR HER ALL NIGHT!
SMACK
RANDALL!
!
ARE YOU SCARED OF RANDALL?
HE MUST BE HER MONSTER.
I'LL FIND THE KID! YOU GO PREPARE THE MACHINE!
shaaa-
MAYBE YOU SHOULD KEEP YOUR VOICE DOWN, TOO.
SHUT UP AND DO AS YOU'RE TOLD!
WHOEVER LET THAT KID OUT IS GOING TO BE VERY SORRY!
.....
HMM?

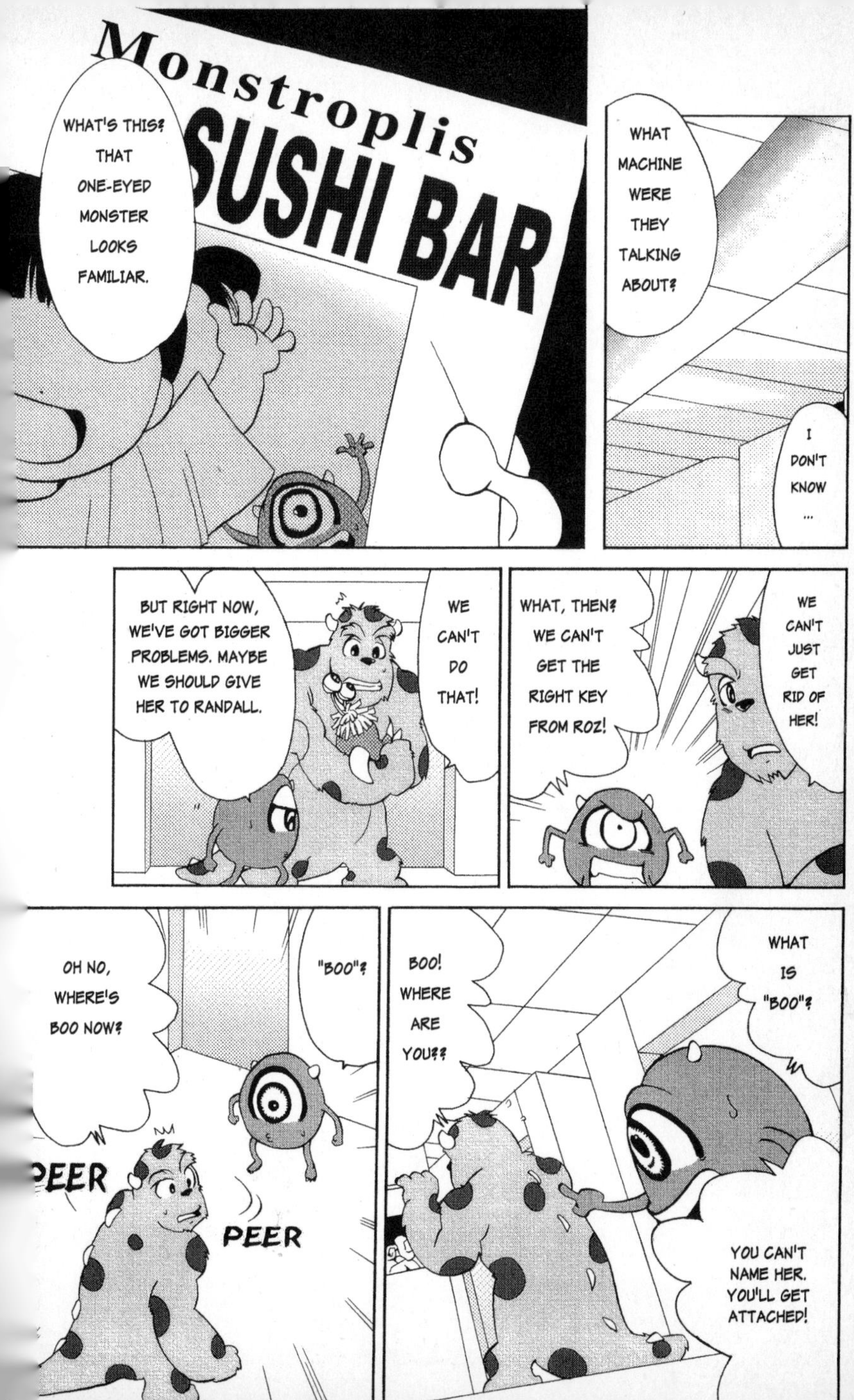
Monstroplis SUSHI BAR
WHAT'S THIS? THAT ONE-EYED MONSTER LOOKS FAMILIAR.
WHAT MACHINE WERE THEY TALKING ABOUT?
I DON'T KNOW ...
BUT RIGHT NOW, WE'VE GOT BIGGER PROBLEMS. MAYBE WE SHOULD GIVE HER TO RANDALL.
WE CAN'T DO THAT!
WHAT, THEN? WE CAN'T GET THE RIGHT KEY FROM ROZ!
WE CAN'T JUST GET RID OF HER!
OH NO, WHERE'S BOO NOW?
"BOO"?
PEER
PEER
BOO! WHERE ARE YOU??
WHAT IS "BOO"?
YOU CAN'T NAME HER. YOU'LL GET ATTACHED!

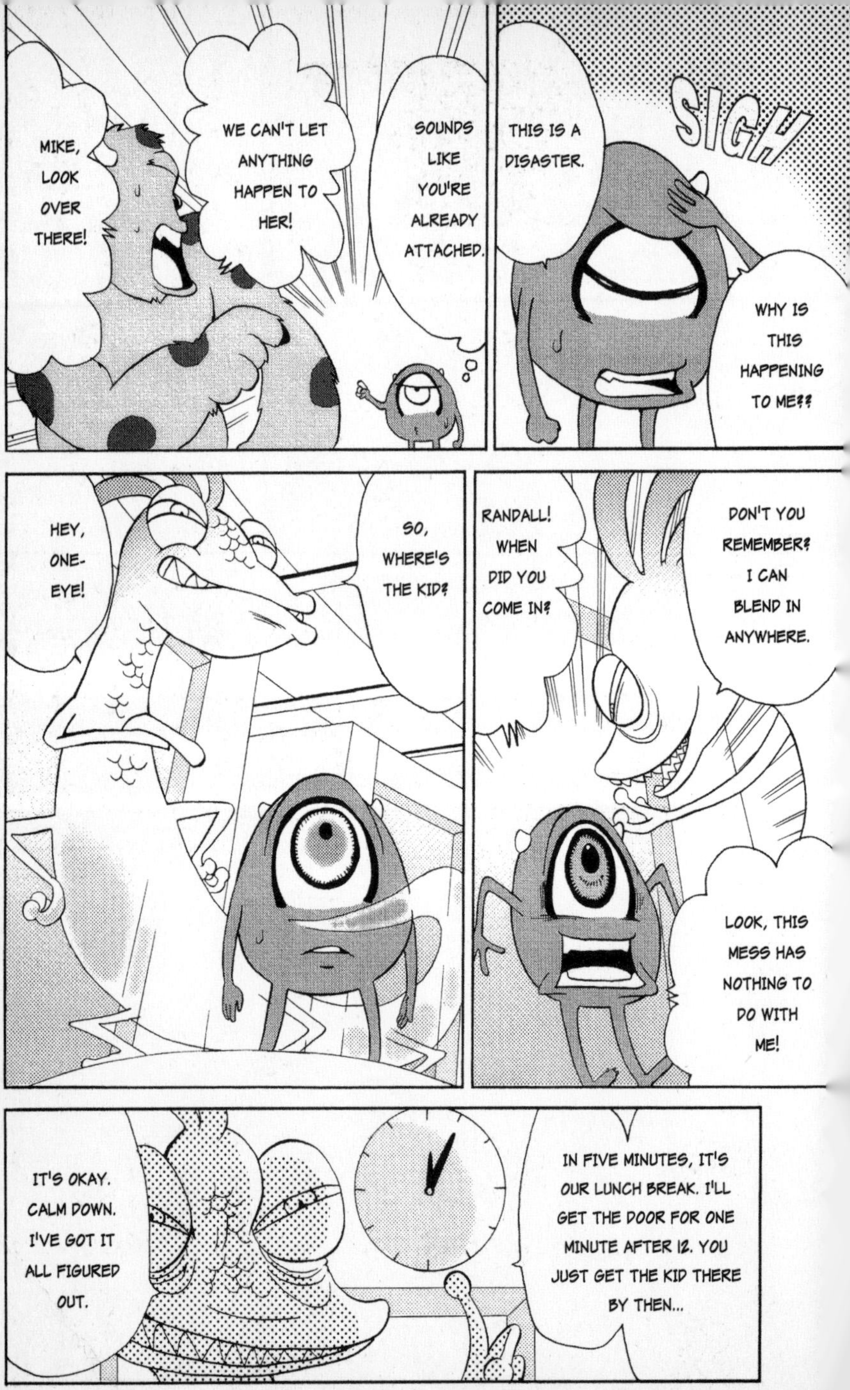
MIKE, LOOK OVER THERE!
WE CAN'T LET ANYTHING HAPPEN TO HER!
SOUNDS LIKE YOU'RE ALREADY ATTACHED.
THIS IS A DISASTER.
SIGH
WHY IS THIS HAPPENING TO ME??
HEY, ONE-EYE!
SO, WHERE'S THE KID?
RANDALL! WHEN DID YOU COME IN?
DON'T YOU REMEMBER? I CAN BLEND IN ANYWHERE.
LOOK, THIS MESS HAS NOTHING TO DO WITH ME!
IT'S OKAY. CALM DOWN. I'VE GOT IT ALL FIGURED OUT.
IN FIVE MINUTES, IT'S OUR LUNCH BREAK. I'LL GET THE DOOR FOR ONE MINUTE AFTER 12. YOU JUST GET THE KID THERE BY THEN...

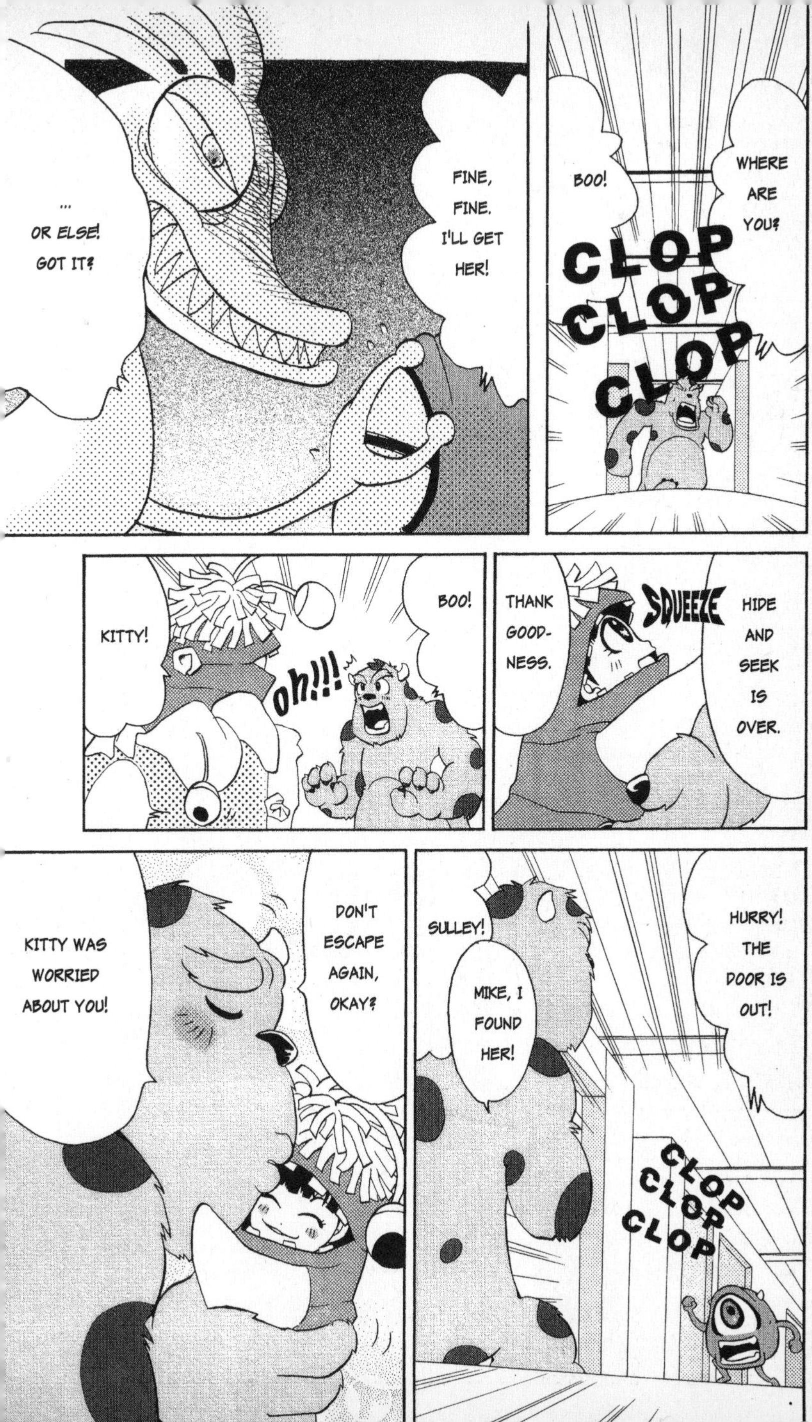
...
OR ELSE! GOT IT?
FINE, FINE. I'LL GET HER!
BOO!
WHERE ARE YOU?
CLOP CLOP CLOP
KITTY!
oh!!!
BOO!
THANK GOOD-NESS.
SQUEEZE
HIDE AND SEEK IS OVER.
KITTY WAS WORRIED ABOUT YOU!
DON'T ESCAPE AGAIN, OKAY?
SULLEY!
MIKE, I FOUND HER!
HURRY! THE DOOR IS OUT!
CLOP CLOP CLOP

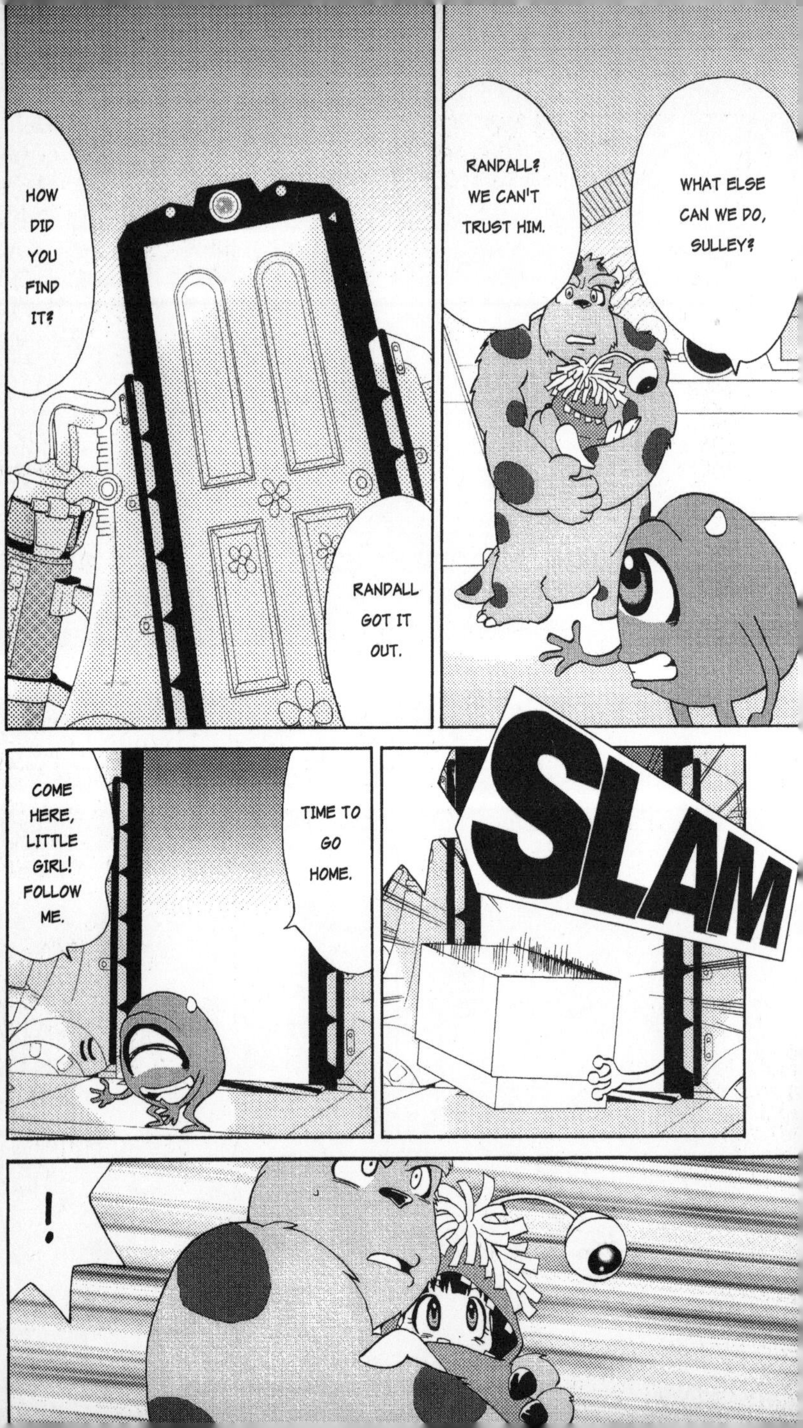
HOW DID YOU FIND IT?
RANDALL GOT IT OUT.
RANDALL? WE CAN'T TRUST HIM.
WHAT ELSE CAN WE DO, SULLEY?
COME HERE, LITTLE GIRL! FOLLOW ME.
TIME TO GO HOME.
SLAM
!

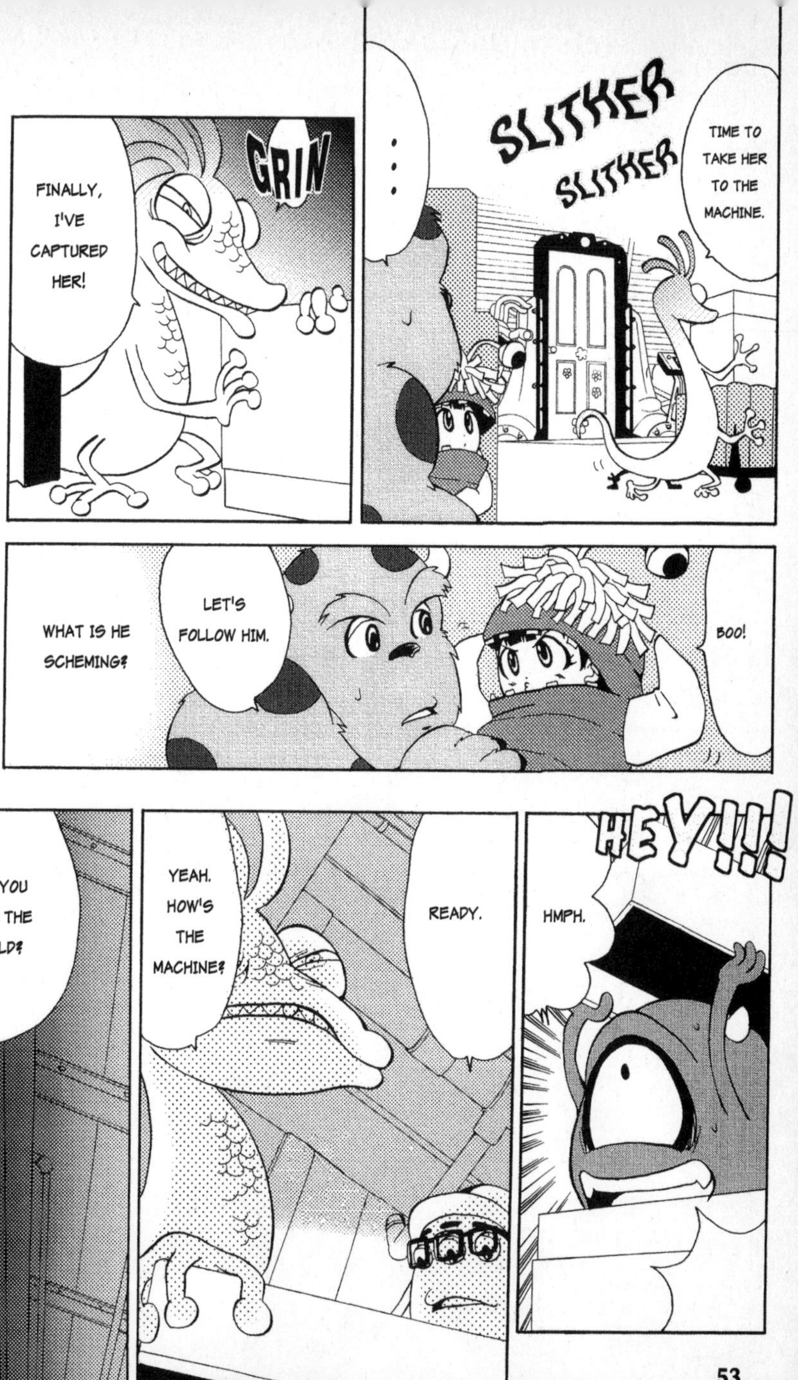
GRIN
FINALLY, I'VE CAPTURED HER!
. . .
SLITHER
SLITHER
TIME TO TAKE HER TO THE MACHINE.
WHAT IS HE SCHEMING?
LET'S FOLLOW HIM.
BOO!
DID YOU FIND THE CHILD?
YEAH. HOW'S THE MACHINE?
READY.
HMPH.
HEY!!!!

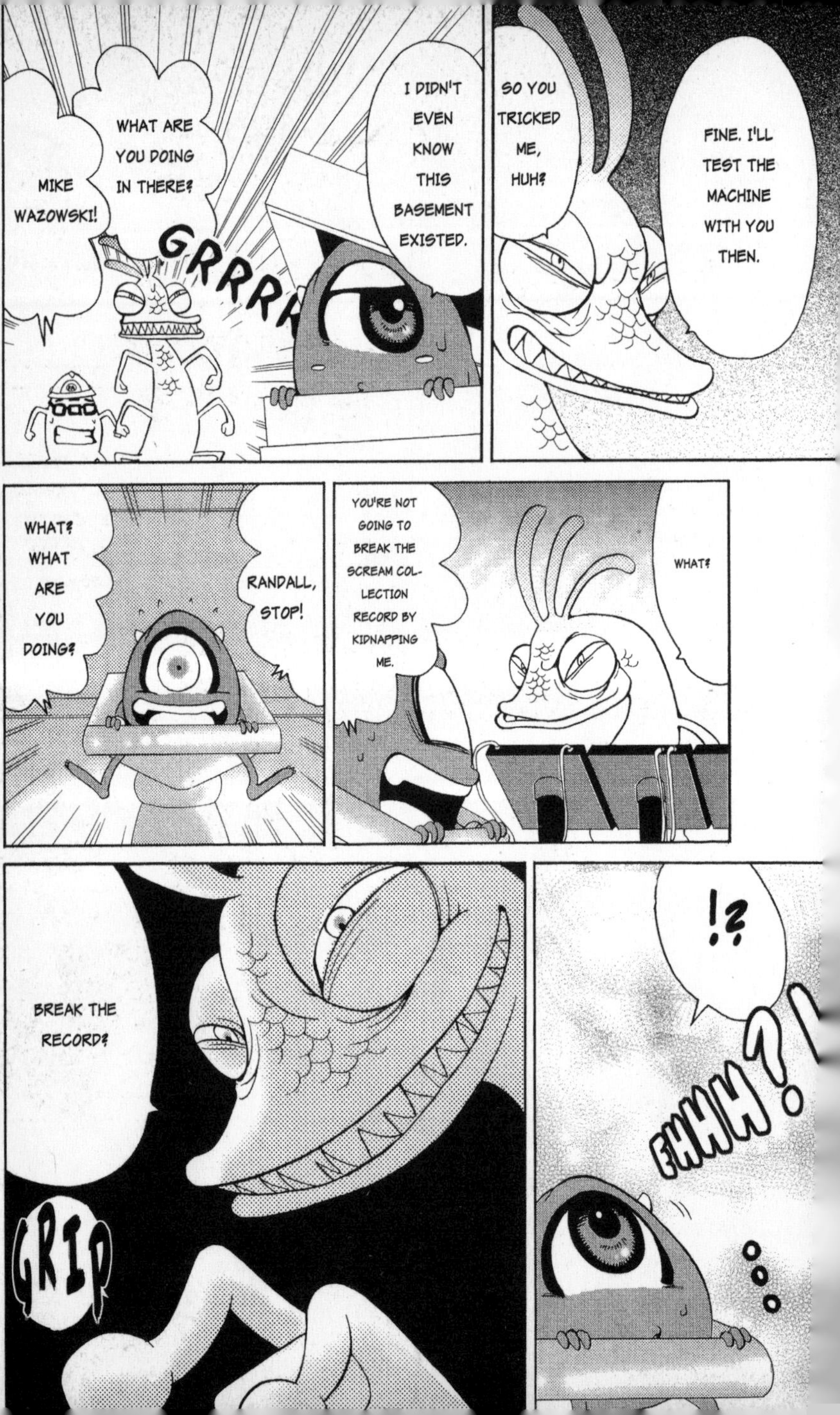
MIKE WAZOWSKI!
WHAT ARE YOU DOING IN THERE?
GRRRR
I DIDN'T EVEN KNOW THIS BASEMENT EXISTED.
SO YOU TRICKED ME, HUH?
FINE. I'LL TEST THE MACHINE WITH YOU THEN.
WHAT? WHAT ARE YOU DOING?
RANDALL, STOP!
YOU'RE NOT GOING TO BREAK THE SCREAM COLLECTION RECORD BY KIDNAPPING ME.
WHAT?
BREAK THE RECORD?
GRIP
!?
EHHHH?!

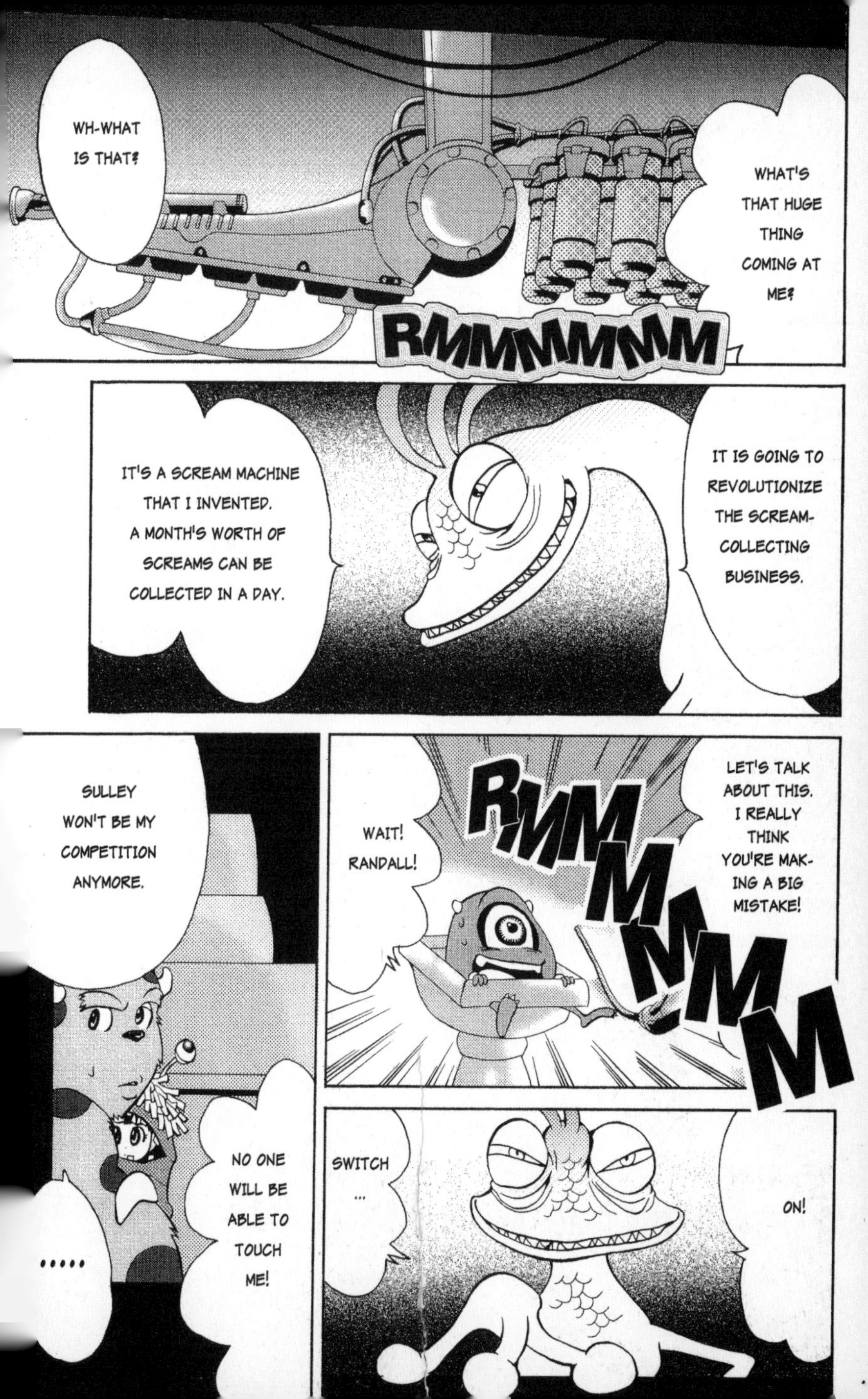
WH-WHAT IS THAT?
WHAT'S THAT HUGE THING COMING AT ME?
RMMMMMMM
IT'S A SCREAM MACHINE THAT I INVENTED. A MONTH'S WORTH OF SCREAMS CAN BE COLLECTED IN A DAY.
IT IS GOING TO REVOLUTIONIZE THE SCREAM-COLLECTING BUSINESS.
SULLEY WON'T BE MY COMPETITION ANYMORE.
NO ONE WILL BE ABLE TO TOUCH ME!
.....
WAIT! RANDALL!
RMMMMMMM
LET'S TALK ABOUT THIS. I REALLY THINK YOU'RE MAKING A BIG MISTAKE!
SWITCH ...
ON!

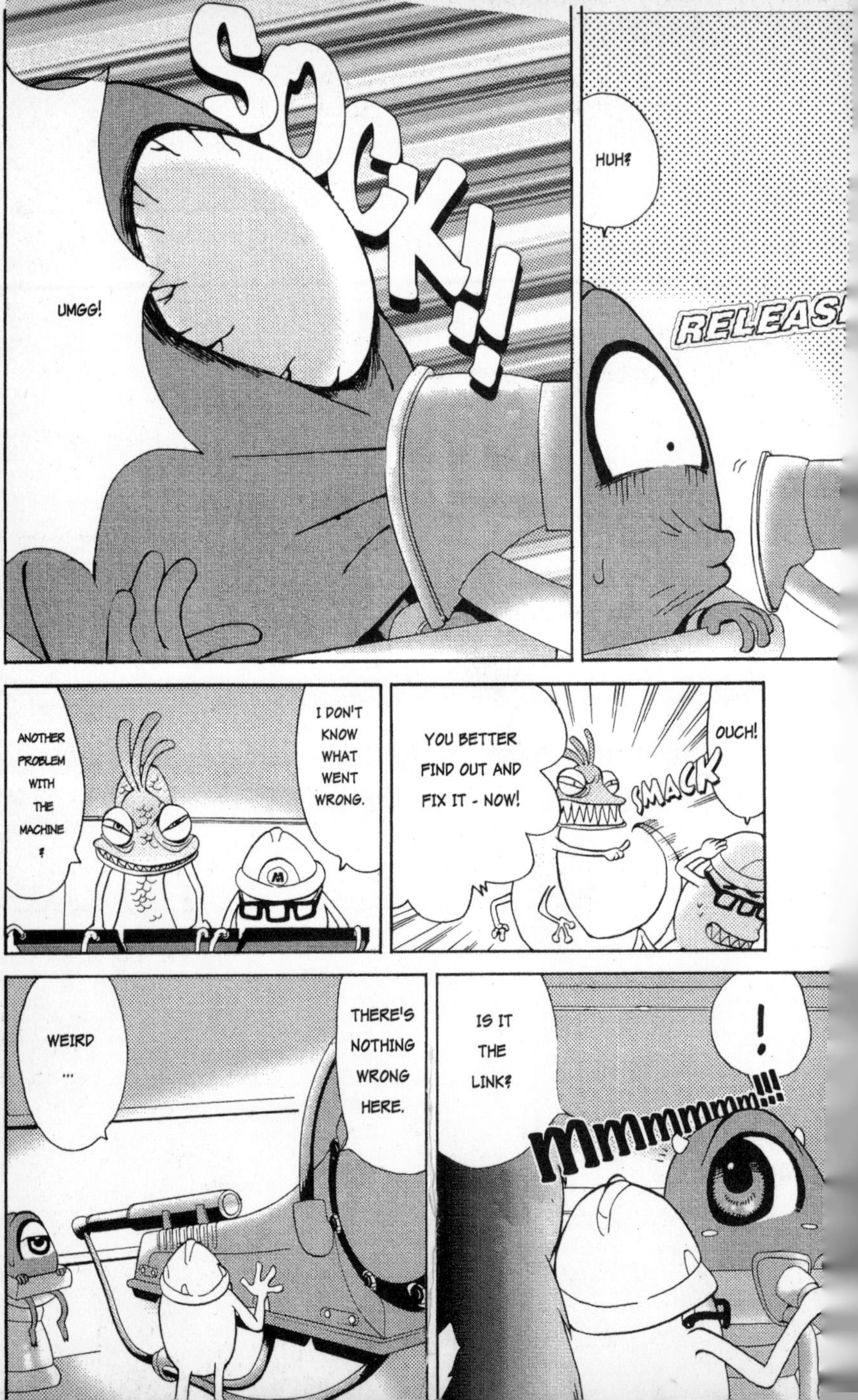
SOCK!!
UMGG!
HUH?
RELEAS
ANOTHER PROBLEM WITH THE MACHINE?
I DON'T KNOW WHAT WENT WRONG.
YOU BETTER FIND OUT AND FIX IT - NOW!
SMACK
OUCH!
WEIRD ...
THERE'S NOTHING WRONG HERE.
IS IT THE LINK?
!
Mmmmmmm!!!

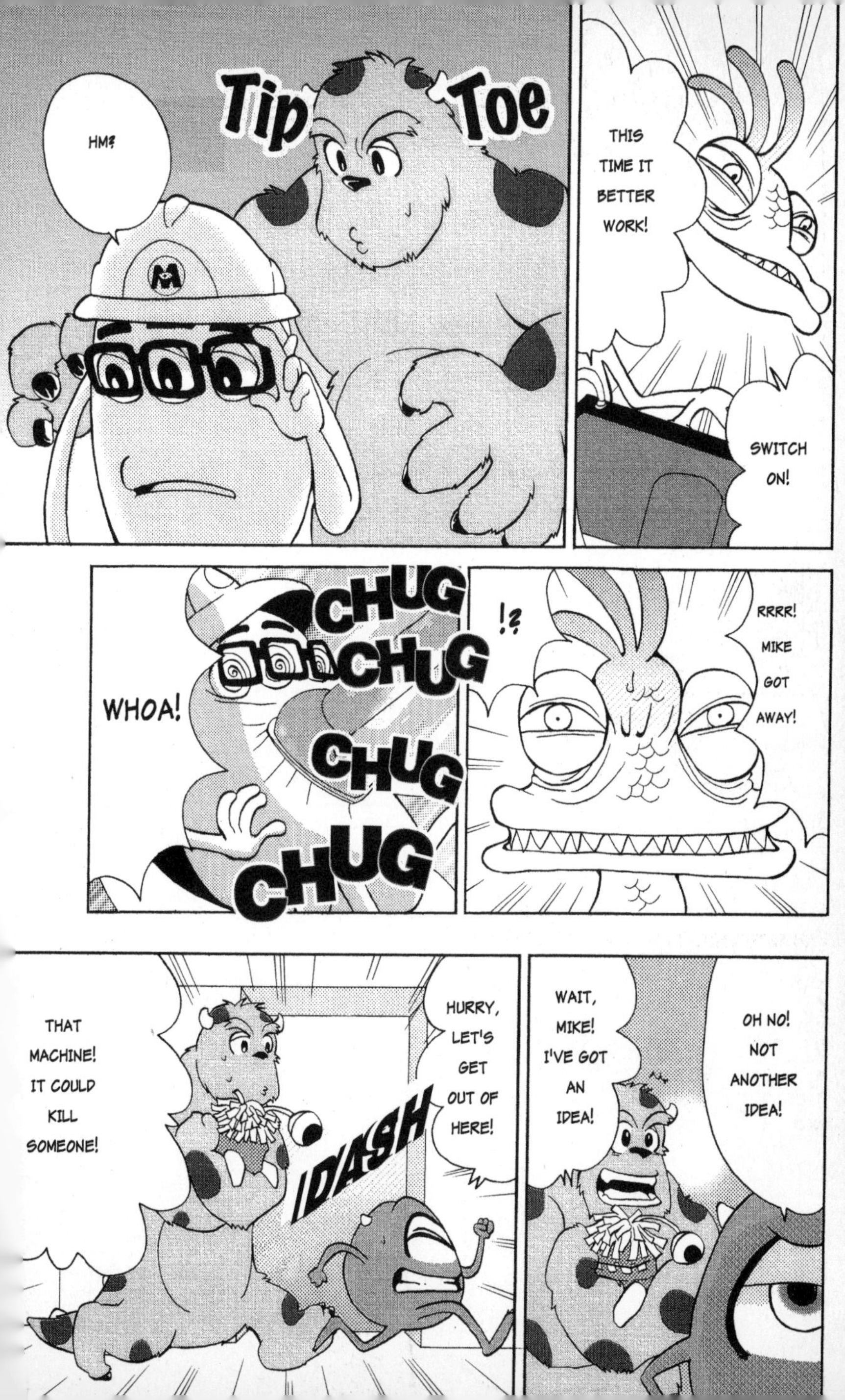
HM?
Tip Toe
THIS TIME IT BETTER WORK!
SWITCH ON!
WHOA!
CHUG CHUG CHUG CHUG
!?
RRRR! MIKE GOT AWAY!
THAT MACHINE! IT COULD KILL SOMEONE!
DASH
HURRY, LET'S GET OUT OF HERE!
WAIT, MIKE! I'VE GOT AN IDEA!
OH NO! NOT ANOTHER IDEA!

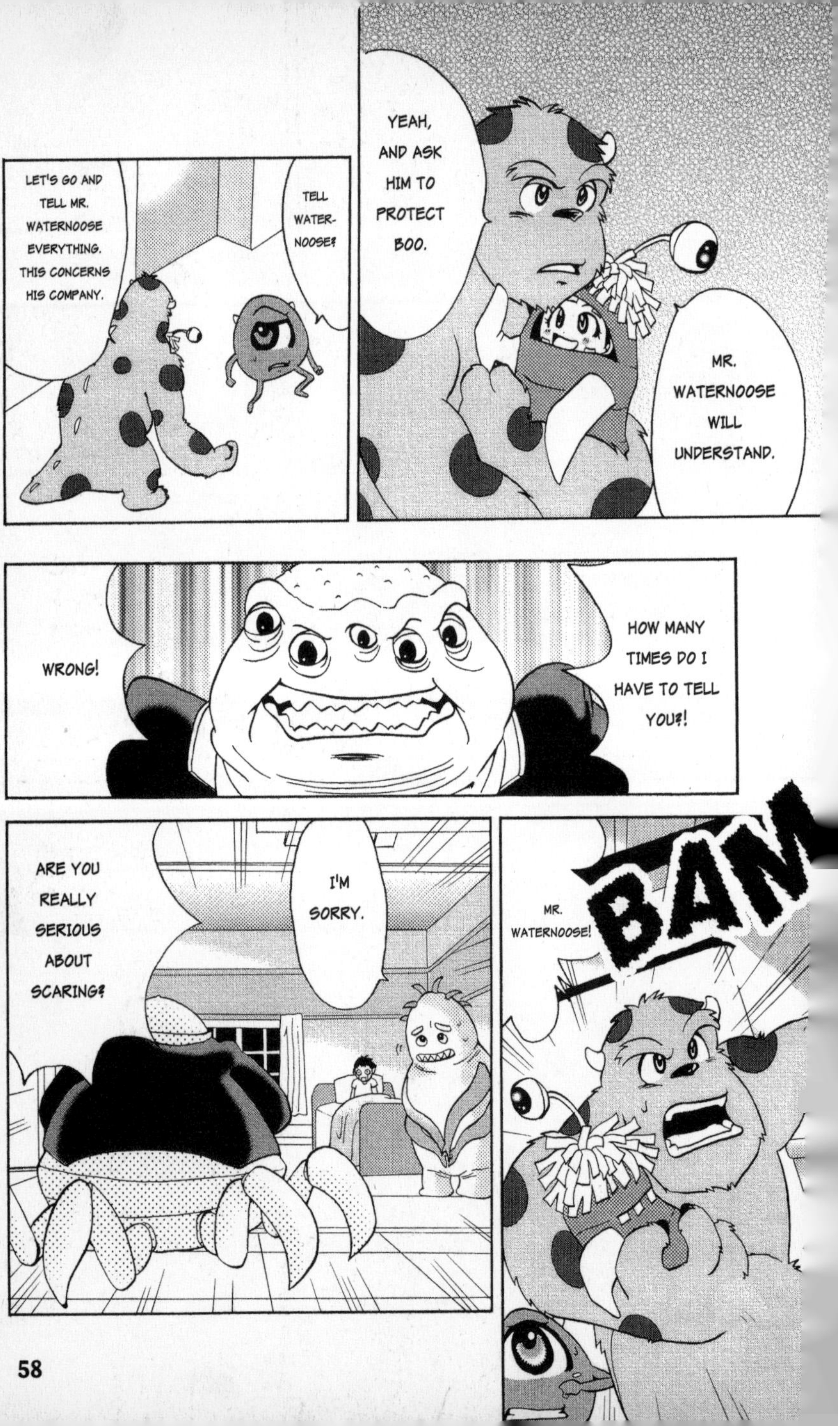
LET'S GO AND TELL MR. WATERNOOSE EVERYTHING. THIS CONCERNS HIS COMPANY.
TELL WATER-NOOSE?
YEAH, AND ASK HIM TO PROTECT BOO.
MR. WATERNOOSE WILL UNDERSTAND.
WRONG!
HOW MANY TIMES DO I HAVE TO TELL YOU?!
ARE YOU REALLY SERIOUS ABOUT SCARING?
I'M SORRY.
MR. WATERNOOSE!
BAM

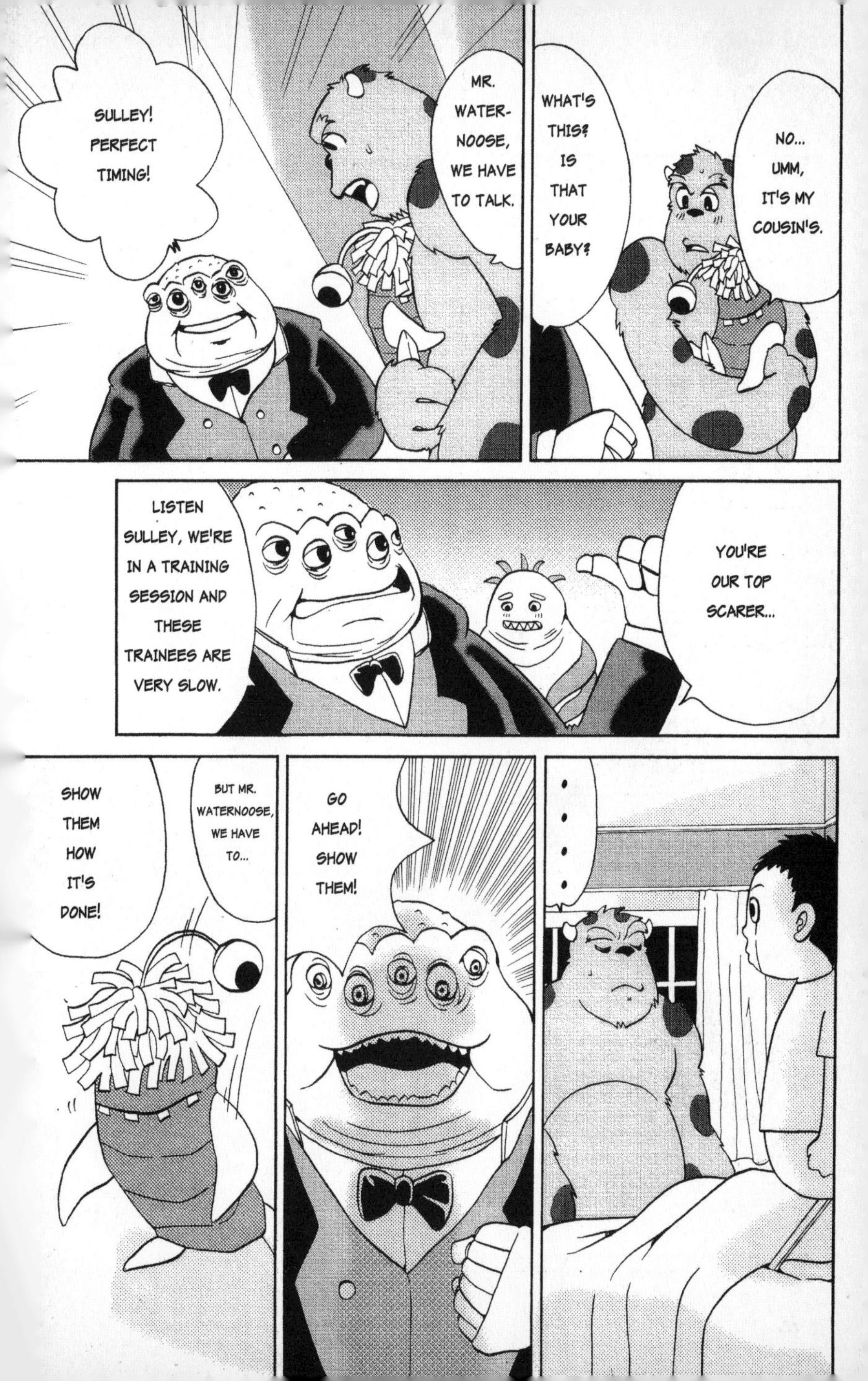
SULLEY! PERFECT TIMING!
MR. WATER-NOOSE, WE HAVE TO TALK.
WHAT'S THIS? IS THAT YOUR BABY?
NO... UMM, IT'S MY COUSIN'S.
LISTEN SULLEY, WE'RE IN A TRAINING SESSION AND THESE TRAINEES ARE VERY SLOW.
YOU'RE OUR TOP SCARER...
SHOW THEM HOW IT'S DONE!
BUT MR. WATERNOOSE, WE HAVE TO...
GO AHEAD! SHOW THEM!
....

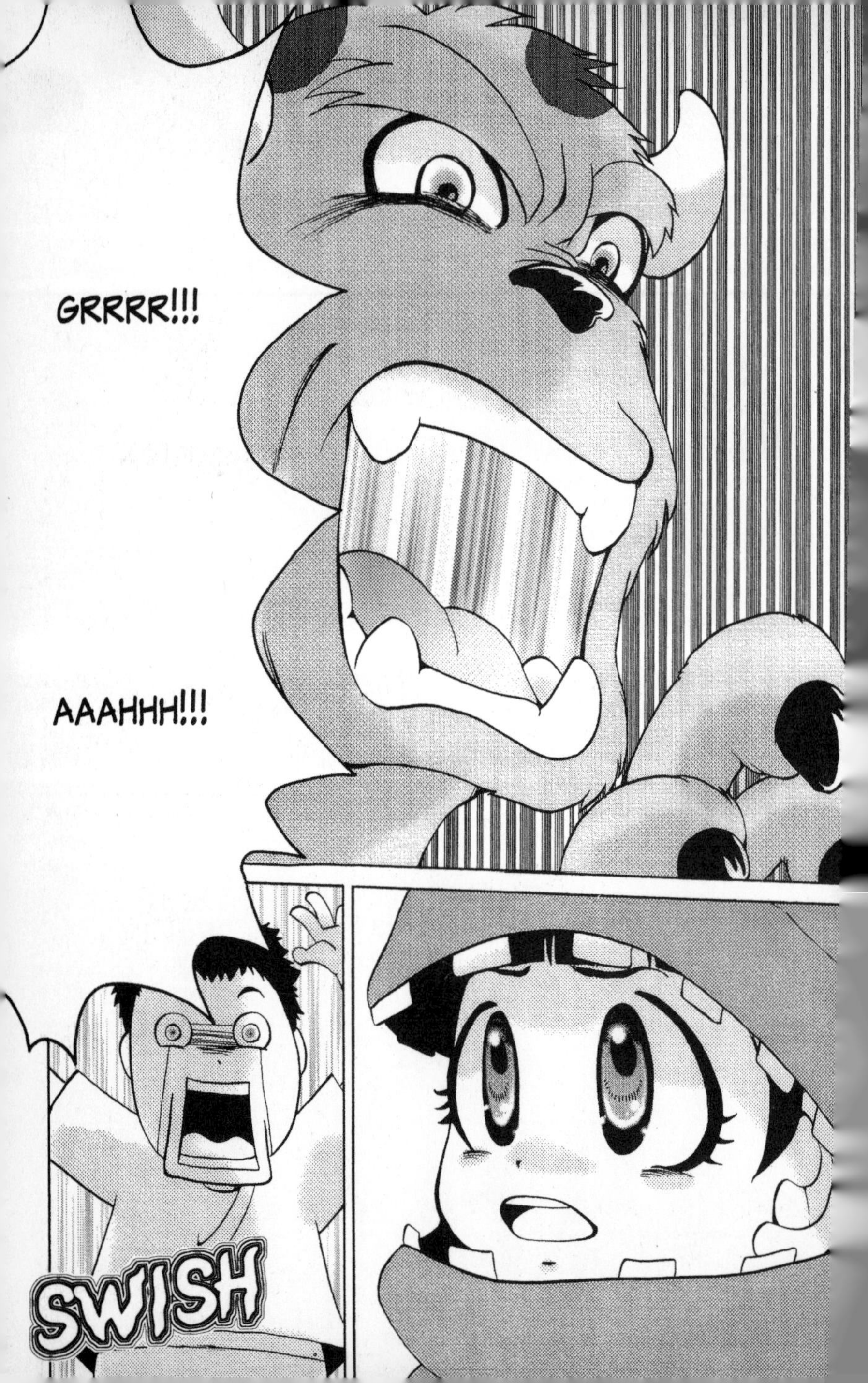
GRRRR!!!
AAAHHH!!!
SWISH

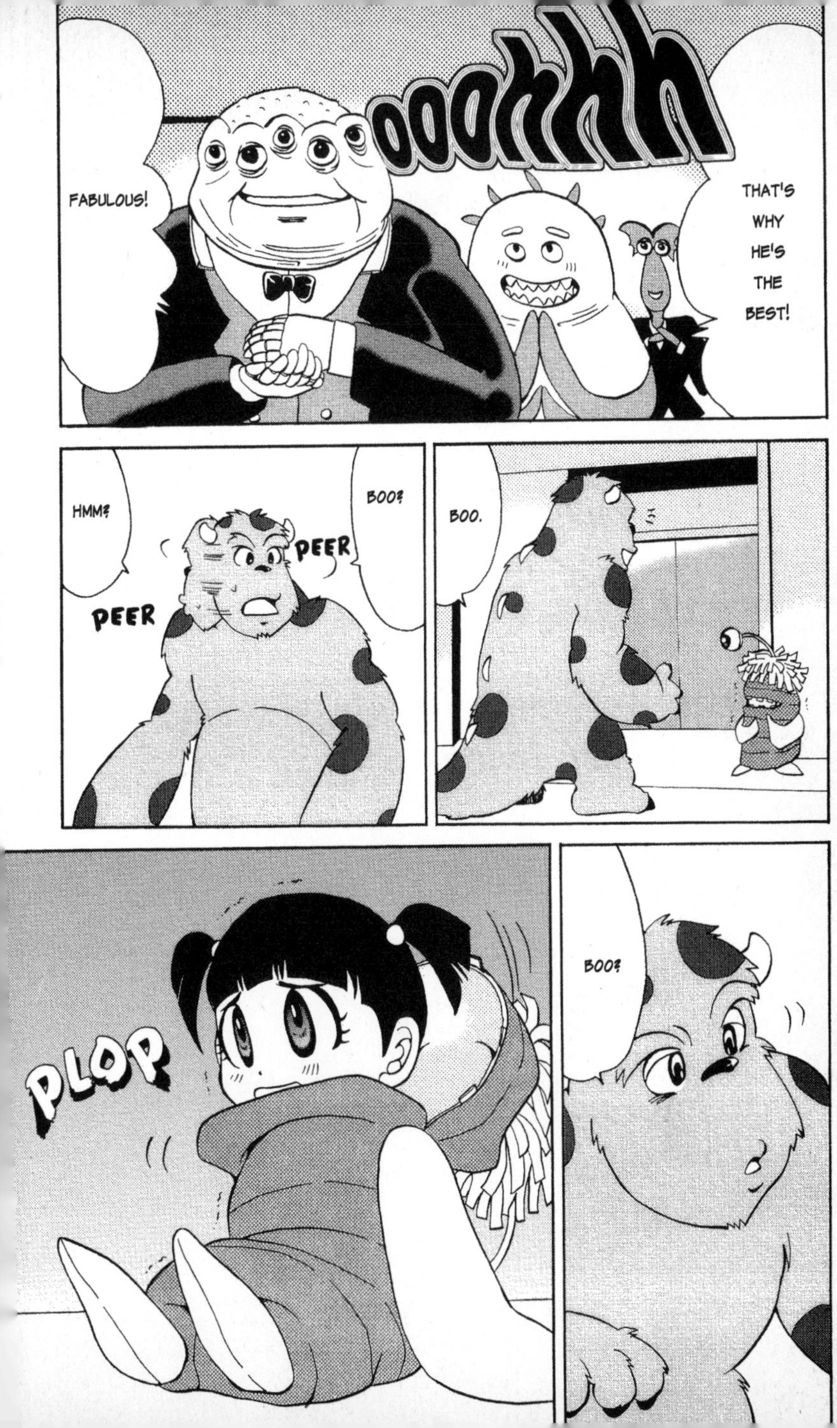
FABULOUS!
OOOHHHH
THAT'S WHY HE'S THE BEST!
HMM?
PEER
PEER
BOO?
BOO.
PLOP
BOO?

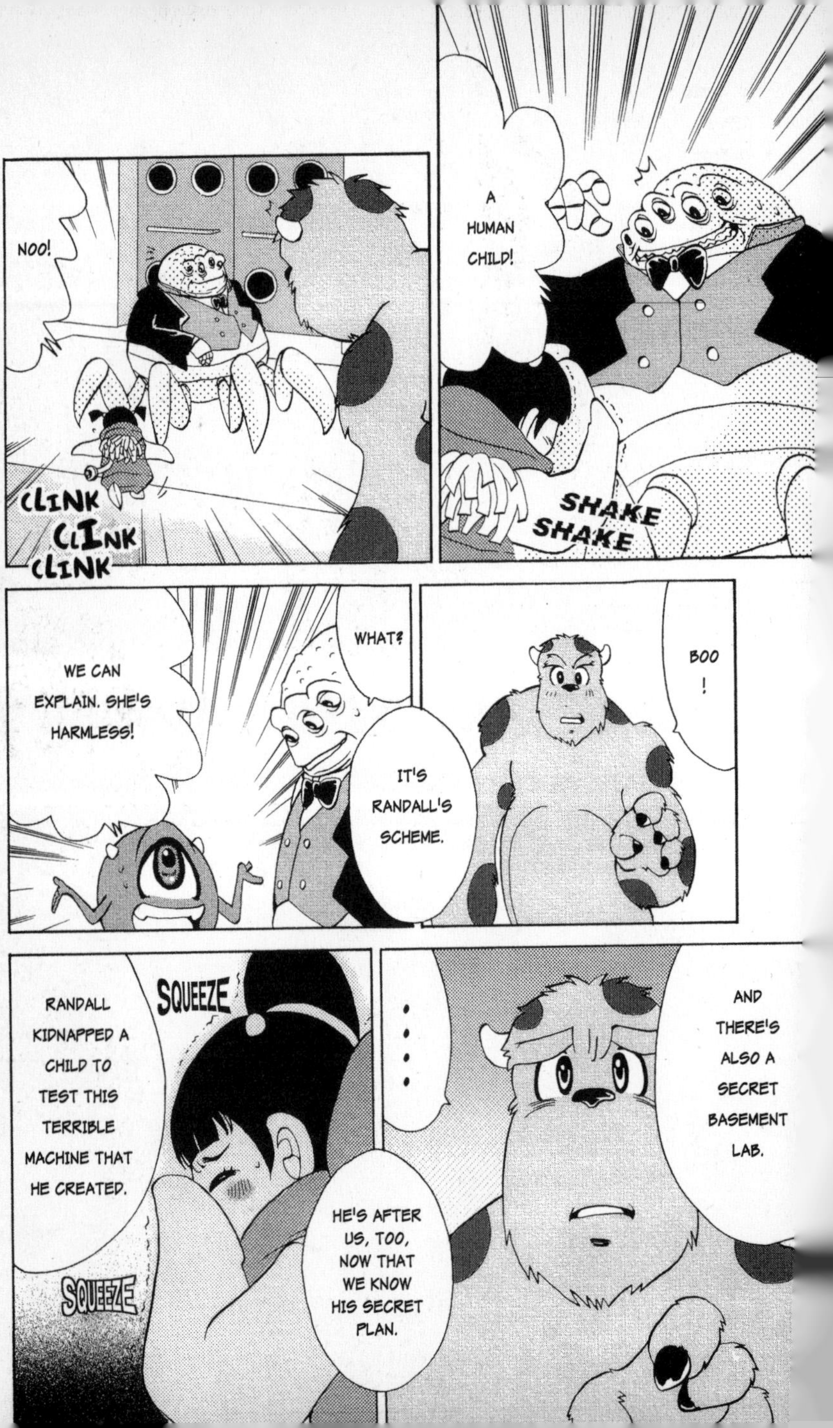
NOO!
CLINK
CLINK
CLINK
A HUMAN CHILD!
SHAKE SHAKE
WE CAN EXPLAIN. SHE'S HARMLESS!
WHAT?
IT'S RANDALL'S SCHEME.
BOO!
RANDALL KIDNAPPED A CHILD TO TEST THIS TERRIBLE MACHINE THAT HE CREATED.
SQUEEZE
SQUEEZE
HE'S AFTER US, TOO, NOW THAT WE KNOW HIS SECRET PLAN.
....
AND THERE'S ALSO A SECRET BASEMENT LAB.

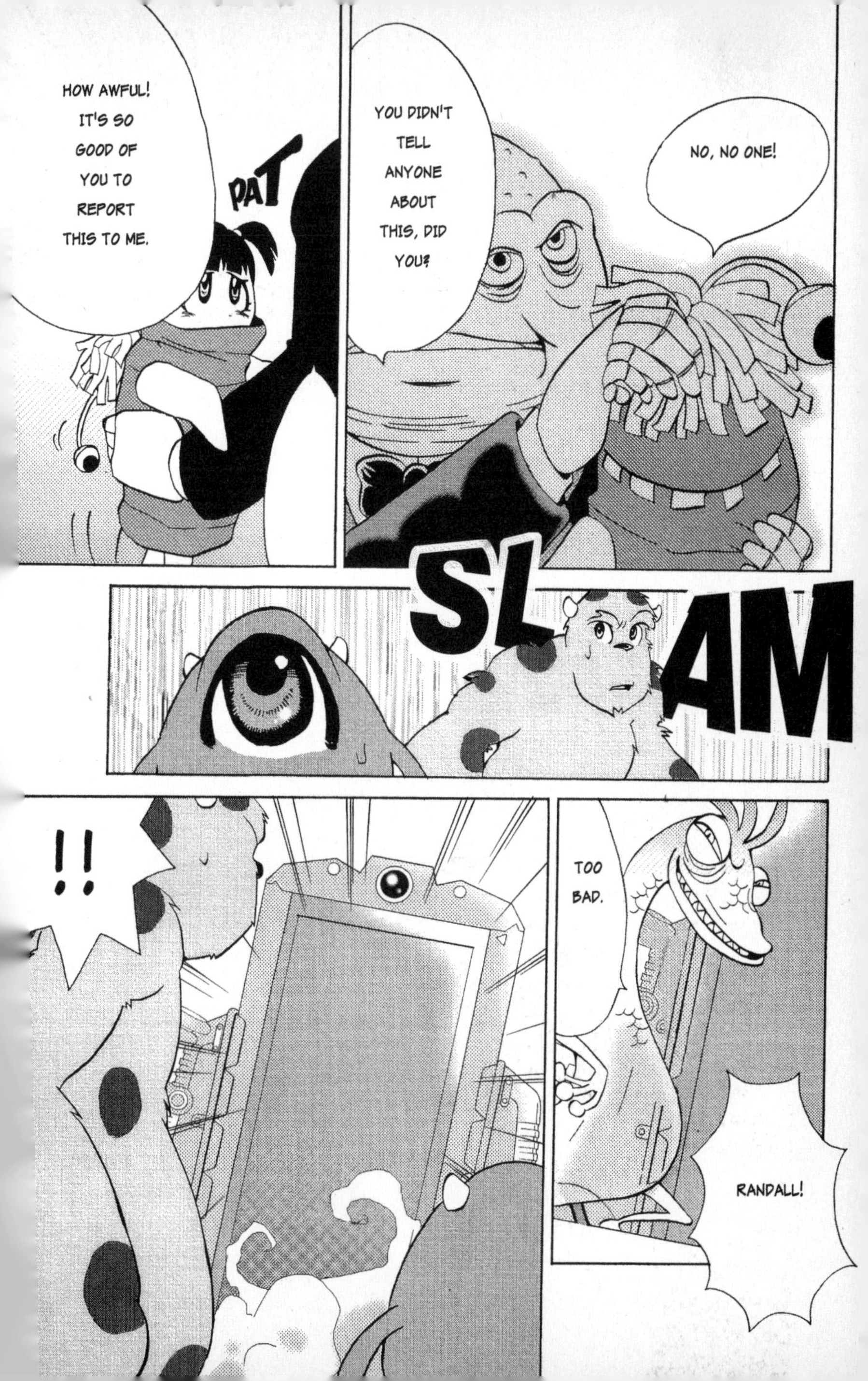
HOW AWFUL! IT'S SO GOOD OF YOU TO REPORT THIS TO ME.
PAT
YOU DIDN'T TELL ANYONE ABOUT THIS, DID YOU?
NO, NO ONE!
SLAM
!!
TOO BAD.
RANDALL!

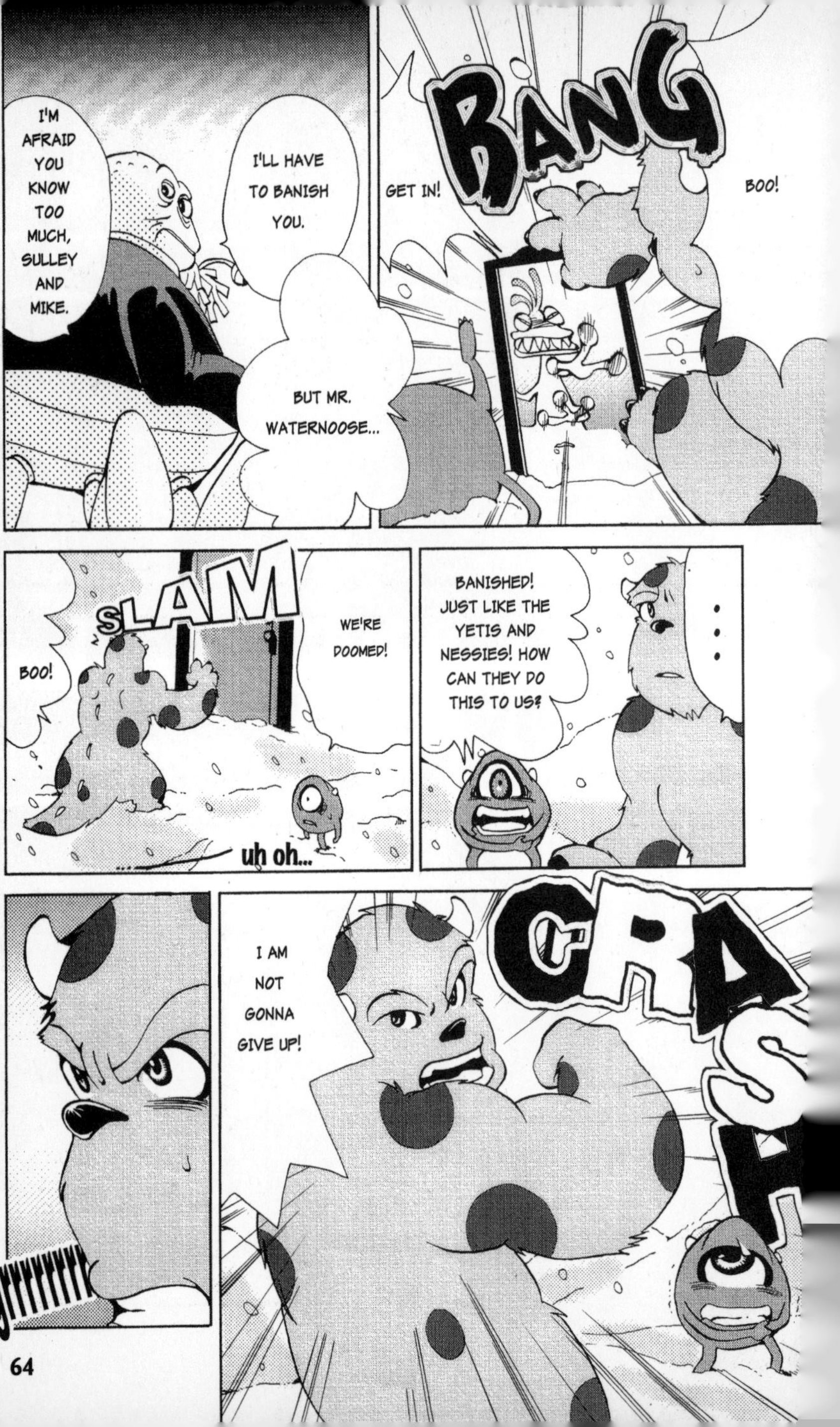
I'M AFRAID YOU KNOW TOO MUCH, SULLEY AND MIKE.
I'LL HAVE TO BANISH YOU.
BUT MR. WATERNOOSE...
GET IN!
BANG
BOO!
BOO!
SLAM
WE'RE DOOMED!
uh oh...
BANISHED! JUST LIKE THE YETIS AND NESSIES! HOW CAN THEY DO THIS TO US?
...
grrrrrrr
I AM NOT GONNA GIVE UP!
CRASH

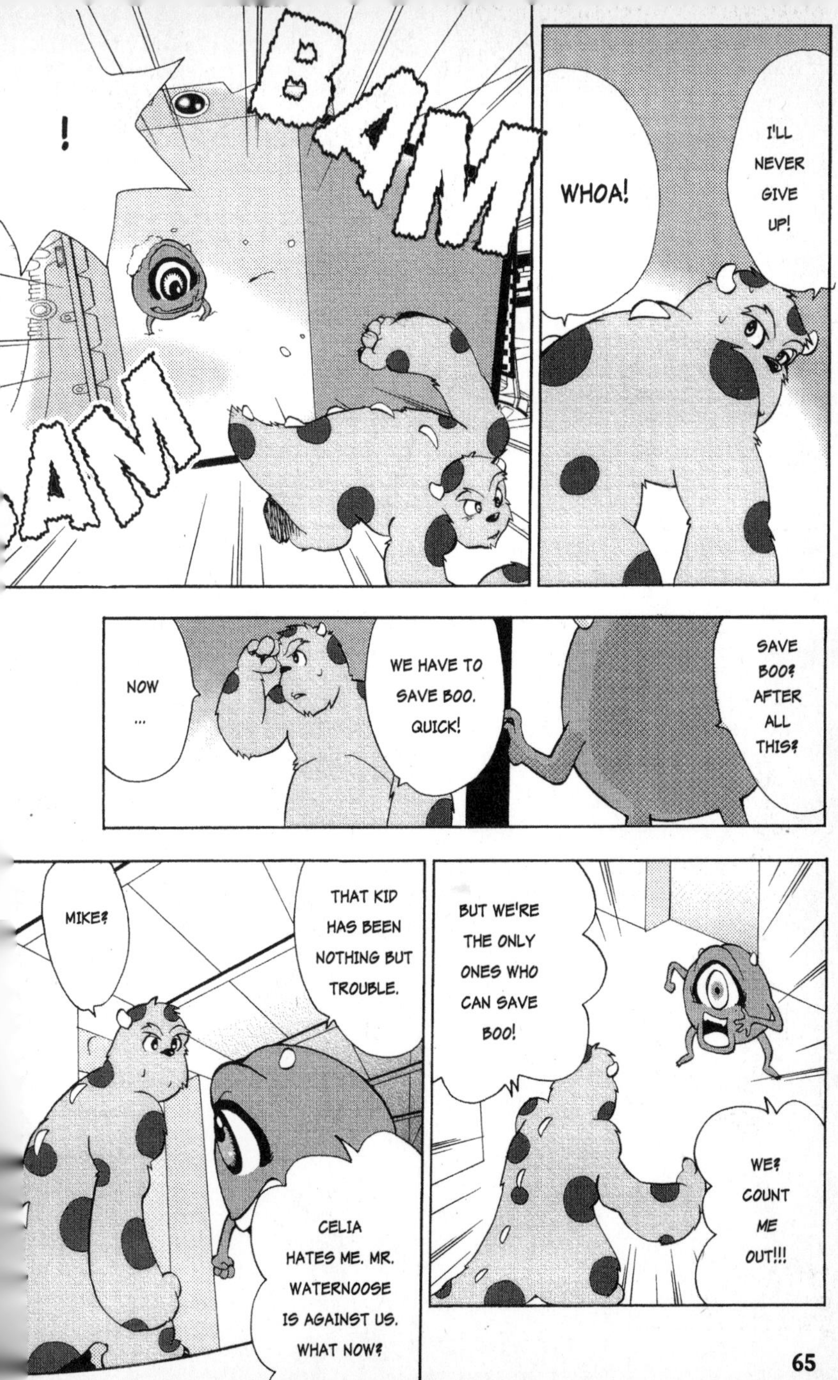
!
BAM
BAM
WHOA!
I'LL NEVER GIVE UP!
NOW ...
WE HAVE TO SAVE BOO. QUICK!
SAVE BOO? AFTER ALL THIS?
MIKE?
THAT KID HAS BEEN NOTHING BUT TROUBLE.
CELIA HATES ME. MR. WATERNOOSE IS AGAINST US. WHAT NOW?
BUT WE'RE THE ONLY ONES WHO CAN SAVE BOO!
WE? COUNT ME OUT!!!

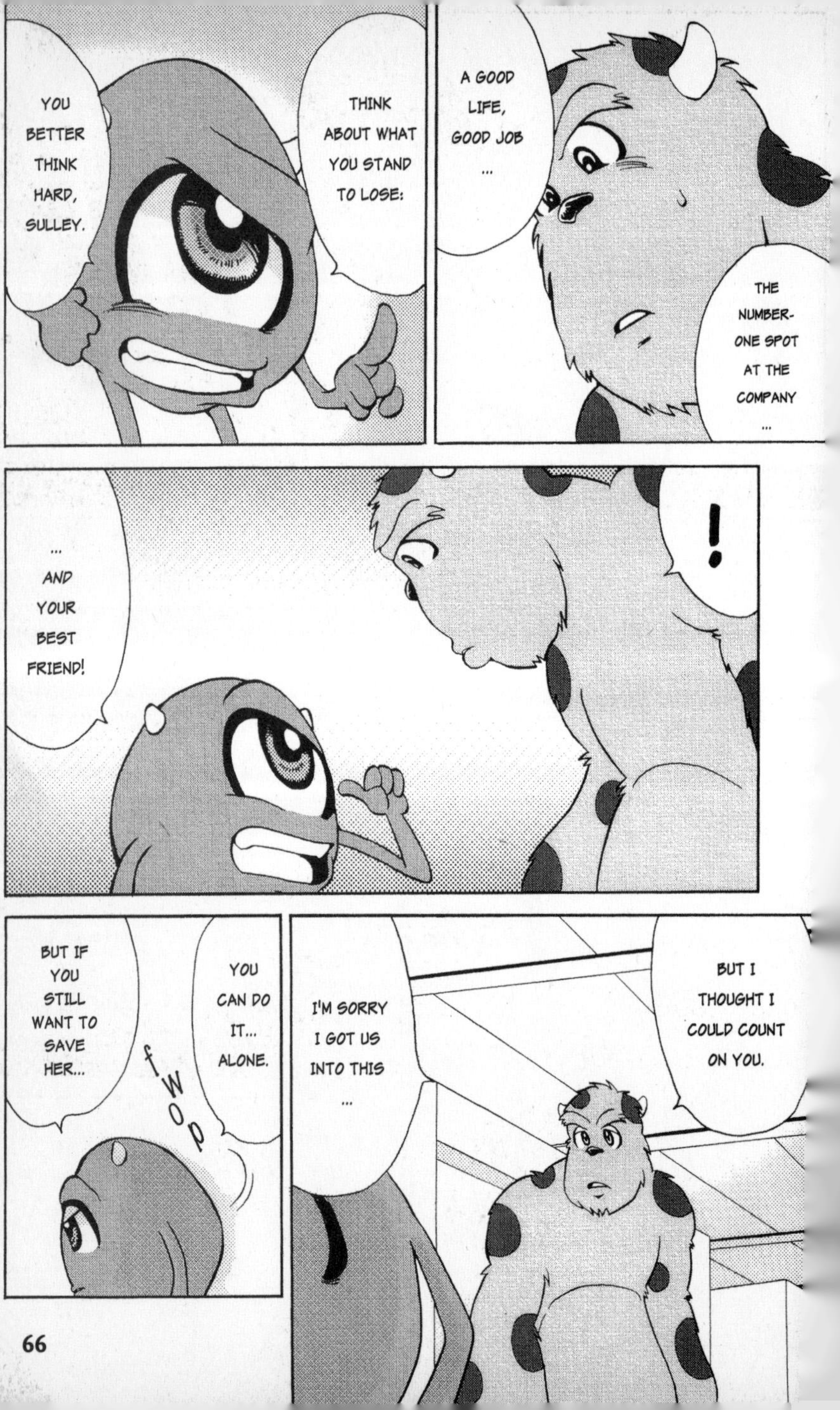
YOU BETTER THINK HARD, SULLEY.
THINK ABOUT WHAT YOU STAND TO LOSE:
A GOOD LIFE, GOOD JOB ...
THE NUMBER-ONE SPOT AT THE COMPANY ...
... AND YOUR BEST FRIEND!
!
BUT IF YOU STILL WANT TO SAVE HER...
fWop
YOU CAN DO IT... ALONE.
I'M SORRY I GOT US INTO THIS ...
BUT I THOUGHT I COULD COUNT ON YOU.

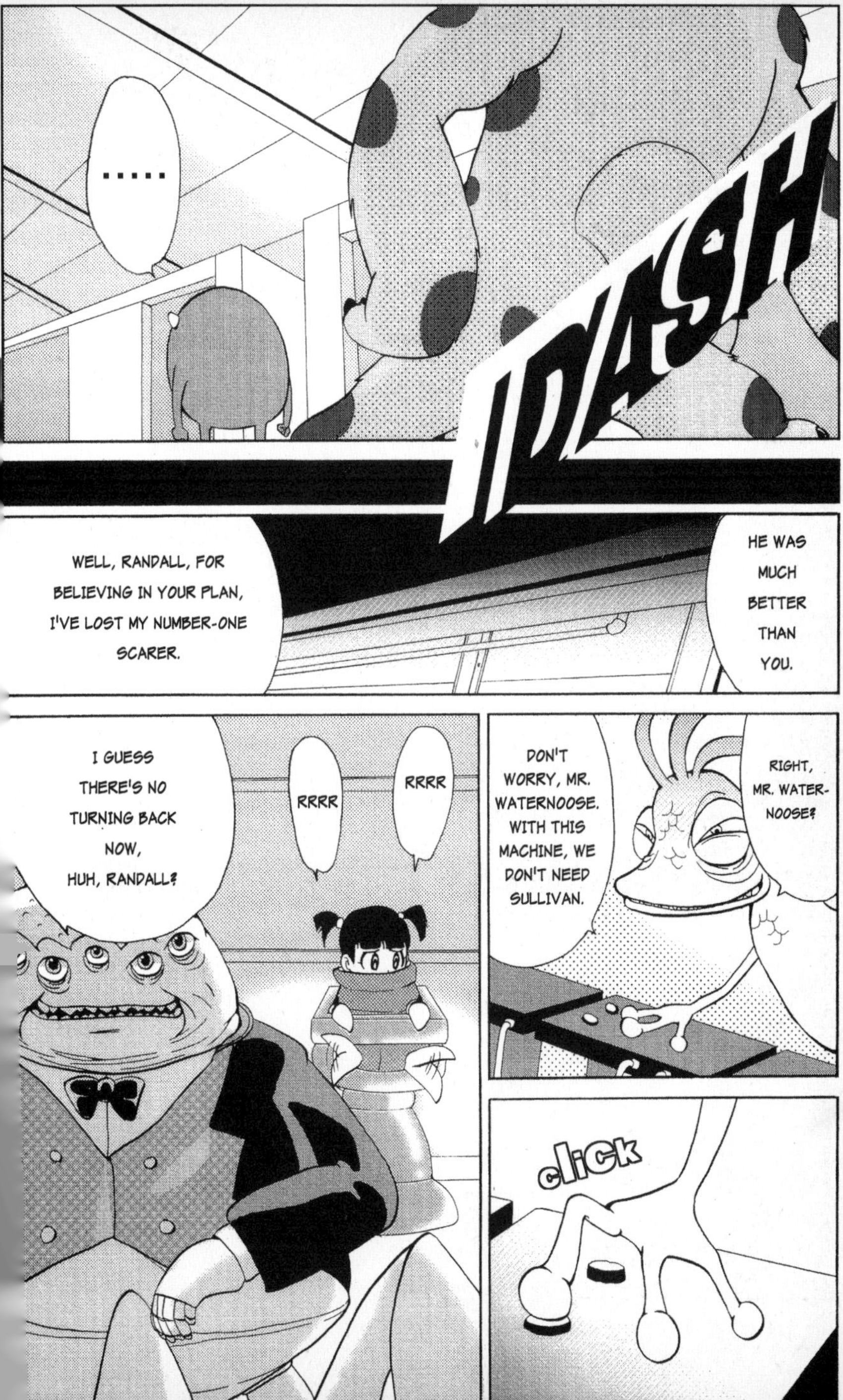
.....
DASH
WELL, RANDALL, FOR BELIEVING IN YOUR PLAN, I'VE LOST MY NUMBER-ONE SCARER.
HE WAS MUCH BETTER THAN YOU.
I GUESS THERE'S NO TURNING BACK NOW, HUH, RANDALL?
RRRR
RRRR
DON'T WORRY, MR. WATERNOOSE. WITH THIS MACHINE, WE DON'T NEED SULLIVAN.
RIGHT, MR. WATER-NOOSE?
click

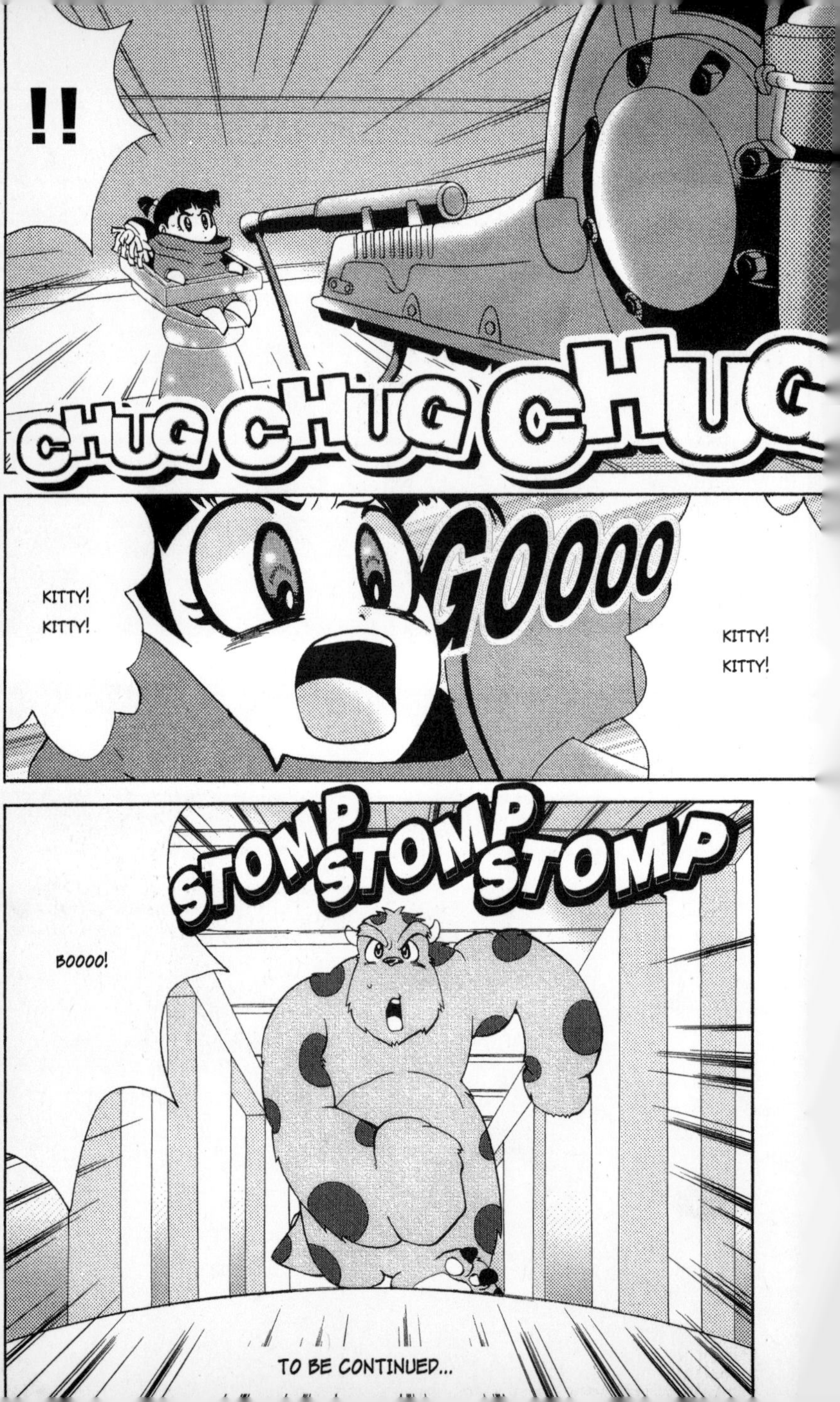
!!
CHUG CHUG CHUG
KITTY! KITTY!
GOOOO
KITTY! KITTY!
STOMP STOMP STOMP
BOOOO!
TO BE CONTINUED...

A MONSTER PLAN

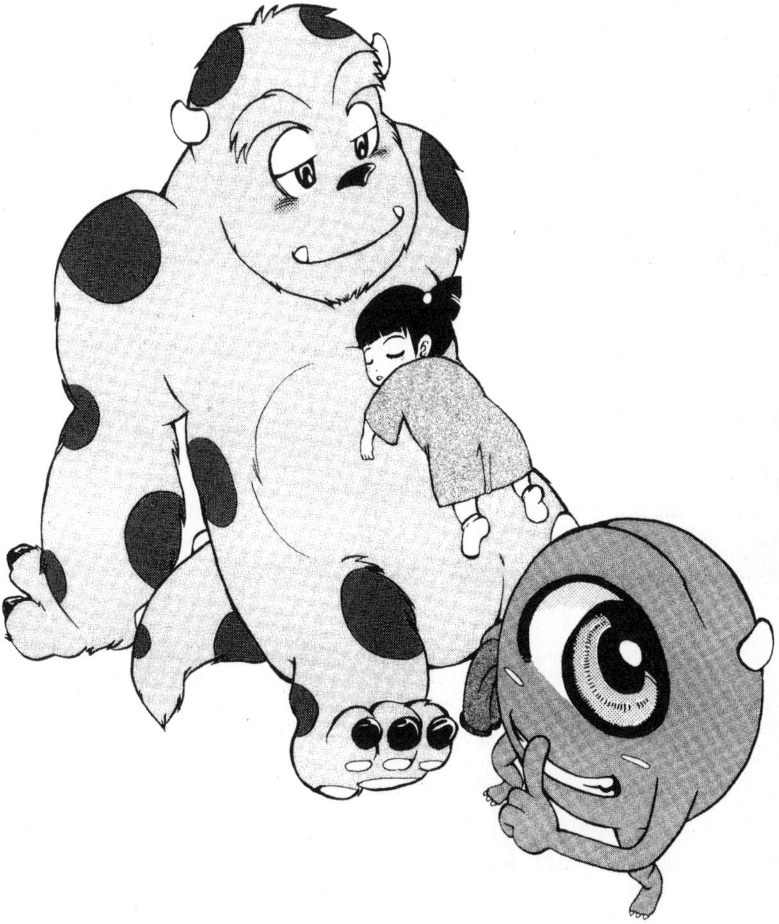

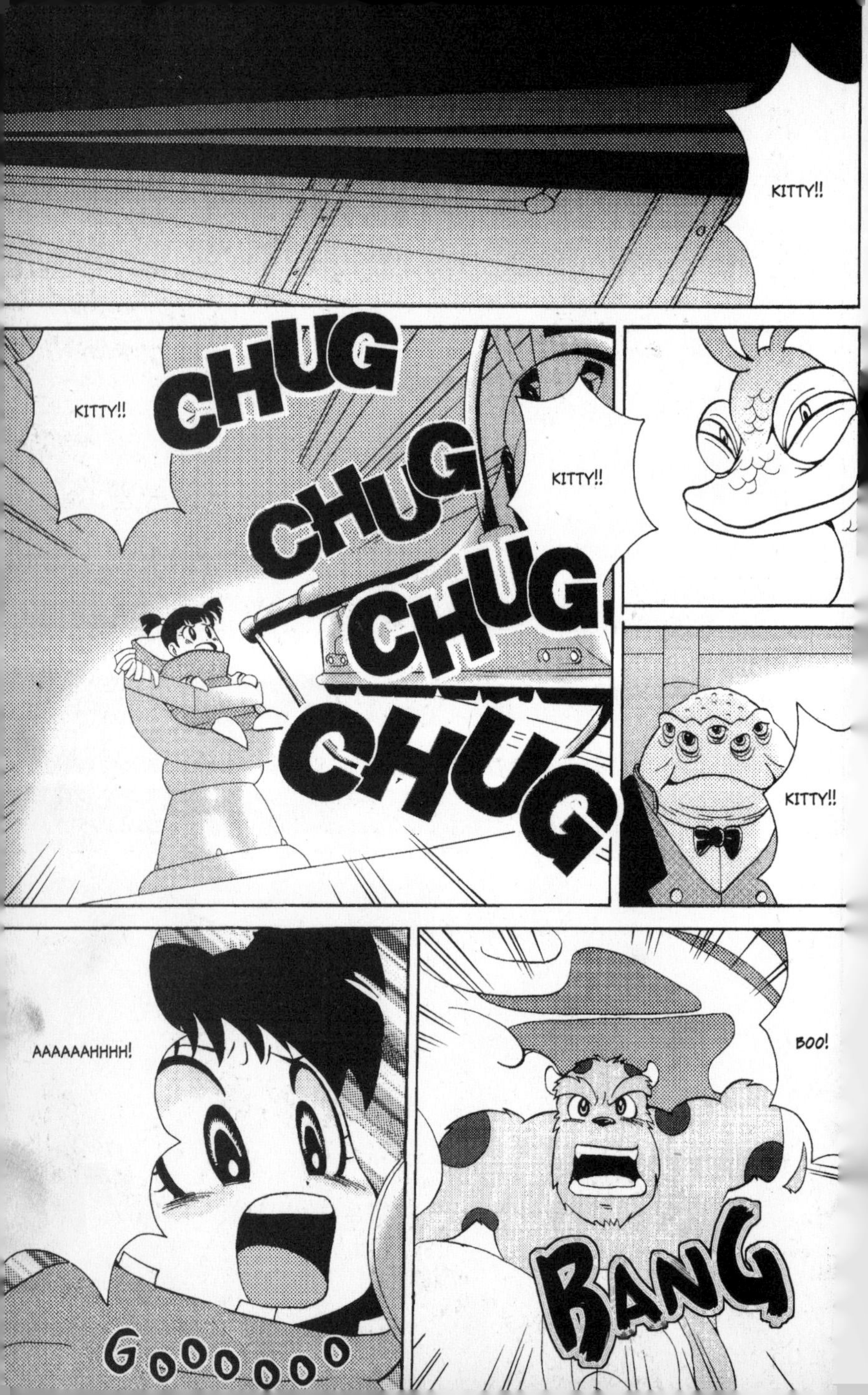
KITTY!!
KITTY!!
CHUG
CHUG
CHUG
CHUG
KITTY!!
KITTY!!
AAAAAAHHHH!
GOOOOOOO
BOO!
BANG

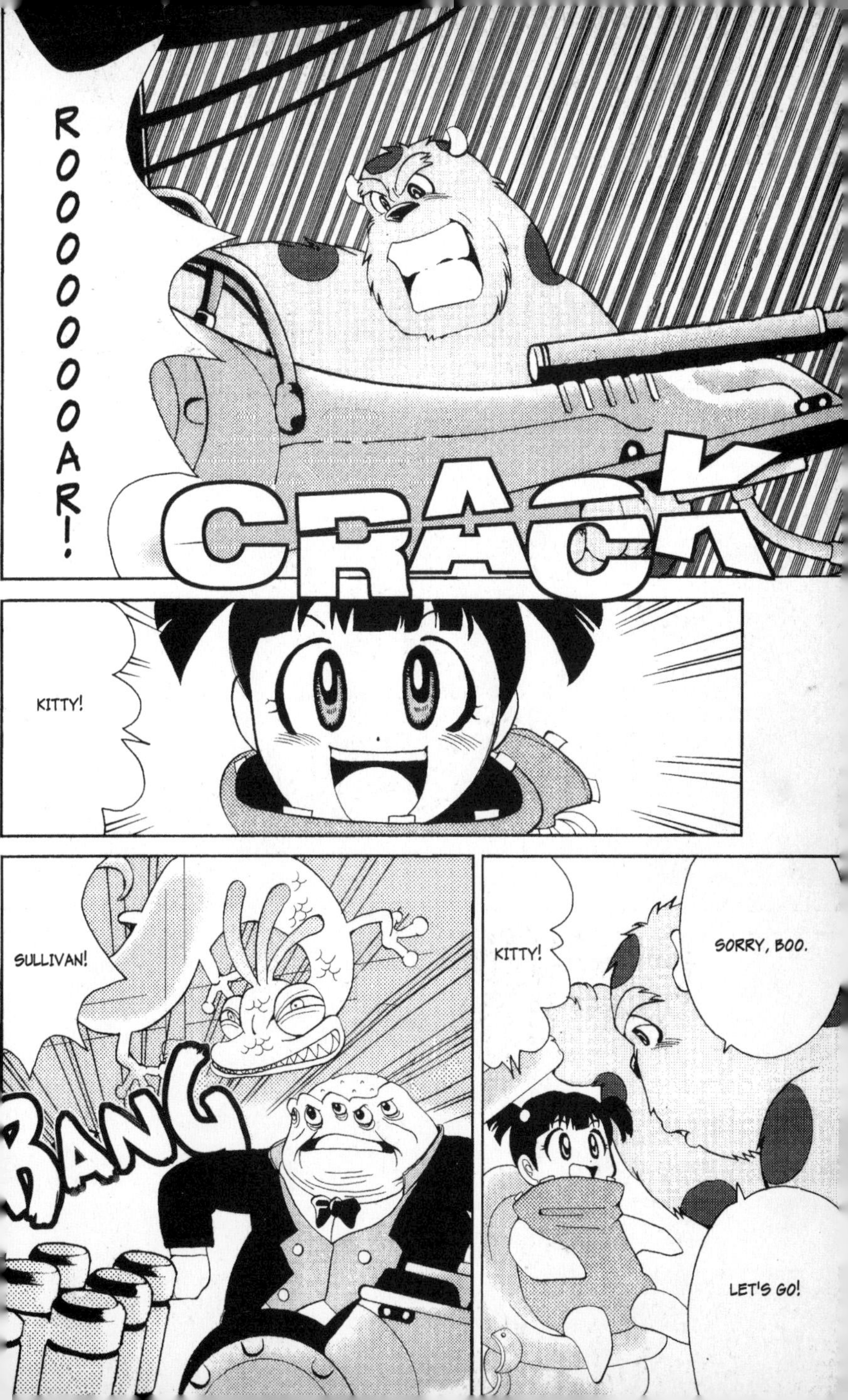
ROOOOOOOOOAR!
CRACK
KITTY!
SULLIVAN!
BANG
KITTY!
SORRY, BOO.
LET'S GO!

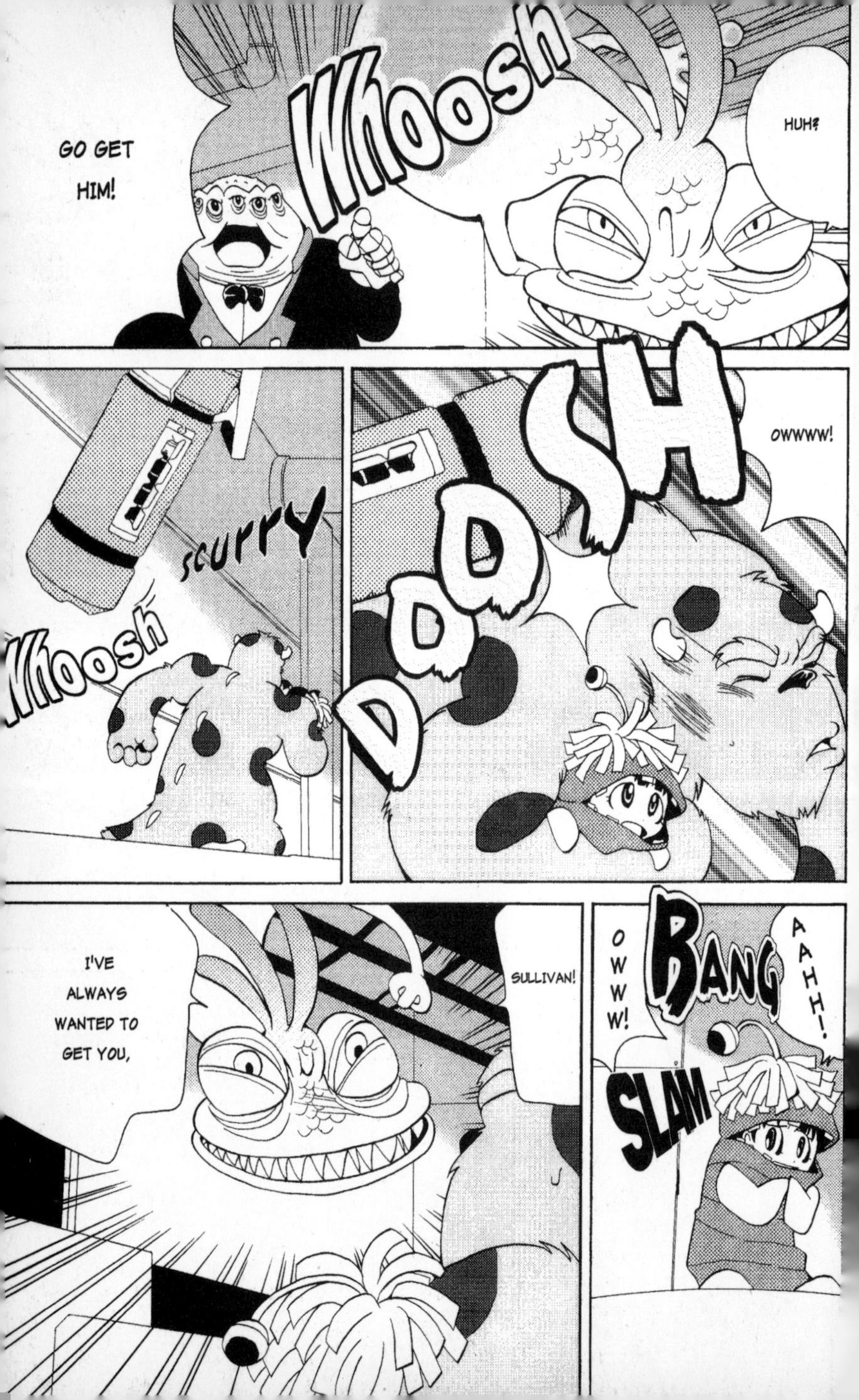
GO GET HIM!
Whoosh
HUH?
scurry
Whoosh
DDDSH
OWWWW!
I'VE ALWAYS WANTED TO GET YOU,
SULLIVAN!
OWWW!
BANG
AAHH!
SLAM

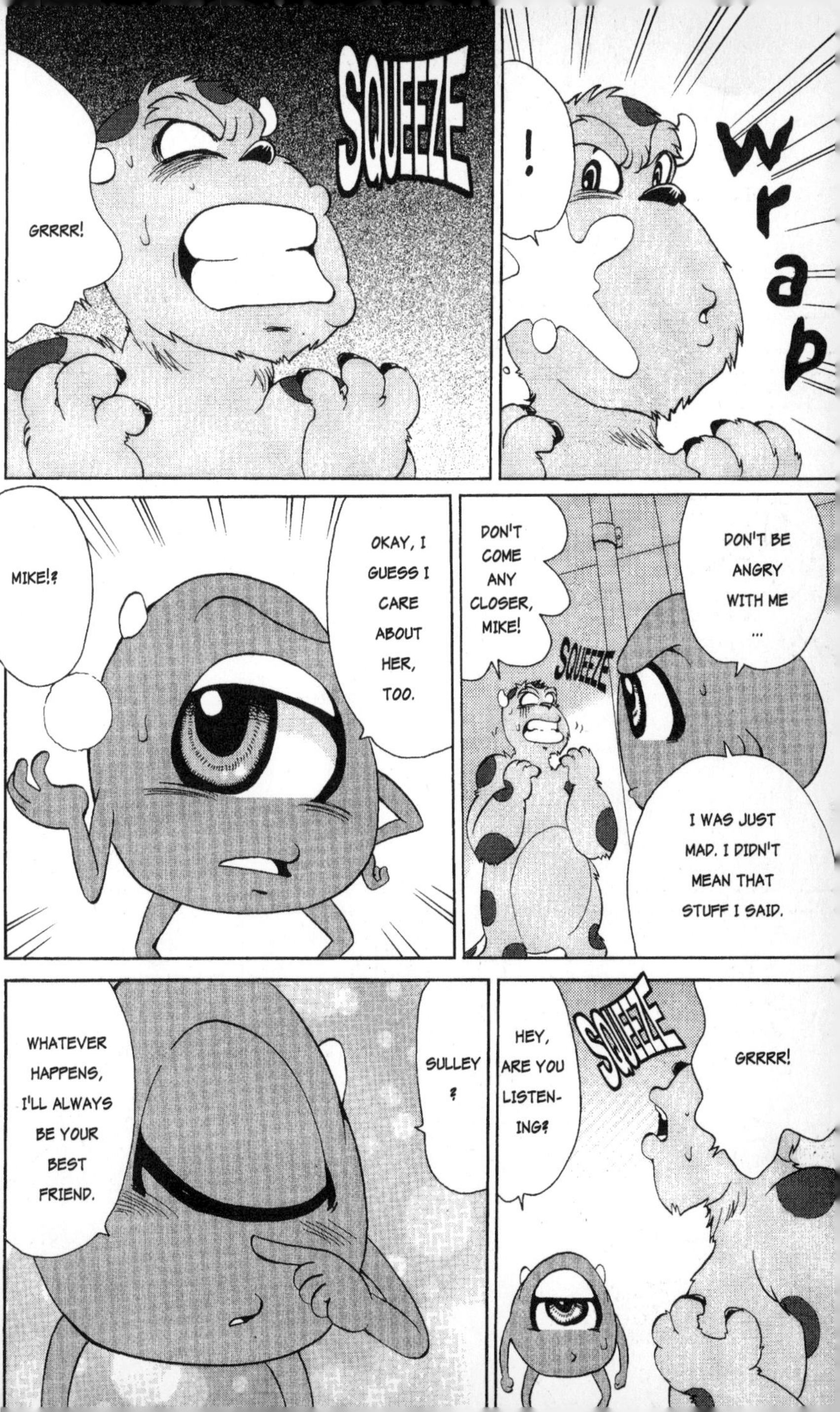
SQUEEZE
GRRRR!
!
wrap
MIKE!?
OKAY, I GUESS I CARE ABOUT HER, TOO.
DON'T COME ANY CLOSER, MIKE!
DON'T BE ANGRY WITH ME ...
SQUEEZE
I WAS JUST MAD. I DIDN'T MEAN THAT STUFF I SAID.
WHATEVER HAPPENS, I'LL ALWAYS BE YOUR BEST FRIEND.
SULLEY?
HEY, ARE YOU LISTENING?
SQUEEZE
GRRRR!

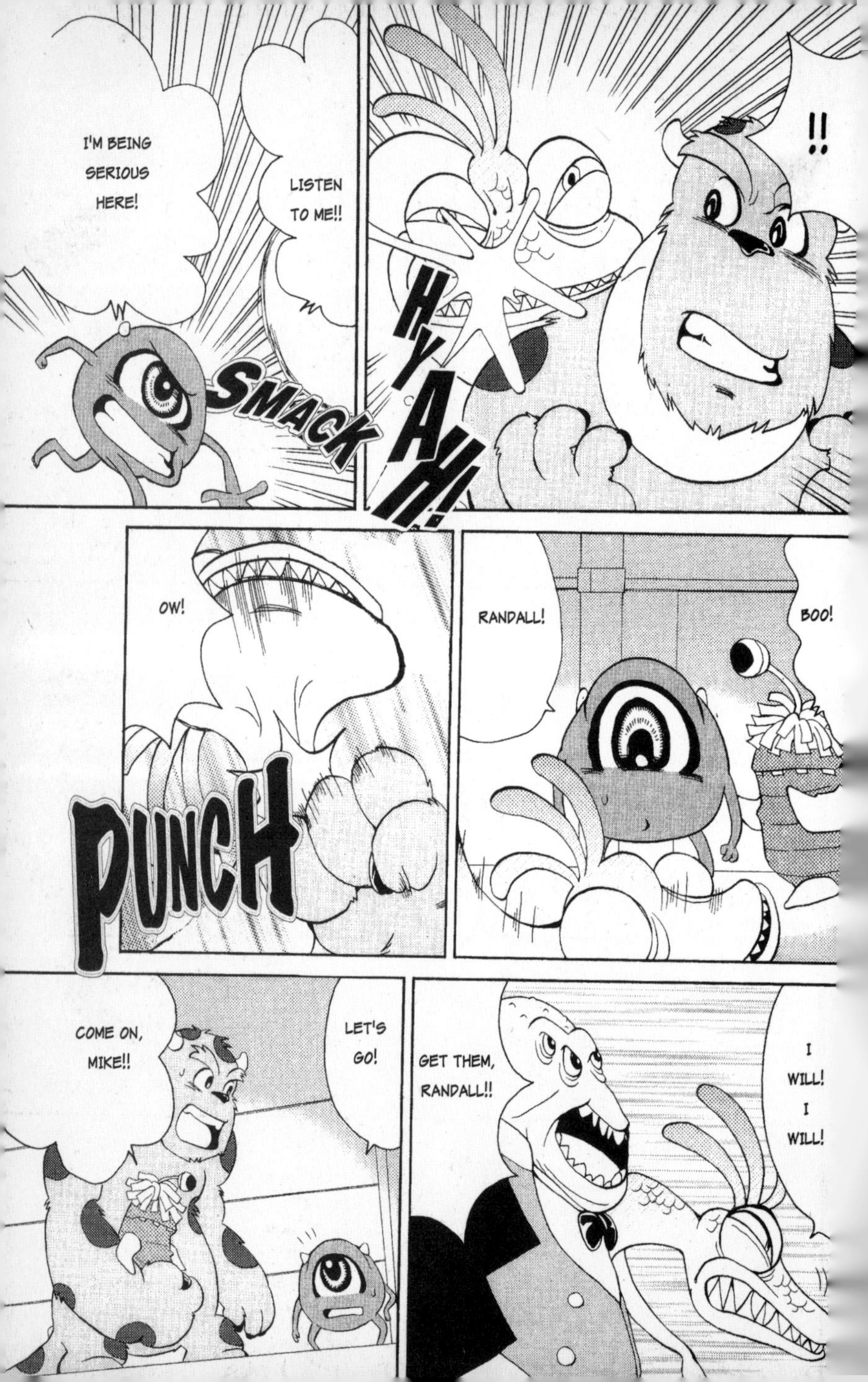
I'M BEING SERIOUS HERE!
LISTEN TO ME!!
SMACK
HYAAH!!
!!
OW!
PUNCH
RANDALL!
BOO!
COME ON, MIKE!!
LET'S GO!
GET THEM, RANDALL!!
I WILL! I WILL!

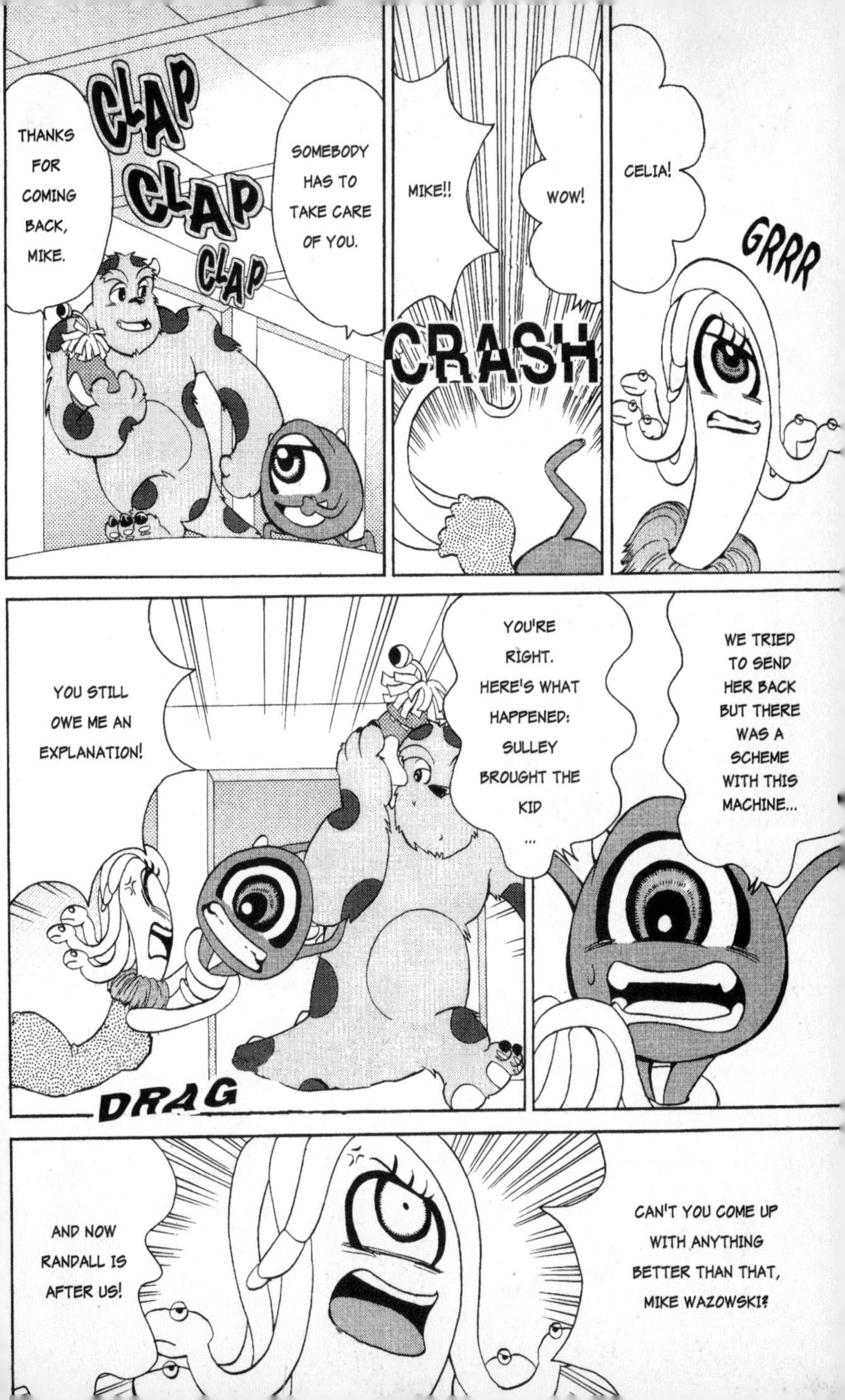
THANKS FOR COMING BACK, MIKE.
CLAP CLAP CLAP
SOMEBODY HAS TO TAKE CARE OF YOU.
MIKE!!
WOW!
CRASH
CELIA!
GRRR
YOU STILL OWE ME AN EXPLANATION!
YOU'RE RIGHT. HERE'S WHAT HAPPENED: SULLEY BROUGHT THE KID ...
DRAG
WE TRIED TO SEND HER BACK BUT THERE WAS A SCHEME WITH THIS MACHINE...
AND NOW RANDALL IS AFTER US!
CAN'T YOU COME UP WITH ANYTHING BETTER THAN THAT, MIKE WAZOWSKI?

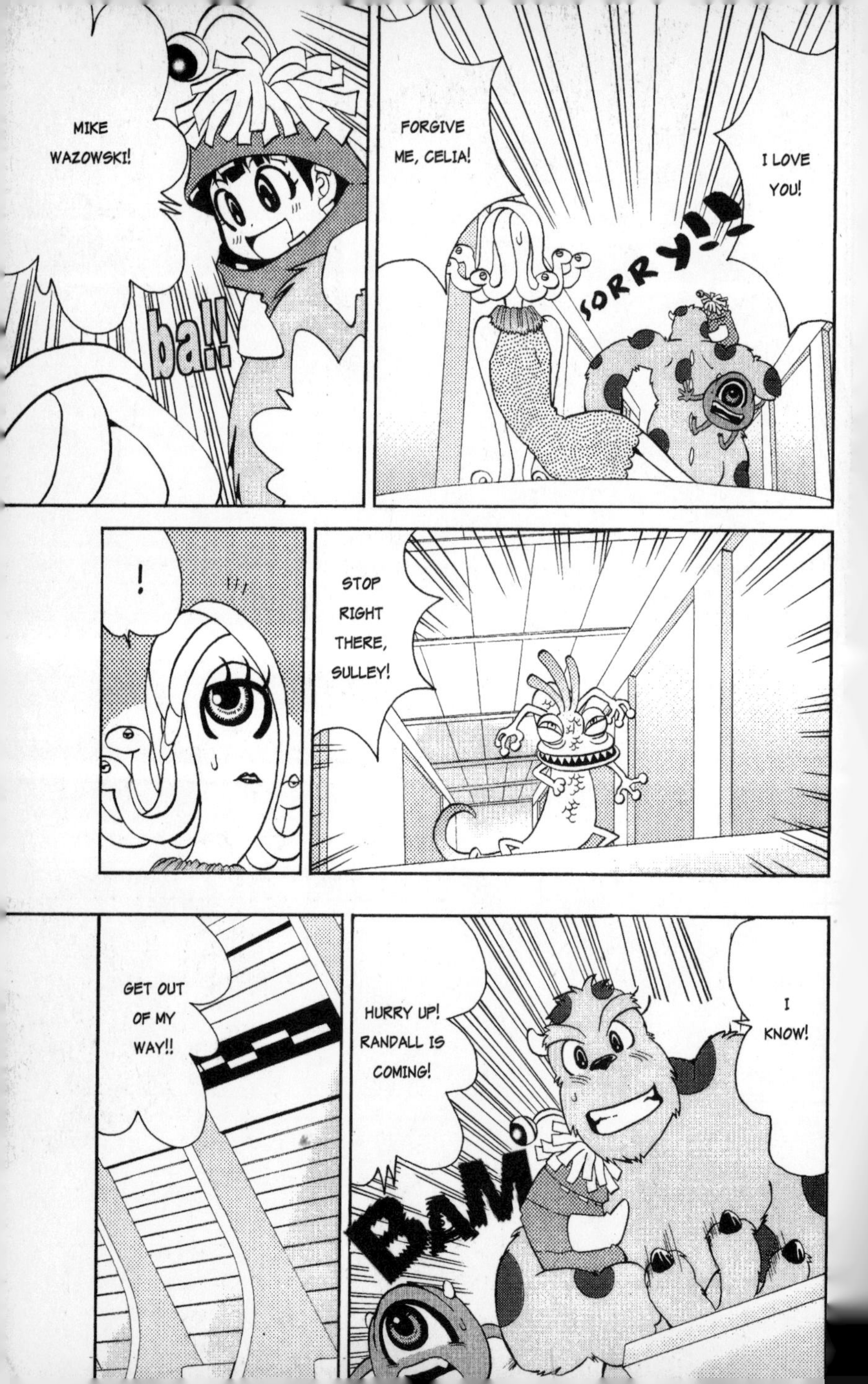
MIKE WAZOWSKI!
ba!!
FORGIVE ME, CELIA!
I LOVE YOU!
SORRY!!
!
STOP RIGHT THERE, SULLEY!
GET OUT OF MY WAY!!
HURRY UP! RANDALL IS COMING!
I KNOW!
BAM

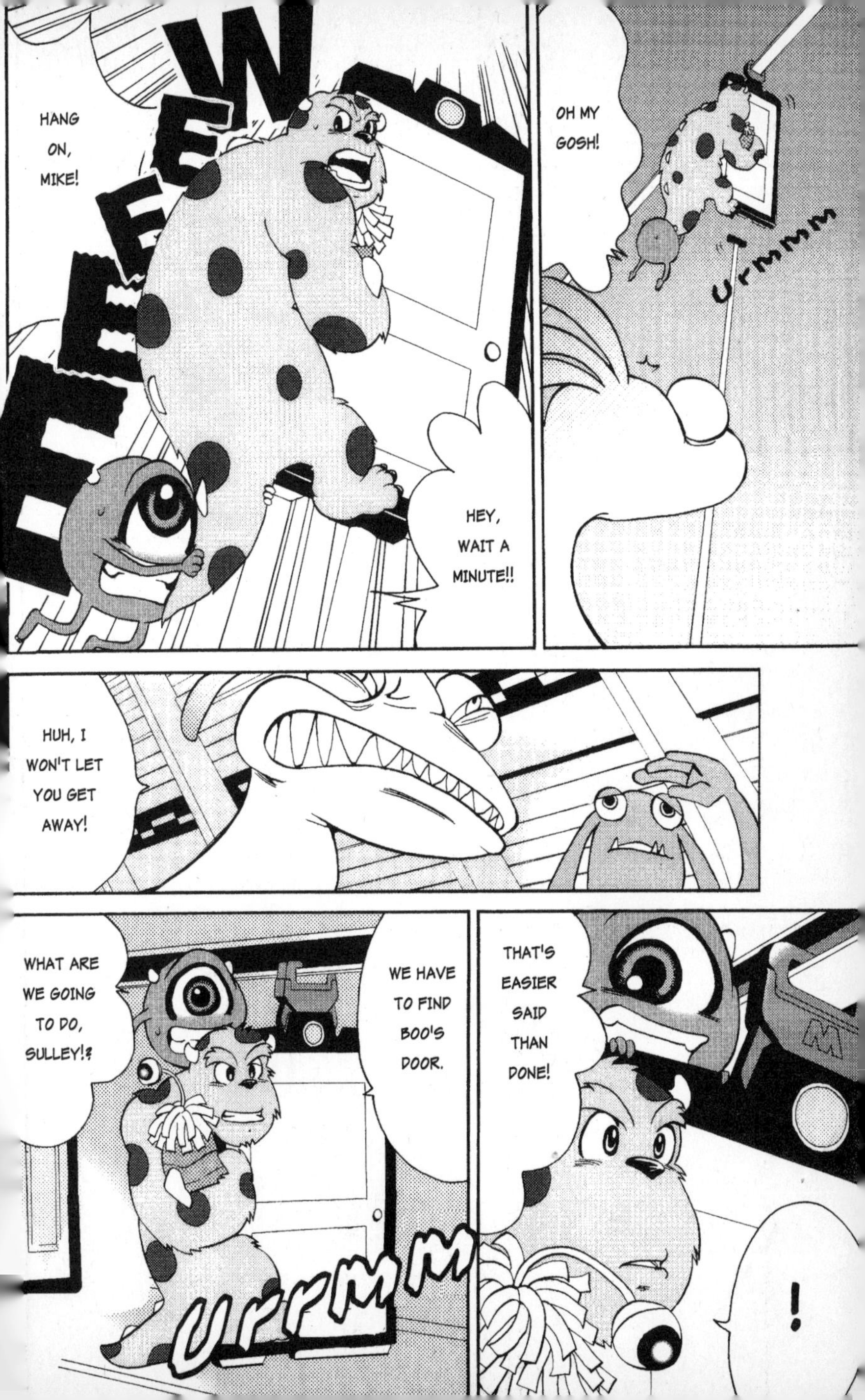
HANG ON, MIKE!
HEY, WAIT A MINUTE!!
OH MY GOSH!
Urmmm
HUH, I WON'T LET YOU GET AWAY!
WHAT ARE WE GOING TO DO, SULLEY!?
WE HAVE TO FIND BOO'S DOOR.
Urrmm
THAT'S EASIER SAID THAN DONE!
!

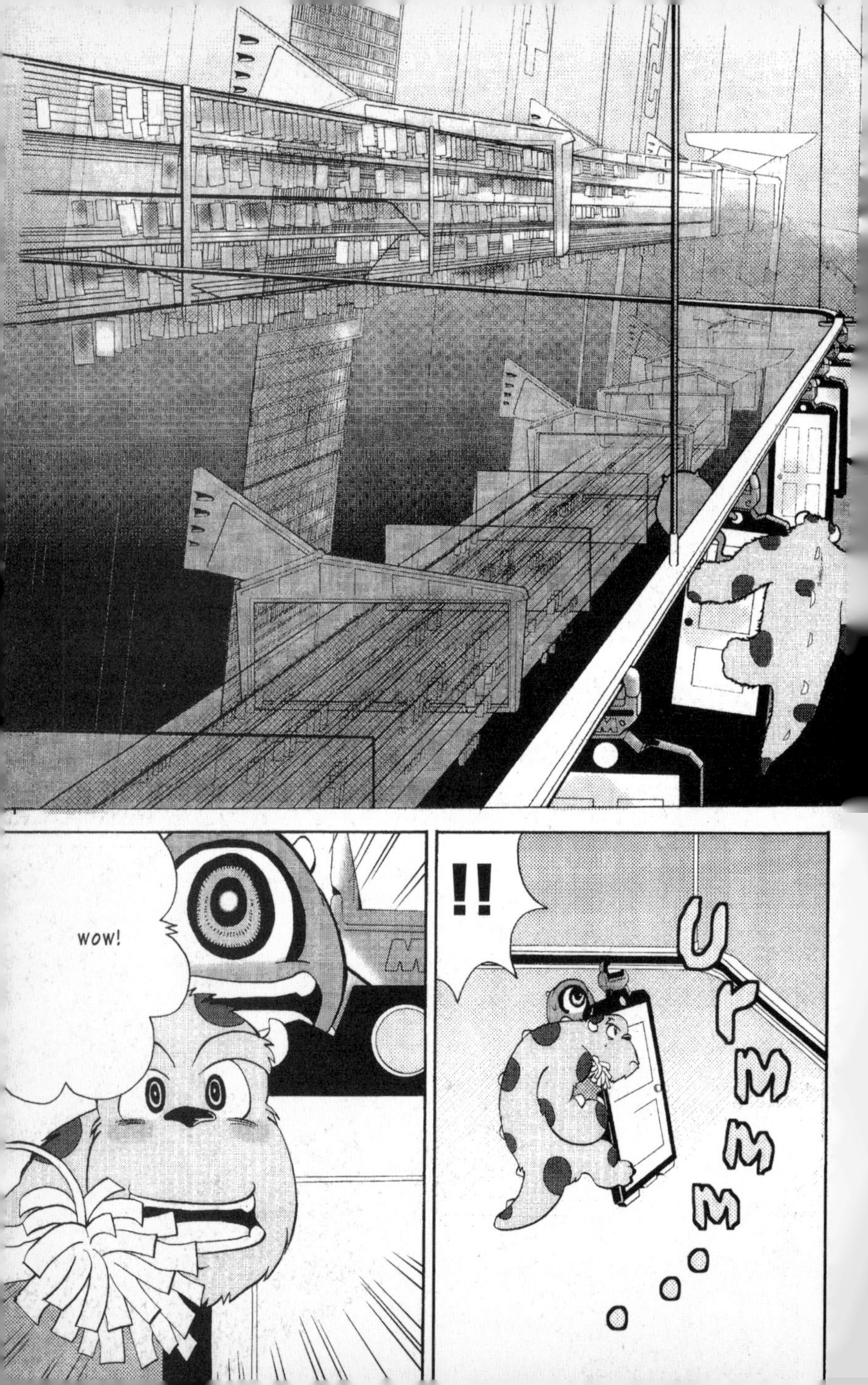
WOW!
!!
URMMM...

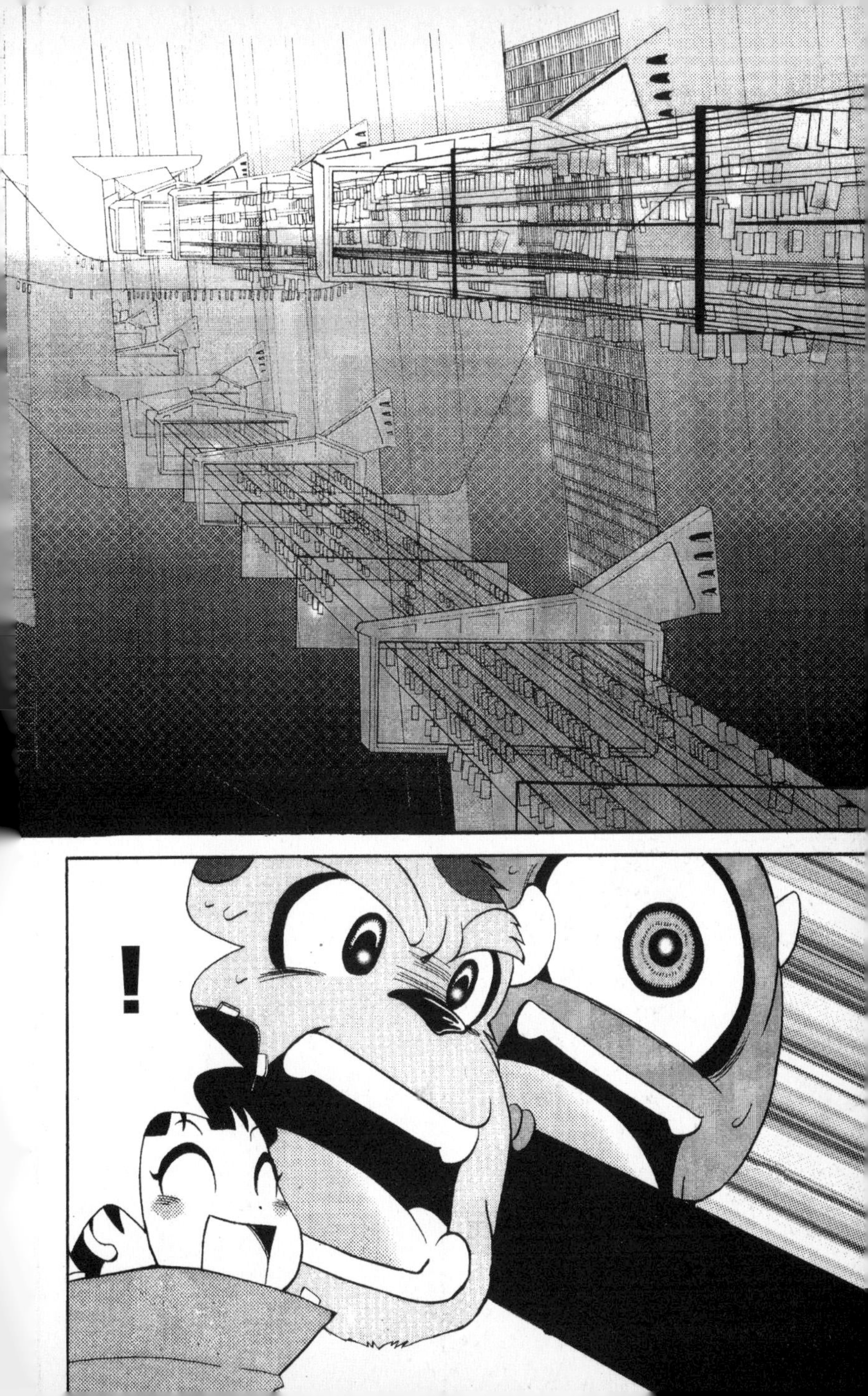
!

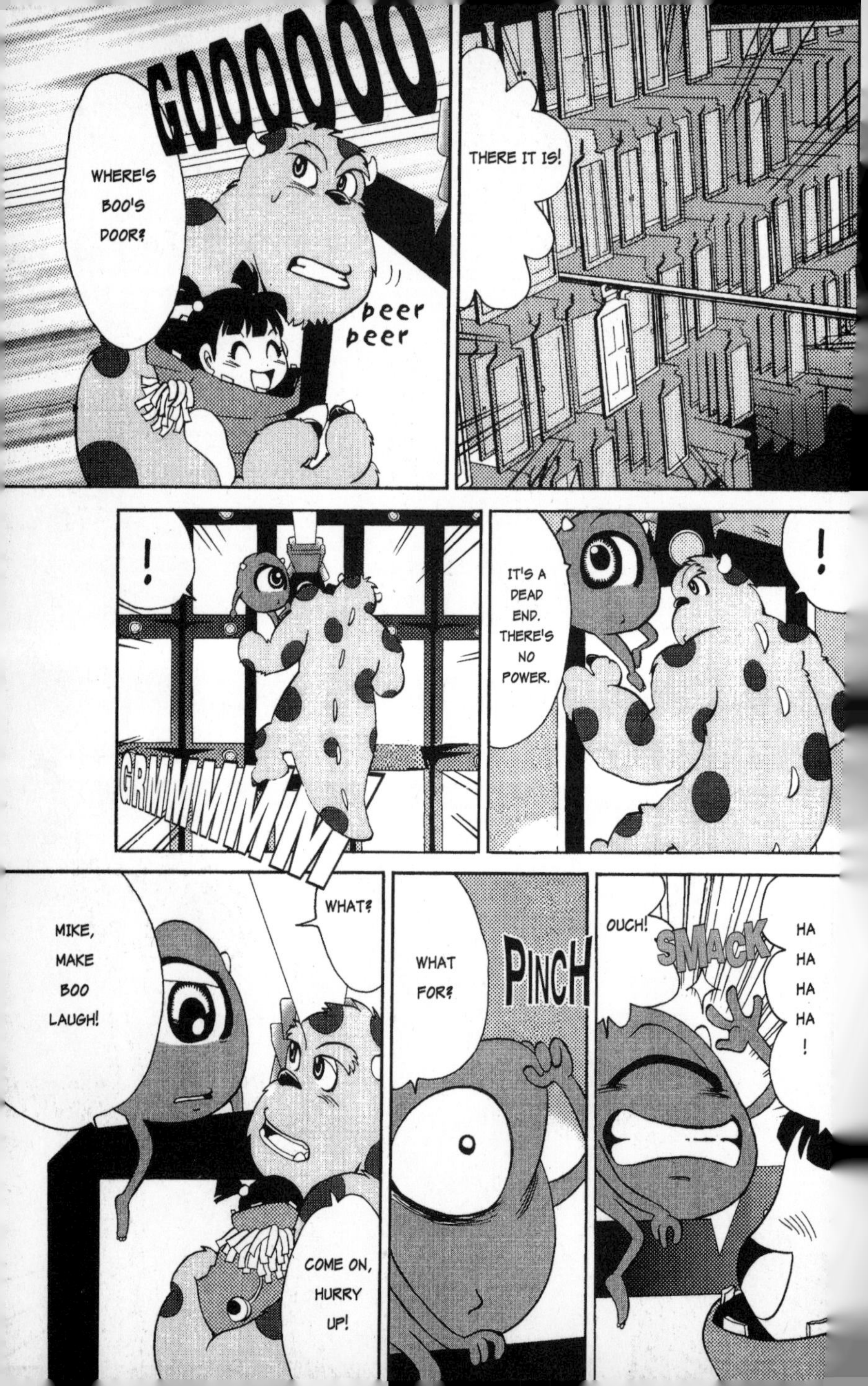
GOOOOOO
WHERE'S BOO'S DOOR?
beer beer
THERE IT IS!
!
GRMMMMMM
IT'S A DEAD END. THERE'S NO POWER.
!
MIKE, MAKE BOO LAUGH!
WHAT?
COME ON, HURRY UP!
WHAT FOR?
PINCH
OUCH!
SMACK
HA HA HA HA!

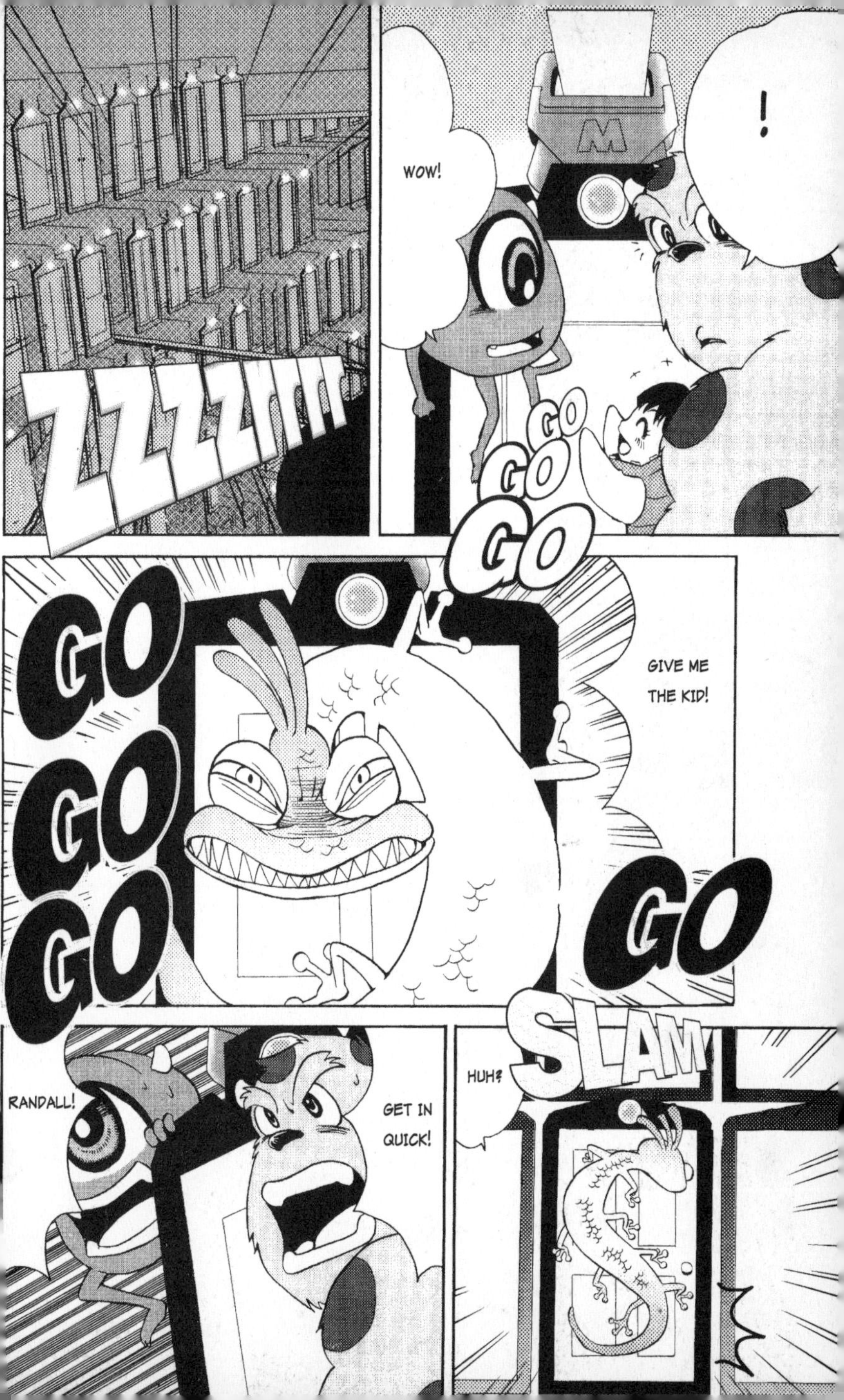
ZZZZrrrr
WOW!
!
GO GO GO GO
GO GO GO
GIVE ME THE KID!
GO
RANDALL!
GET IN QUICK!
SLAM
HUH?

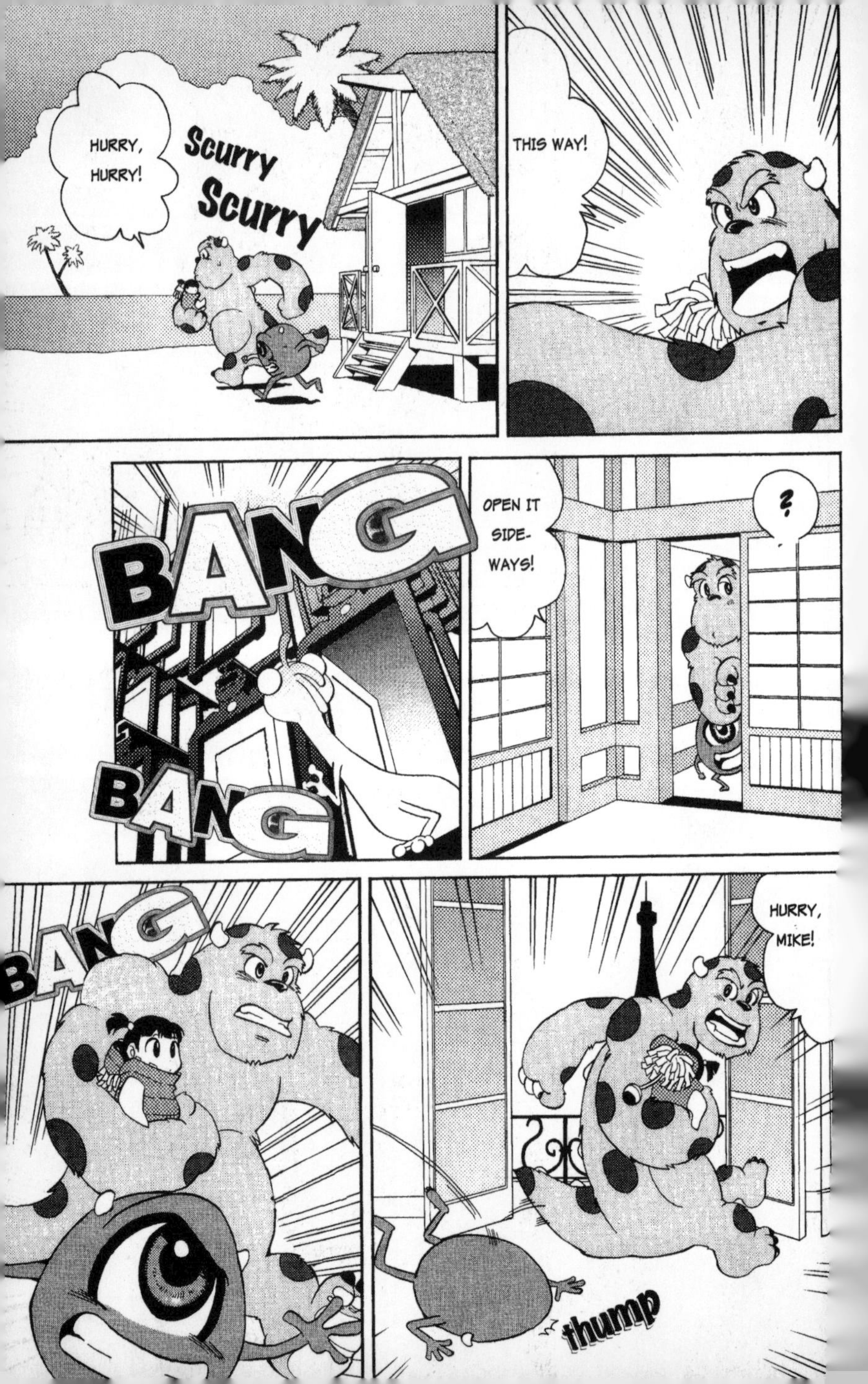
HURRY, HURRY!
Scurry Scurry
THIS WAY!
BANG
BANG
OPEN IT SIDE-WAYS!
?
BANG
HURRY, MIKE!
thump

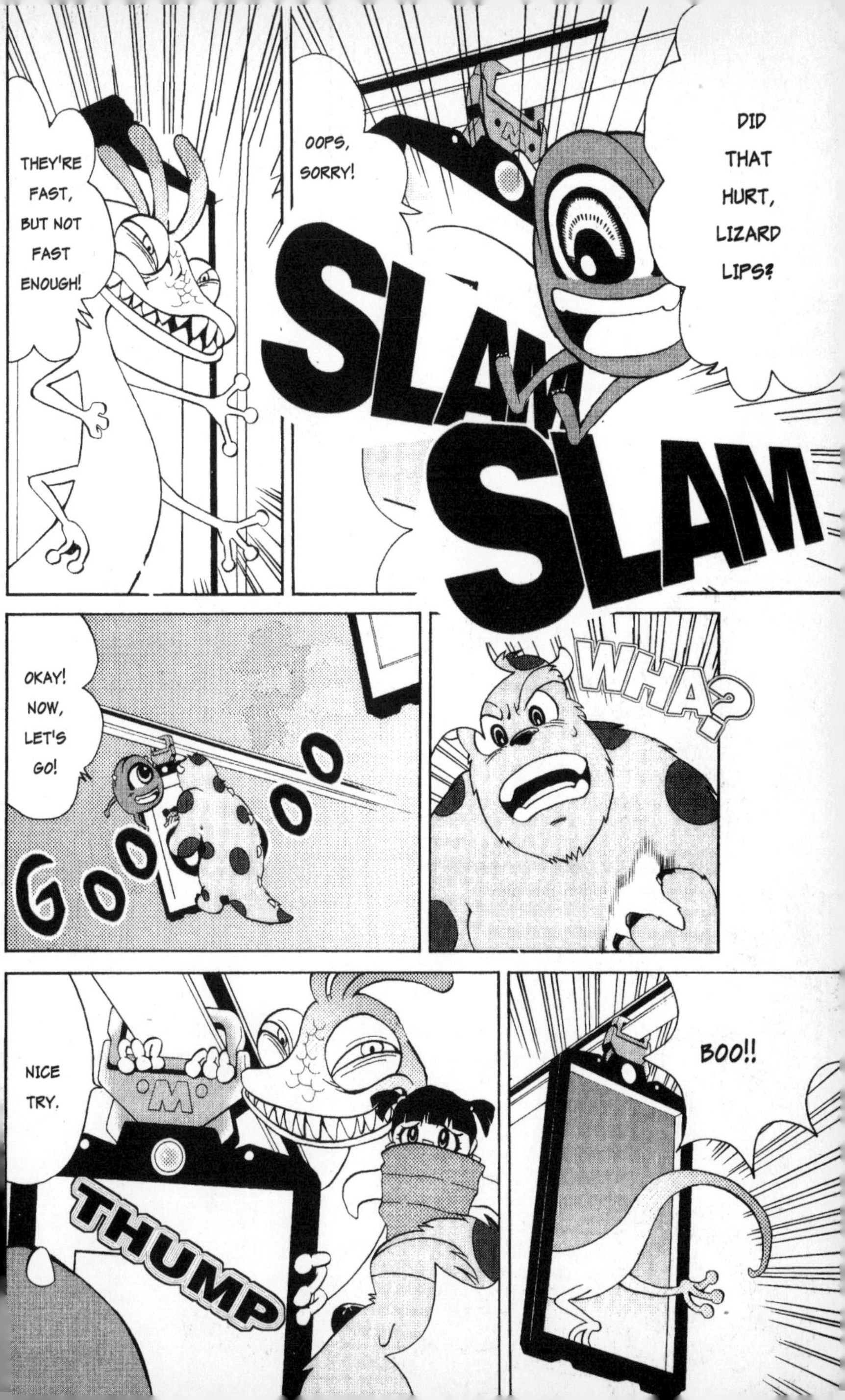
THEY'RE FAST, BUT NOT FAST ENOUGH!
OOPS, SORRY!
SLAM
SLAM
DID THAT HURT, LIZARD LIPS?
OKAY! NOW, LET'S GO!
GOOOOO
WHA?
NICE TRY.
THUMP
BOO!!

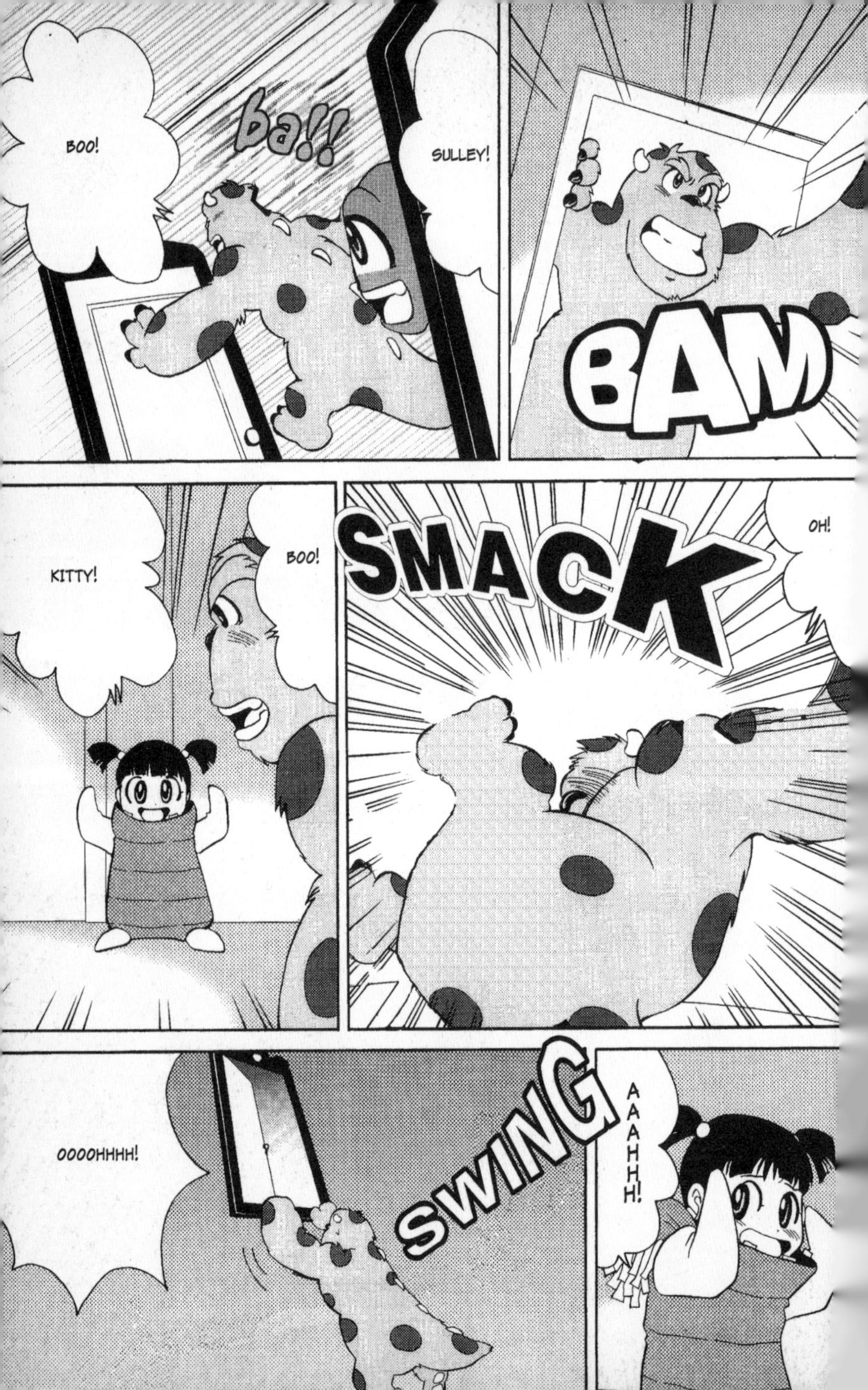
BOO!
ba!!
SULLEY!
BAM
KITTY!
BOO!
SMACK
OH!
OOOOHHHH!
SWING
AAAAHHH!

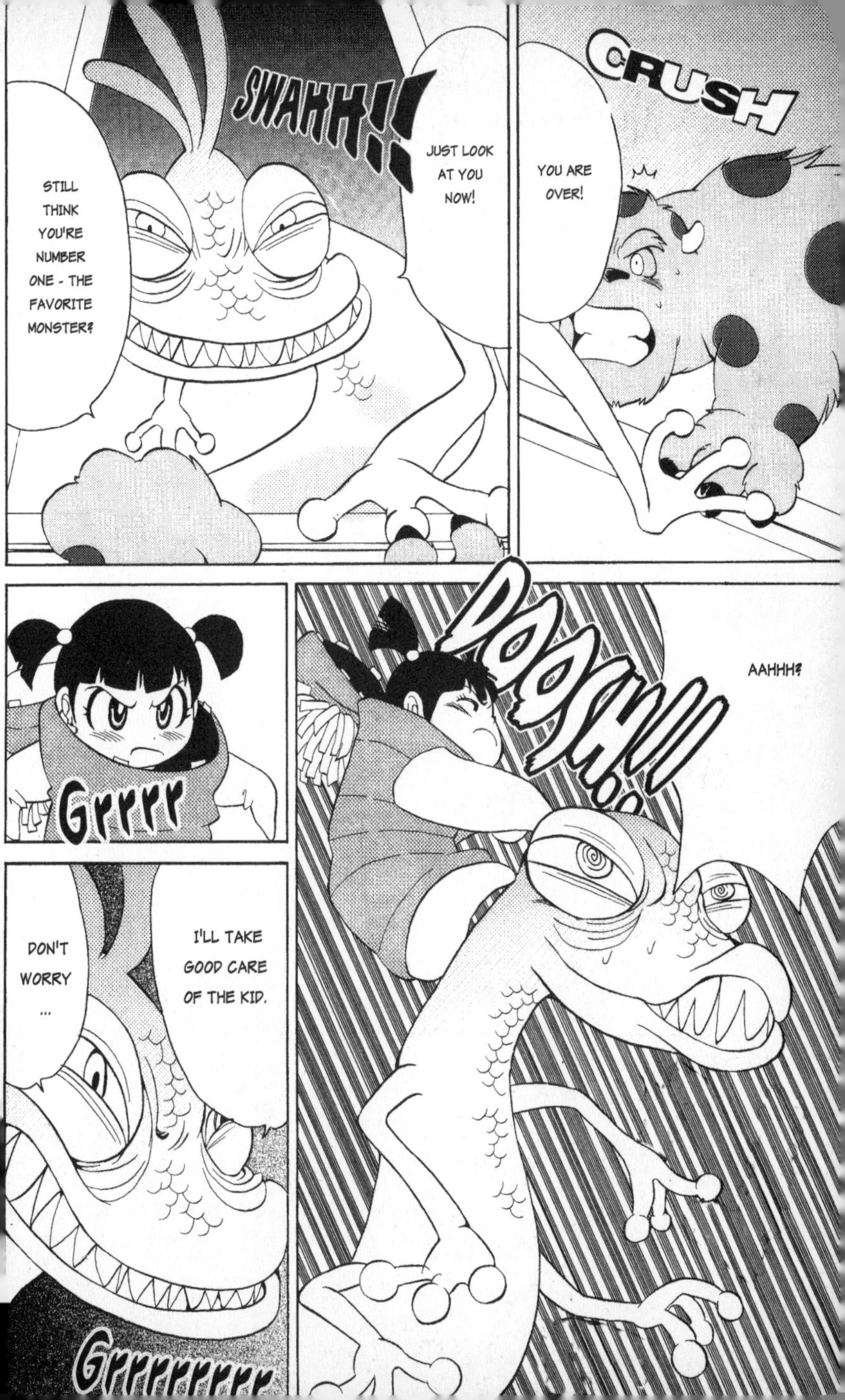
STILL THINK YOU'RE NUMBER ONE - THE FAVORITE MONSTER?
SWAHH!!
JUST LOOK AT YOU NOW!
CRUSH
YOU ARE OVER!
Grrrr
DOOSH!!
AAHHH?
DON'T WORRY ...
I'LL TAKE GOOD CARE OF THE KID.
Grrrrrrrrr

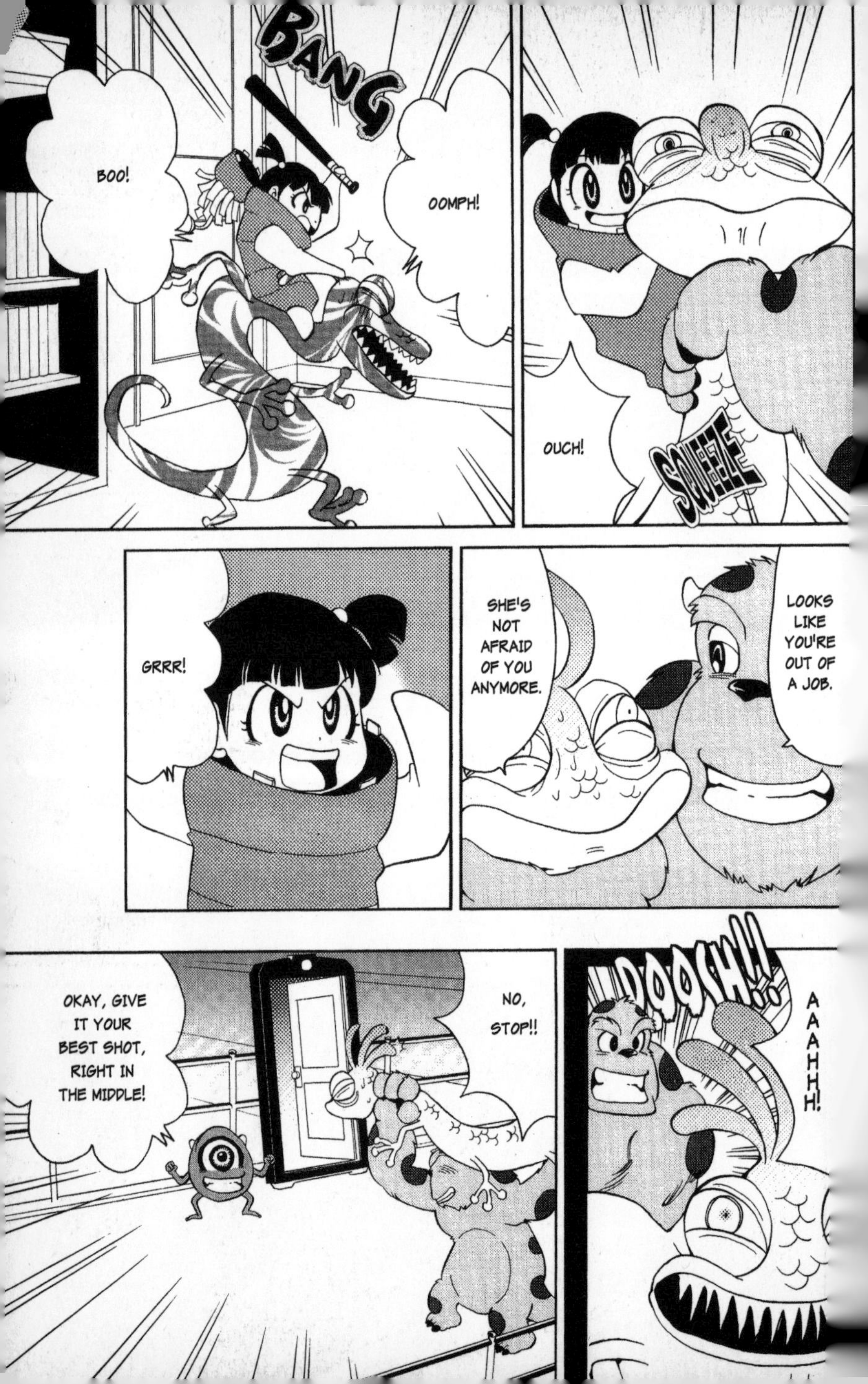
BANG
BOO!
OOMPH!
OUCH!
SQUEEZE
GRRR!
SHE'S NOT AFRAID OF YOU ANYMORE.
LOOKS LIKE YOU'RE OUT OF A JOB.
OKAY, GIVE IT YOUR BEST SHOT, RIGHT IN THE MIDDLE!
NO, STOP!!
OOOCH!!
AAAAHHH!

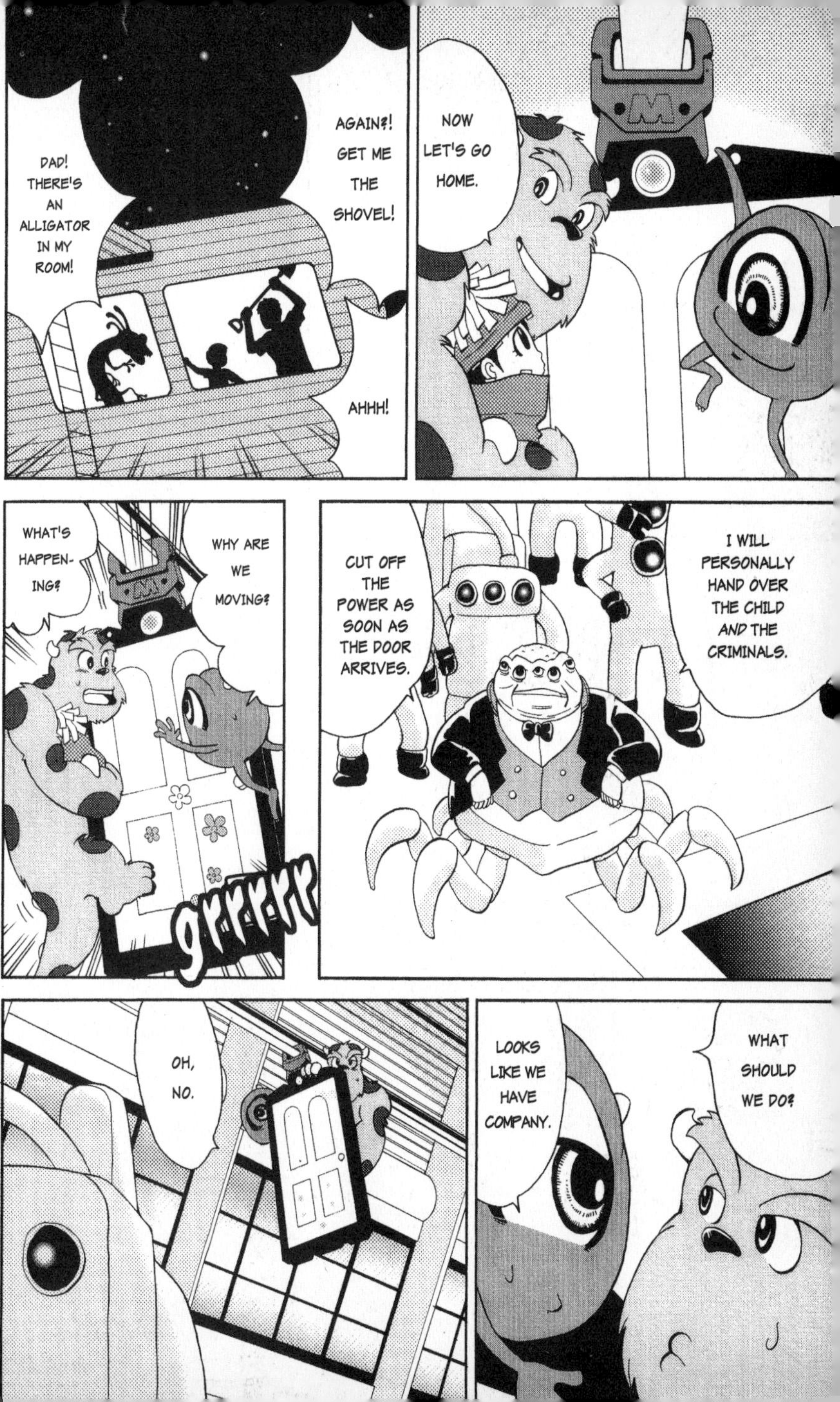
DAD! THERE'S AN ALLIGATOR IN MY ROOM!
AGAIN?! GET ME THE SHOVEL!
AHHH!
NOW LET'S GO HOME.
WHAT'S HAPPEN-ING?
WHY ARE WE MOVING?
grrrrr
CUT OFF THE POWER AS SOON AS THE DOOR ARRIVES.
I WILL PERSONALLY HAND OVER THE CHILD AND THE CRIMINALS.
OH, NO.
LOOKS LIKE WE HAVE COMPANY.
WHAT SHOULD WE DO?

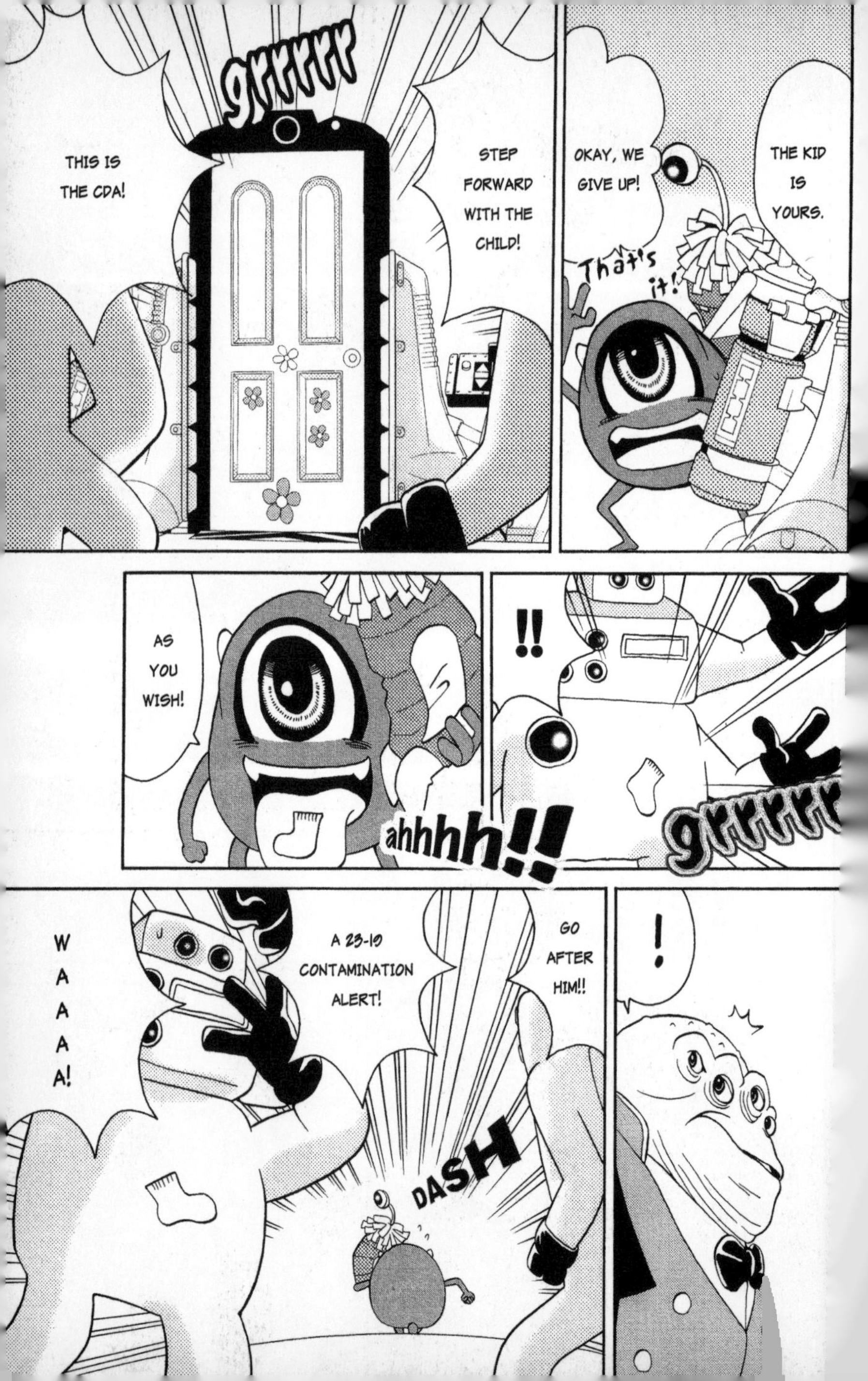
grrrrr
THIS IS THE CDA!
STEP FORWARD WITH THE CHILD!
OKAY, WE GIVE UP!
THE KID IS YOURS.
That's it!
AS YOU WISH!
!!
ahhhh!!
grrrrr
WAAAA!
A 23-19 CONTAMINATION ALERT!
GO AFTER HIM!!
DASH
!

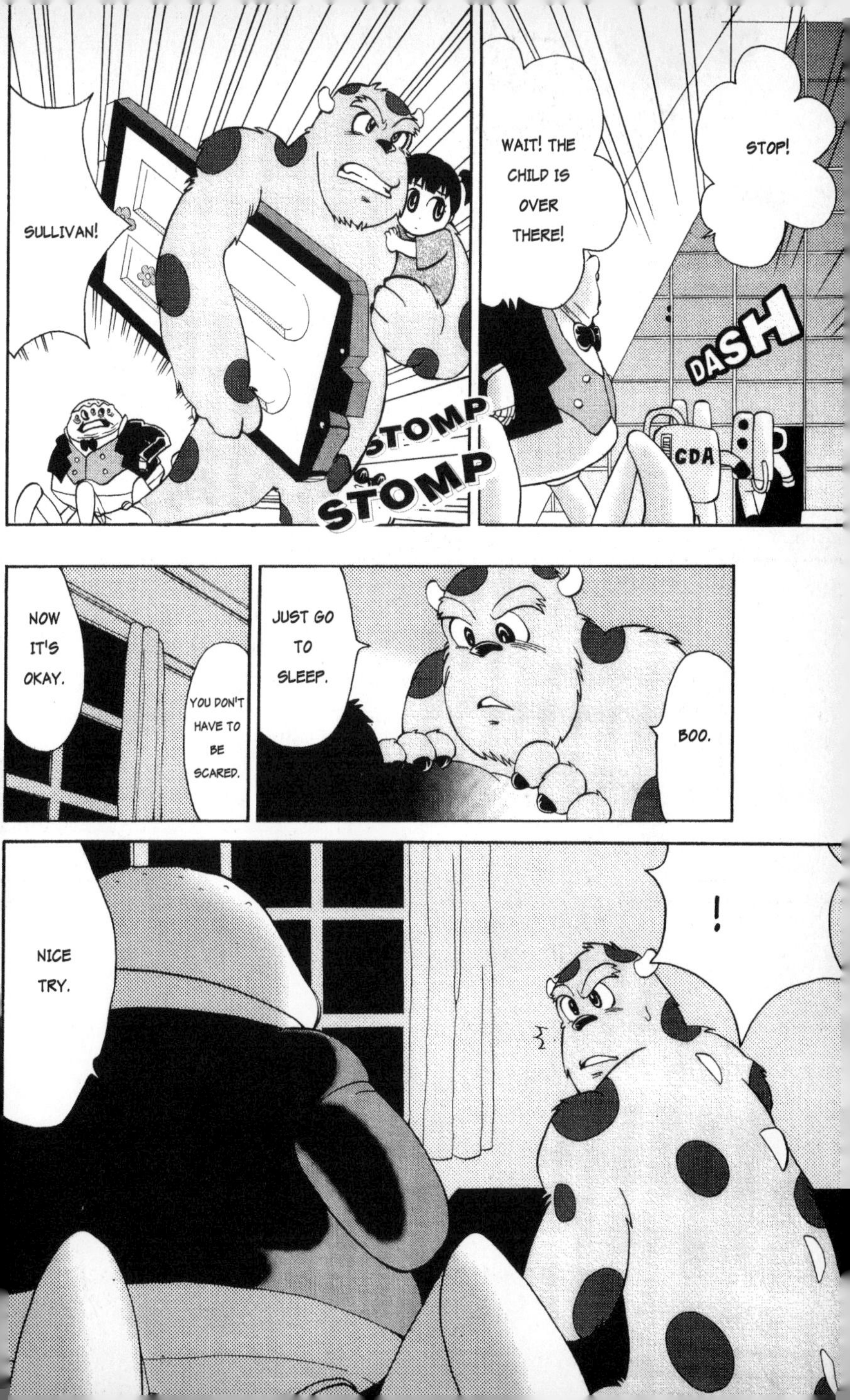
SULLIVAN!
STOMP
STOMP
WAIT! THE CHILD IS OVER THERE!
STOP!
DASH
CDA
NOW IT'S OKAY.
YOU DON'T HAVE TO BE SCARED.
JUST GO TO SLEEP.
BOO.
NICE TRY.
!

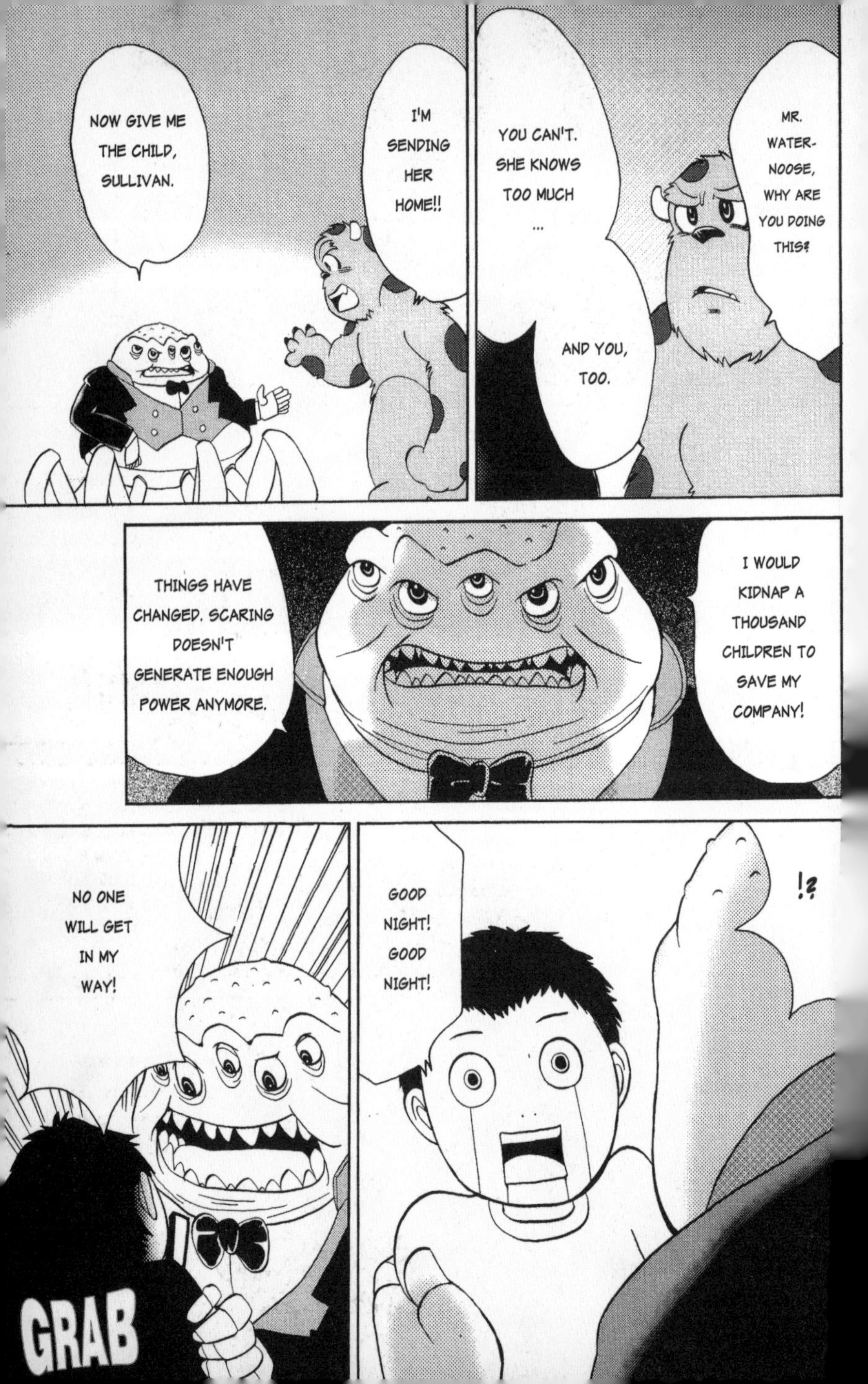
NOW GIVE ME THE CHILD, SULLIVAN.
I'M SENDING HER HOME!!
YOU CAN'T. SHE KNOWS TOO MUCH ...
AND YOU, TOO.
MR. WATER-NOOSE, WHY ARE YOU DOING THIS?
THINGS HAVE CHANGED. SCARING DOESN'T GENERATE ENOUGH POWER ANYMORE.
I WOULD KIDNAP A THOUSAND CHILDREN TO SAVE MY COMPANY!
NO ONE WILL GET IN MY WAY!
GRAB
GOOD NIGHT! GOOD NIGHT!
!?

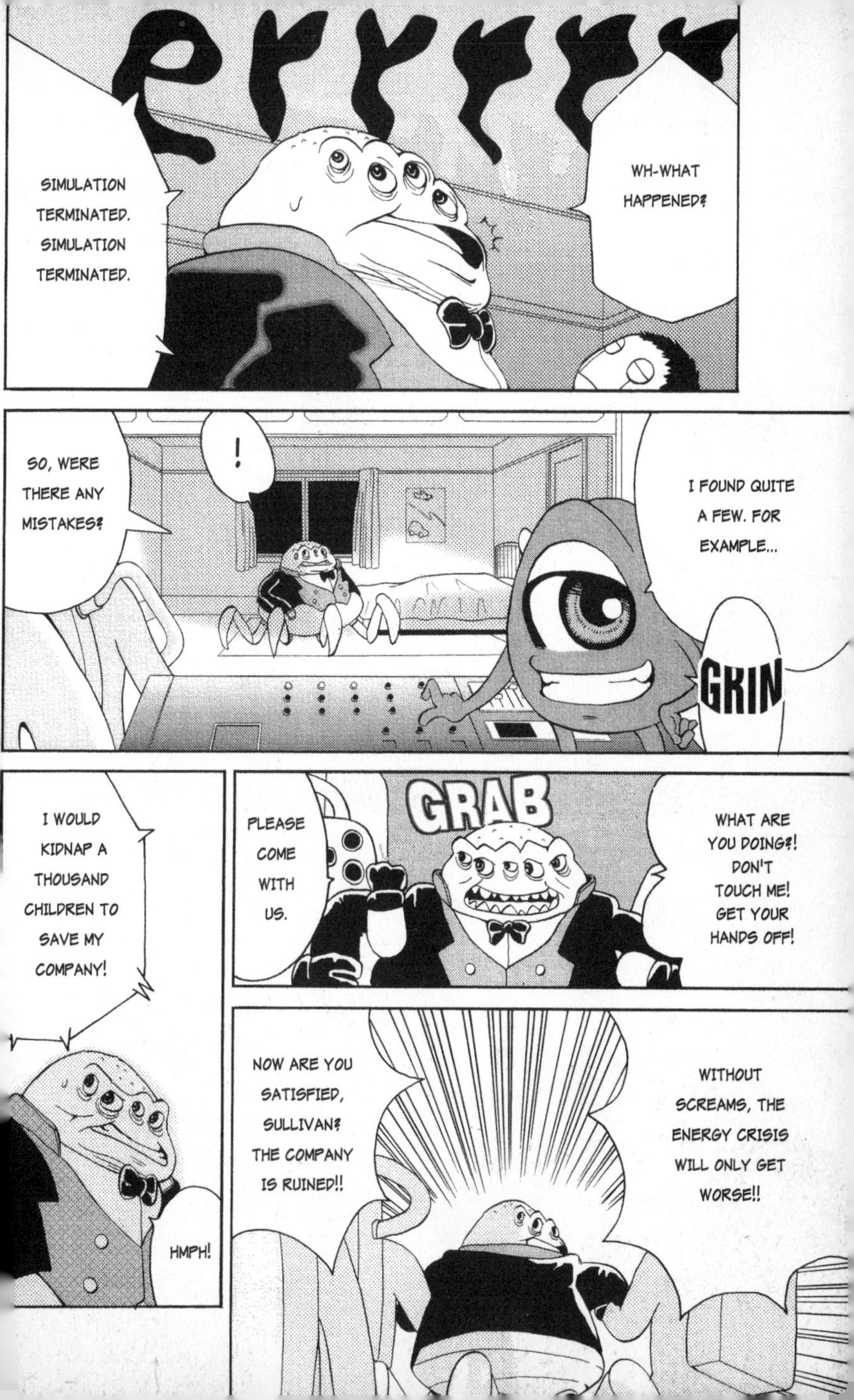
PFFFFF
SIMULATION TERMINATED. SIMULATION TERMINATED.
WH-WHAT HAPPENED?
SO, WERE THERE ANY MISTAKES?
!
I FOUND QUITE A FEW. FOR EXAMPLE...
GRIN
I WOULD KIDNAP A THOUSAND CHILDREN TO SAVE MY COMPANY!
GRAB
PLEASE COME WITH US.
WHAT ARE YOU DOING?! DON'T TOUCH ME! GET YOUR HANDS OFF!
HMPH!
NOW ARE YOU SATISFIED, SULLIVAN? THE COMPANY IS RUINED!!
WITHOUT SCREAMS, THE ENERGY CRISIS WILL ONLY GET WORSE!!

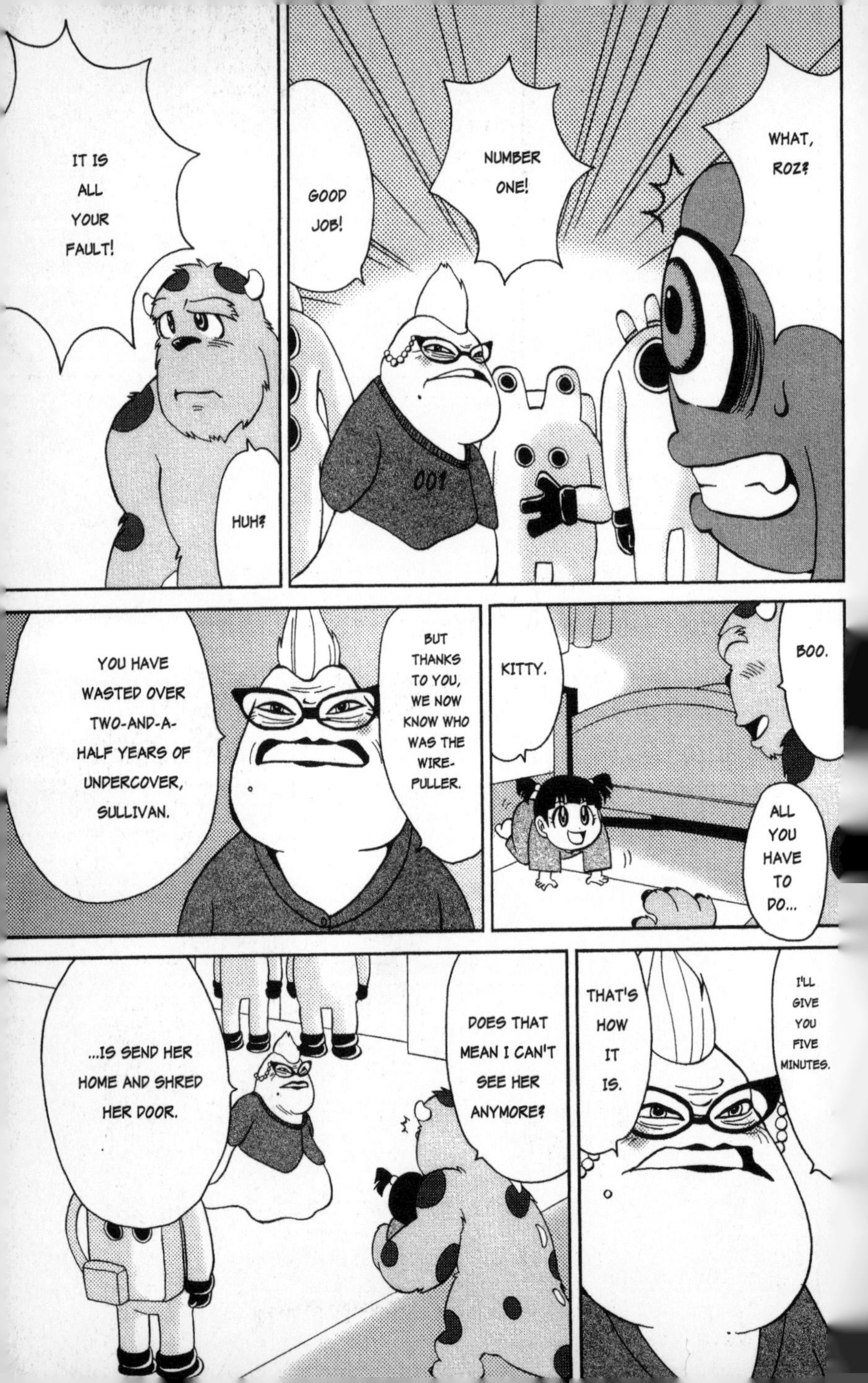
IT IS ALL YOUR FAULT!
HUH?
GOOD JOB!
NUMBER ONE!
WHAT, ROZ?
YOU HAVE WASTED OVER TWO-AND-A-HALF YEARS OF UNDERCOVER, SULLIVAN.
BUT THANKS TO YOU, WE NOW KNOW WHO WAS THE WIRE-PULLER.
KITTY.
BOO.
ALL YOU HAVE TO DO...
...IS SEND HER HOME AND SHRED HER DOOR.
DOES THAT MEAN I CAN'T SEE HER ANYMORE?
THAT'S HOW IT IS.
I'LL GIVE YOU FIVE MINUTES.

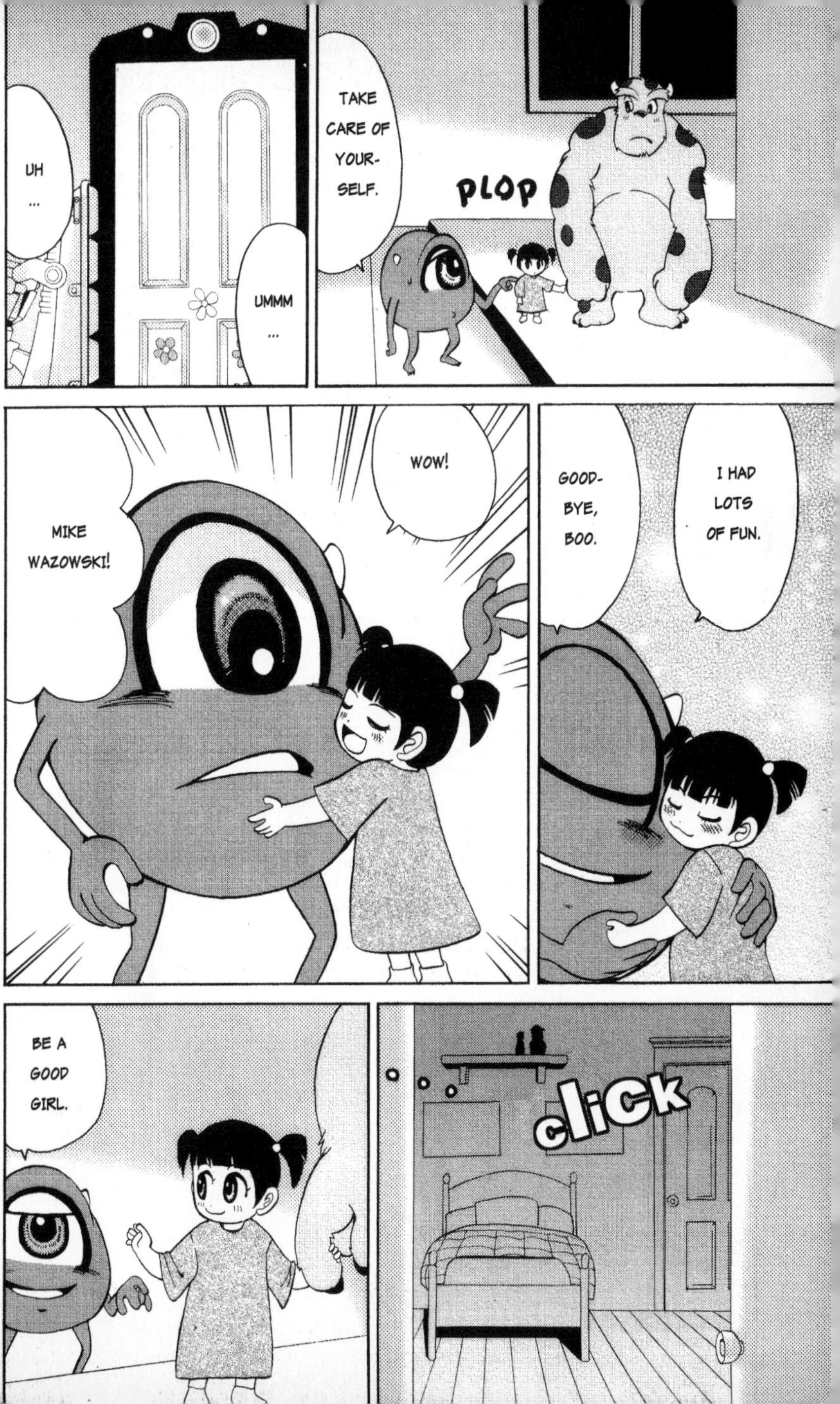
UH ...
UMMM ...
TAKE CARE OF YOUR-SELF.
PLOP
MIKE WAZOWSKI!
WOW!
GOOD-BYE, BOO.
I HAD LOTS OF FUN.
BE A GOOD GIRL.
click

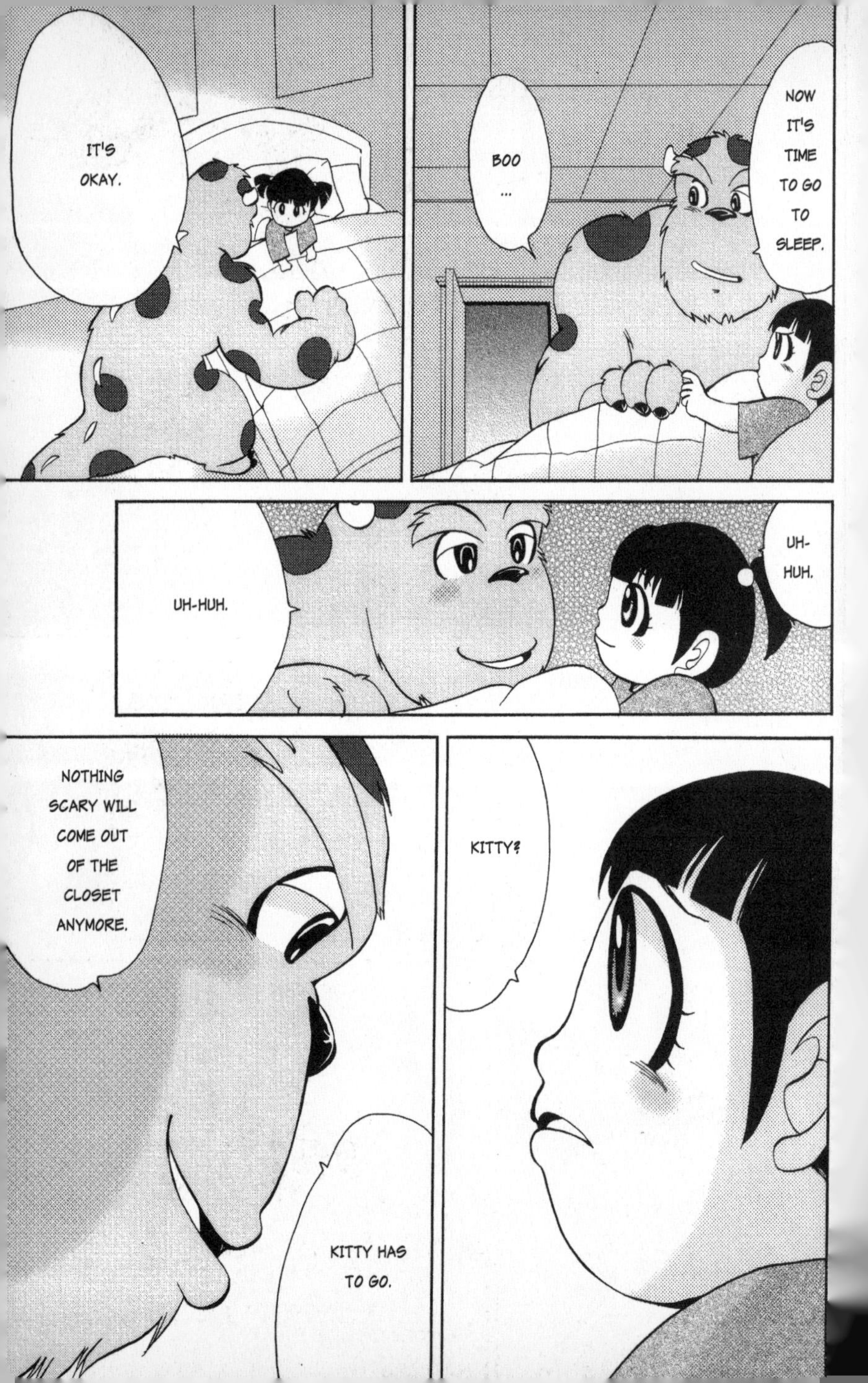
IT'S OKAY.
BOO ...
NOW IT'S TIME TO GO TO SLEEP.
UH-HUH.
UH-HUH.
NOTHING SCARY WILL COME OUT OF THE CLOSET ANYMORE.
KITTY HAS TO GO.
KITTY?

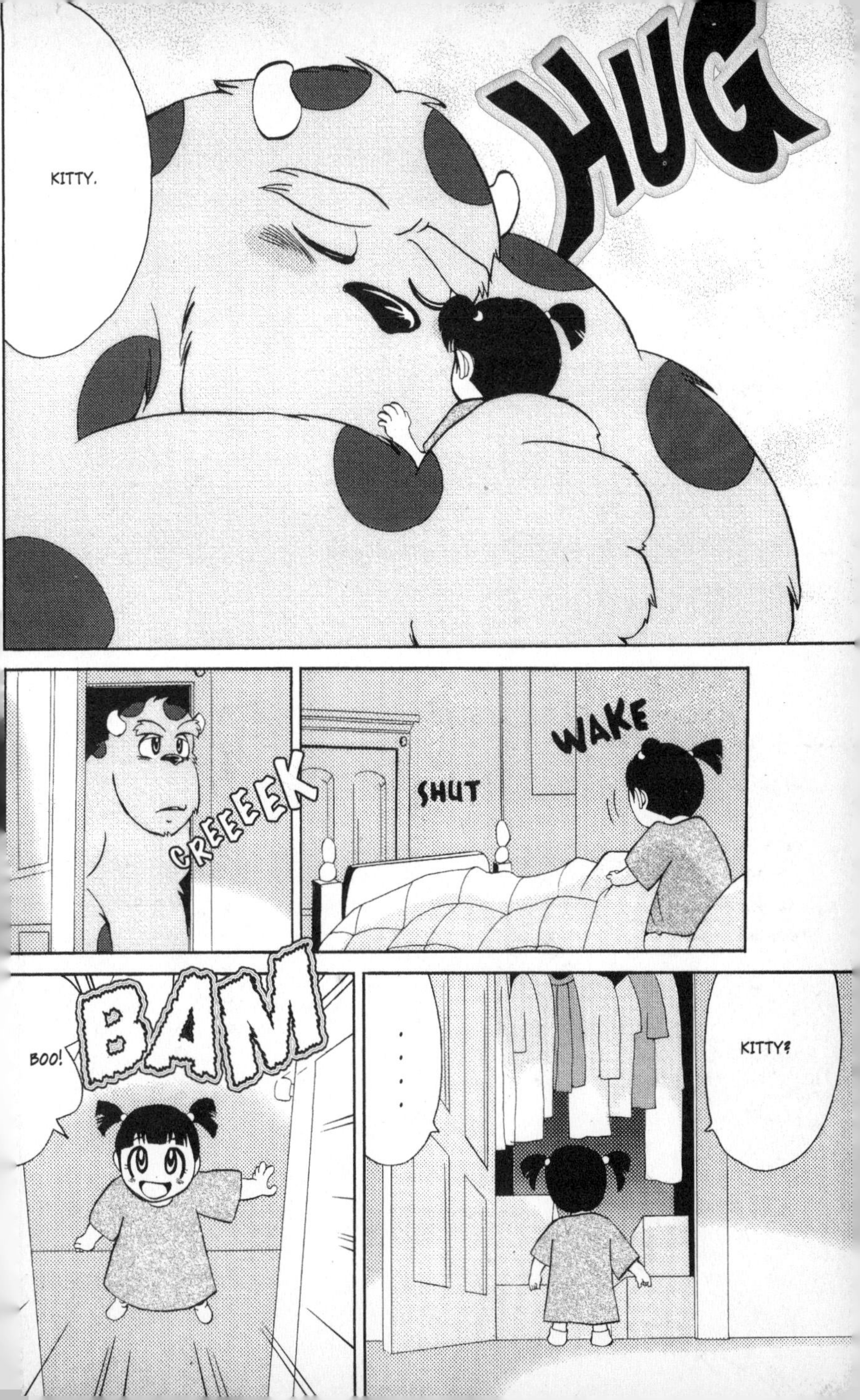
KITTY.
HUG
CREEEEK
SHUT
WAKE
BOO!
BAM
. . . .
KITTY?

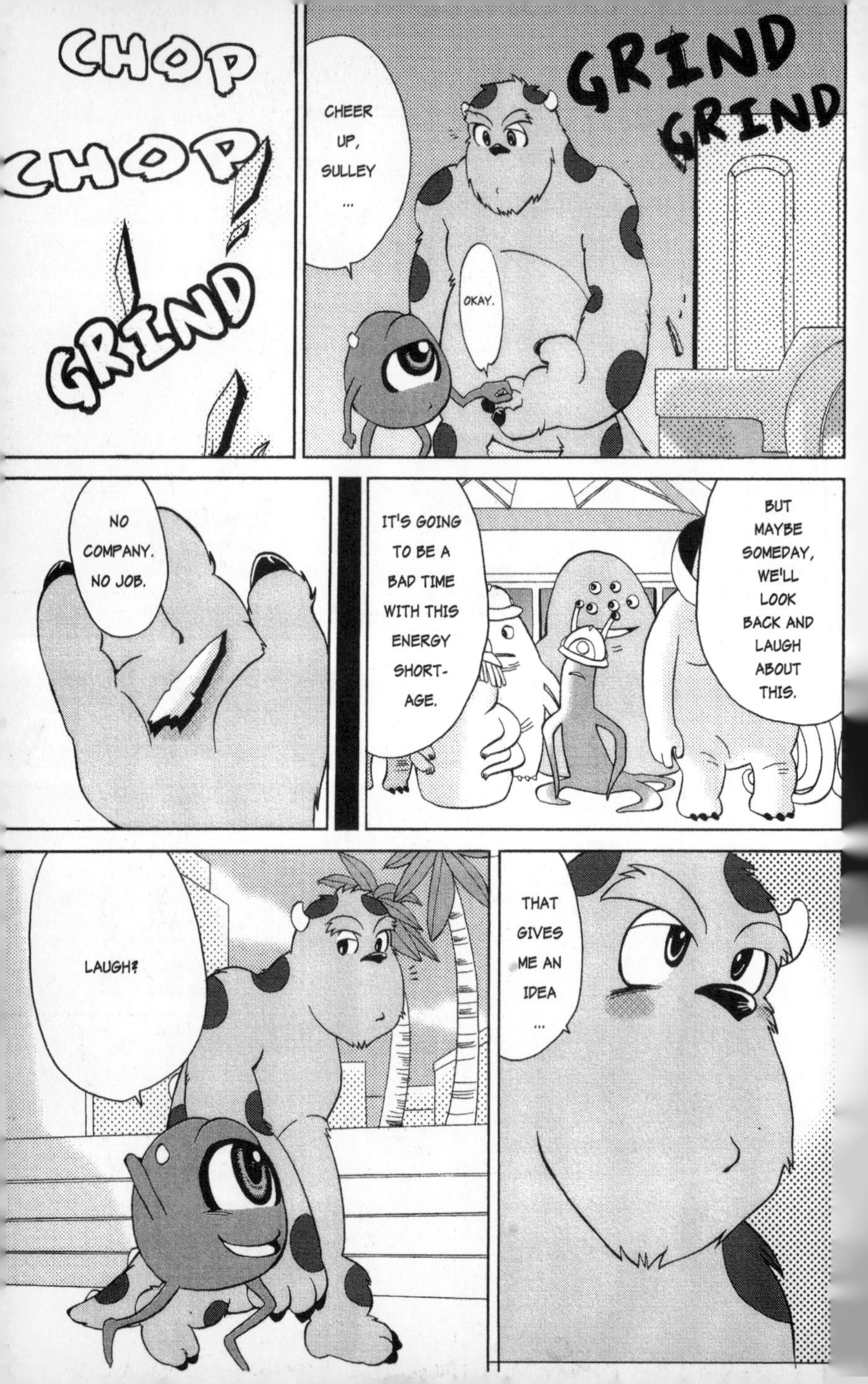
CHOP
CHOP
GRIND
CHEER UP, SULLEY ...
GRIND GRIND
OKAY.
NO COMPANY. NO JOB.
IT'S GOING TO BE A BAD TIME WITH THIS ENERGY SHORT-AGE.
BUT MAYBE SOMEDAY, WE'LL LOOK BACK AND LAUGH ABOUT THIS.
LAUGH?
THAT GIVES ME AN IDEA ...

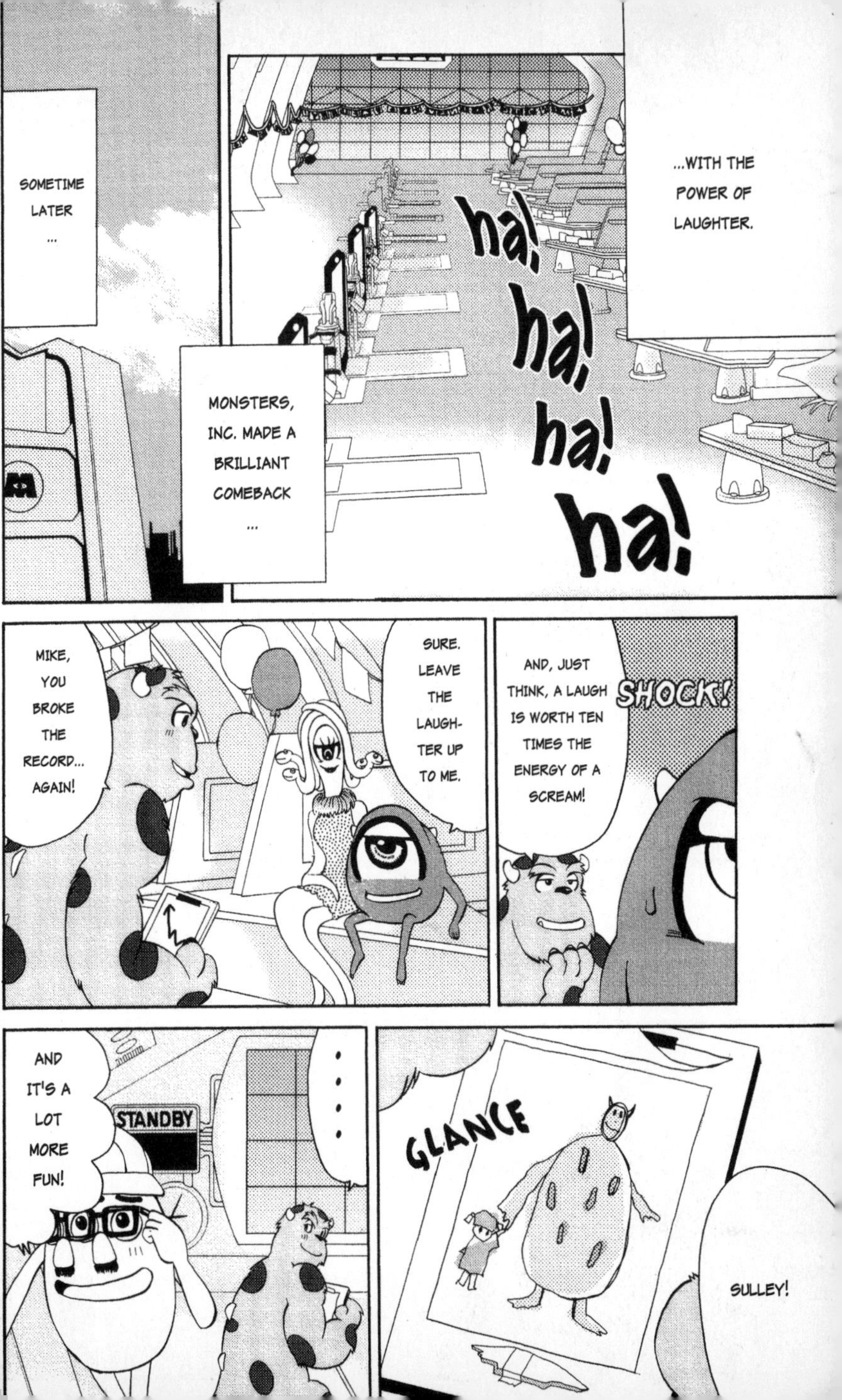
SOMETIME LATER ...
MONSTERS, INC. MADE A BRILLIANT COMEBACK ...
ha! ha! ha! ha!
...WITH THE POWER OF LAUGHTER.
MIKE, YOU BROKE THE RECORD... AGAIN!
SURE. LEAVE THE LAUGH-TER UP TO ME.
AND, JUST THINK, A LAUGH IS WORTH TEN TIMES THE ENERGY OF A SCREAM!
SHOCK!
AND IT'S A LOT MORE FUN!
STANDBY
....
GLANCE
SULLEY!

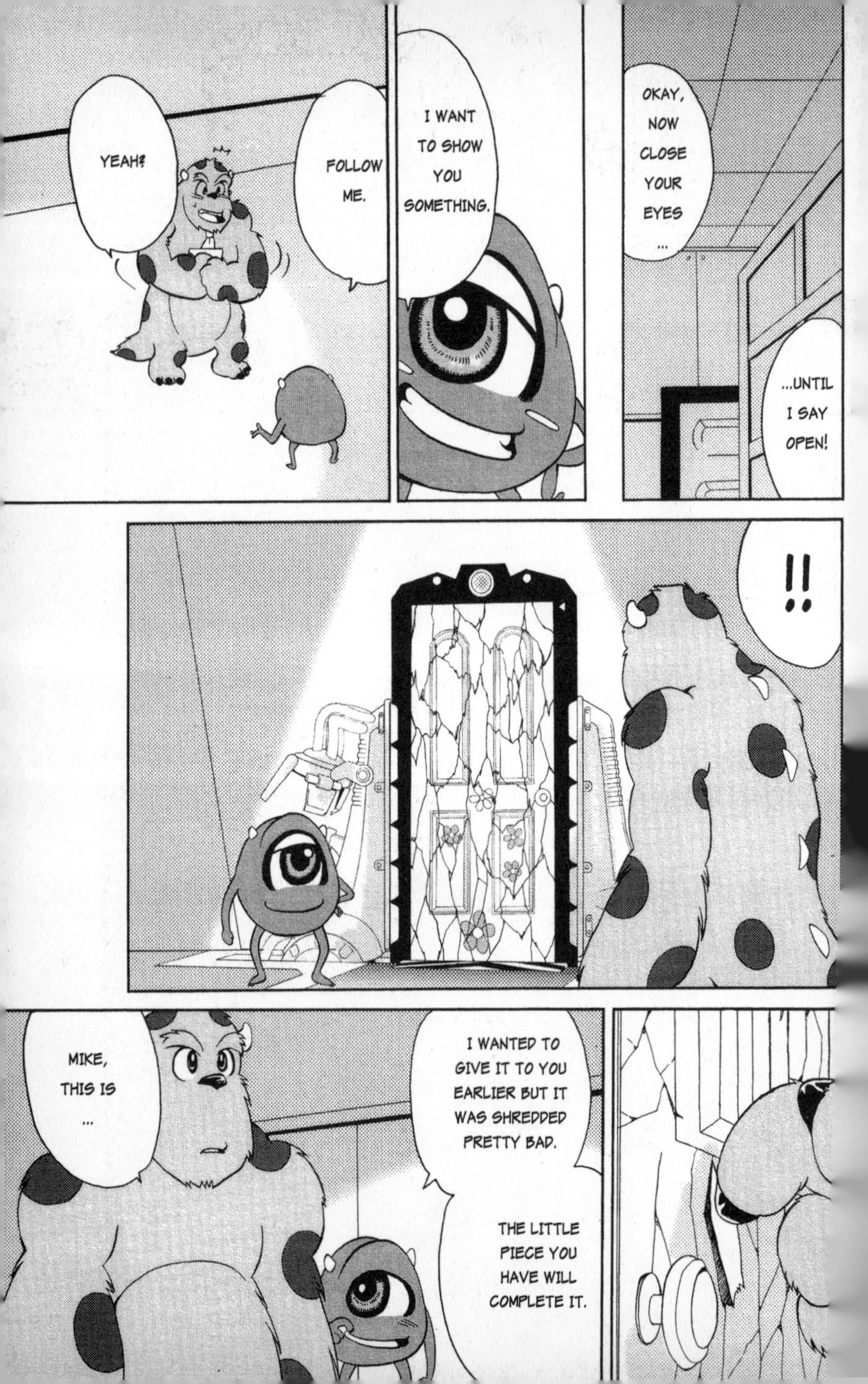
YEAH?
FOLLOW ME.
I WANT TO SHOW YOU SOMETHING.
OKAY, NOW CLOSE YOUR EYES ...
...UNTIL I SAY OPEN!
!!
MIKE, THIS IS ...
I WANTED TO GIVE IT TO YOU EARLIER BUT IT WAS SHREDDED PRETTY BAD.
THE LITTLE PIECE YOU HAVE WILL COMPLETE IT.

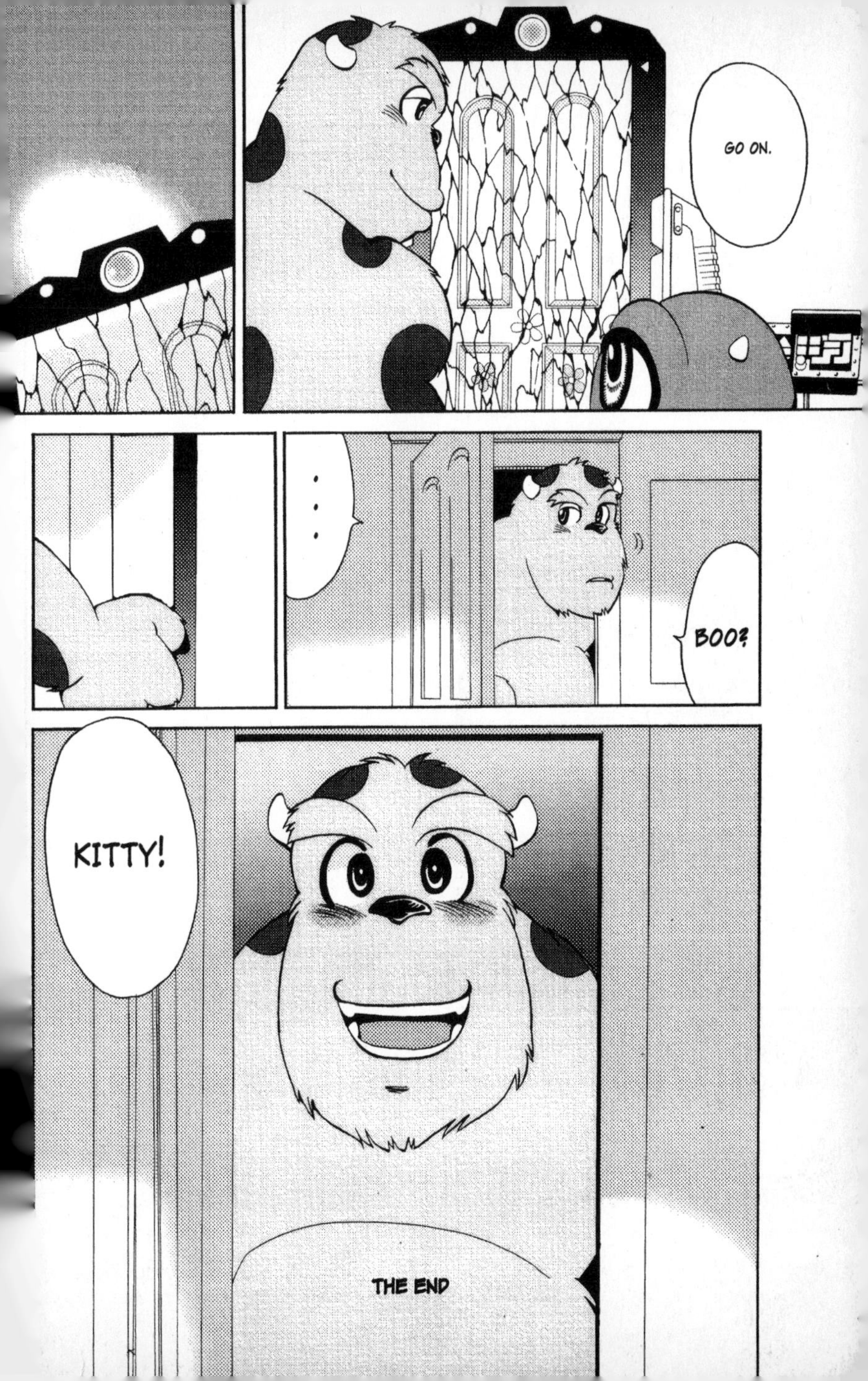
GO ON.
...
BOO?
KITTY!
THE END

CARDCAPTORS

Don't just watch the anime.... Read it! On-Sale now!

See TOKYOPOP.com for more CLAMP titles.

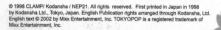

© 1998 CLAMP/ Kodansha / NEP21. All rights reserved. First printed in Japan in 1998 by Kodansha Ltd., Tokyo, Japan. English Publication rights arranged through Kodansha, Ltd. English text © 2002 by Mixx Entertainment, Inc. TOKYOPOP is a registered trademark of Mixx Entertainment, Inc.

TOKYOPO

Meet Misaki, the Prodigy.

A lighting-fast fighting doll.
An insane mentor.
A pinky promise to be the best.

ANGELIC LAYER

**The new manga from CLAMP,
creators of Cardcaptor Sakura.**

Volume 1 & 2 available now!

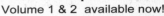

Angelic Layer © 1999 CLAMP. All Rights Reserved. First published in Japan by KADOKAWA SHOTEN PUBLISHING CO., LTD., Tokyo.
English translation rights arranged with KADOKAWA SHOTEN PUBLISHING CO. LTD., Tokyo through TUTTLE-MORI AGENCY, INC., Tokyo.
TOKYOPOP is a registered tradmark of Mixx Entertainment, Inc.

SAILOR MOON

Sailor Moon
Everyone's favorite
schoolgirl-turned-superhero!
In Bookstores Everywhere.

ff 1999 Naoko Takeuchi, Kodansha Ltd., Toei Animation Co., Ltd. © 1995 DIC Productions,
TOKYOPOP is a registered trademark of Mixx Entertainment.

STRAY SHEEP

TOKYOPOP®

Wandering into your child's heart
In Stores 2003

Stray Sheep © FUJI TELEVISION / ROBOT. TOKYPOP is a registered tradmark of Mixx Entertainment, Inc.

MOBILE SUIT

GUNDAM

THE LAST OUTPOST

ANOTHER EXCITING ADVENTURE
IN THE GUNDAM UNIVERSE

© 2002 Yoshiyuki Tomino, Hajime & Koichi Tokita © 2002 Sunrise & Sotsu Agency. All Rights Reserved. First published in Japan as New Mobile Chronicles Gundam W: G-UNIT in 2002 by Kodansha Ltd. Tokyo. English publication rights arranged through Kodansha Ltd.
TOKYOPOP is a registered trademark of Mixx Entertainment, Inc.